InvAsian

Asian Sisters Represent

Editor
Marjorie Beggs, San Francisco Study Center

Cover Design
Marlino Bitanga

Interior Design
Don McCartney Design

Production
Carl Angel, San Francisco Study Center

ISBN: 1-888956-06-2

© 2003 Asian Women United of California
www.asianwomenunited.org

Contents

CHAPTER 1

Sharing Ambivalence: Who Am I?

CHAPTER 2

Circles: Family

Acknowledgments:
We Are Grateful

Asian Women United of California is grateful to the girls and young women who participated in focus groups that were held in Berkeley, San Francisco, Long Beach, San Diego, Washington, D.C., New York and Minneapolis. They read and discussed stories, poems and memoirs, and helped our editorial committee decide what should be included in *InvAsian: Asian Sisters Represent.*

Many thanks to Cecilia Awayan, Adrienne C. Baker, Sherry Carlay, Ciera Carter, Monica Ching, Catherine Dayrit, Rotha Dom, Rosalind Kam, Lamphou Keomanyvong, Melissa Lindemann, Jessica Lowman, Linda Lowman, Ashley Mallory, Sothary Meas, Jessica Munivong, Gladys Murphy, Cindy Nguyen, Hoa Nguyen, Salie Nham, Puthea On, Marjie Palacios, Leah Park, Olivia Pham, Katherine Phoutthaphaphone, Kimberly Quinto, Eman Rimawi, Veronica Serrano, Vilay Soukphaly, Anna Thepkaisone, Phatty Thorn, Kunther Thy, Lena Tong, Diana Tran, Lisa Tran, Phuong Tran, Joi Turner, Soria Ul, Michi Ushio, Carroll Vongsouthi, Tu-Anh Vu, Amelia Workman, Maisue Xiong and Elaine Yoon.

We also want to thank the many people who made suggestions all along the way and helped organize focus groups, including Mary E. Adams and Kathy Jones of Monroe Clark School, San Diego; Diep Tran and Que Dang of Asians and Pacific Islanders for Reproductive Health, Long Beach; Melanie Fontanilla of Filipinos for Affirmative Action, Oakland; Julie Ha and Anna Rhee of Washington Alliance of Korean American Women, Washington, D.C.; Katherine Cowy Kim of Pacific News Service in San Francisco; Peter Kim of East Bay Asian Youth Center; Bryna Storch-Woodcock of Sarah Lawrence College; Bernadette Racelis, cinematographer; and David Rothbun of South High School, Minneapolis. Finally, we are grateful to Christina Cha and Iyko Day, who helped us with editing.

Foreword: To Asian Girls

I couldn't sleep the night before my 20th birthday. I just knew that the next morning, when the "-teen" dropped from my age, I would be forever transformed into someone more mature, more responsible, more. . .well, into an ADULT. I'd encountered the same restlessness rumbling under my chest many times before: in the still and nervous moments before my house awakened each Christmas morning, as I clutched the steering wheel before my driver's test, as I stared at the clover on the soccer field before my first kiss, when the door clicked as my parents walked out of my dorm room the day I moved into college.

So you can imagine my surprise when I awoke the next morning, feeling like the exact same girl. That was six years ago, and some things still haven't changed.

Don't get me wrong — there have been plenty of new things to excite me, to break my heart, to worry about, and to hope for. But I still read fashion magazines and wonder what I'd do with Gwyneth Paltrow's wardrobe, or a runway model's height. I now live 600 miles away, but when I go home, my parents still ask me where I've been, who I was with, and when I will become a doctor. I still get butterflies when I'm around someone I like. I still get zits (aargh!). I still have dreams.

Thank goodness growing up doesn't have to happen overnight. It's overwhelming enough already. And if you've grown up with parents or grandparents from another country, or with strangers always asking you where you're from, without seeing too many actresses, or senators, or singers or athletes who look like you, then you know it can seem overwhelming, TIMES TEN. That's why this book is for YOU.

You won't find what we've collected here in beauty magazines or music videos. Your teachers aren't going to tell you about the thoughts and emotions you'll encounter within these pages. This book is about the things that we see and understand as only Asian girls do. It affirms what you've known deep down, all along — that our identities pit us against challenges that other people don't have to deal with, but that we are more than capable of conquering them with attitude and with grace, because we are female and we are Asian in America.

Be forewarned. Once you choose to flip through these pages, you make the decision to come face to face with the complicated and the diverse, the painful and the beautiful — to confront the courageous and unforgettable emotions, images and voices of your Asian American sisters. You'll begin to envision yourself and the heritages you've inherited in new ways. You'll laugh and cry out loud seeing your pain, your anxieties, your exhilaration, your confusion and your pride reflected in our stories and poems. You will be infuriated, comforted, inspired. Your inner creator/artist/ storyteller will be awakened, and she will invade your soul and stir your imagination.

A-ha! We've got you already! There's no turning back now. Just sit back, and enjoy this ride while it lasts.

Evelyn I. Rodriguez
Asian Women United Board Member
InvAsian Editorial Board Member

CHAPTER 1

Sharing
Ambivalence

Who Am I?

Ching Chong Chinaman

BY ANGELA ROSARIO

Ching Chong Chinaman sittin' on a bench,
tryin' to make a dollar out of fifteen cents.

I remember the song.
I remember the little girls at recess
standing in a circle,
their pigtails bouncing up and down
as they clapped their hands together
and they sang the song.

I remember I used to sing it with them
sometimes,
and we laughed at the end
because the Chinaman couldn't do it
and it sounded so silly
to try and make a dollar
out of fifteen cents.

But one day,
my laughter stopped
when I became the Chinaman,
and they continued to laugh
without me.

And it occurred to me
how much pain there must have been
and how desperate the situation would have to be
that would lead a man
to sit on a bench
and try to make a dollar out of fifteen cents.

Irish Red, Korean Blues

FRANCES KIM RUSSELL

This is a story my mother likes to remind me of: *When you were a baby— oh, you were such a pretty baby!— you were born with a full head of black hair. Thick, black hair. But when you turned three months old, all your hair fell out. I said, "Oh no! Is she gonna be bald her whole life?" But then your hair grew back, and it was red like your granddaddy's hair. That's where you get your temper from— your red, Irish hair.*

My grandfather's picture sits on the mantel. It is an amber portrait on thick photographic paper, with his features colored in with pastels. His rosy-cheeked face smiles out from an Air Force uniform. I study his closely cropped hair, a soft auburn color. In the bathroom, I study my own hair in the mirror. A mixture of brown with blond highlights and red lowlights, my hair seems to me a strange thing of multiple colors and subtle hues that shifted with the seasons. My brother and sister were jealous that I got the "good hair" while they were stuck with boring, dark hair.

When I was growing up, the color of my hair was a magic thing that conjured up dreams of really being Irish. I associated it with leprechauns and hidden gold. My hair had the power of rage; I believed my mother when she told me my hot temper came from my hair color. My hair also had the power to resurrect my grandfather, who had died when my father was only six years old.

When my father's mother came all the way from Georgia to visit, my mother said, "Look, she has her granddaddy's hair." And for the first time, my grandmother looked at my slightly slanted eyes, round moon face, and light hair and didn't raise her hand to strike me as she had threatened to so many times before. I told myself that it was him protecting me, that the inherited color of my hair could protect me from my grandmother's racism.

For years, my hair fell straight and long to the small of my back, almost long enough to tuck into the back of my pants. On school days, my mother would comb it into a tight ponytail, pulling the hair hard so that the skin on my face stretched toward my temples. My eyes were pulled into a tight, feline slant.

In high school, other Korean kids would approach me and ask why I kept dyeing my hair. They didn't believe me when I told them it was natural. Sometimes strange white women would approach me just to ask what color I was using and to say they were trying to dye their hair that color, too. They never believed me either, but would look at me cynically, as if I just didn't want to be found out. Only when I would tell them that I was half Irish would they tilt their heads to one side and sigh, "Ooh, how interesting!" then stare at me and my hair for a moment.

As I began cutting it shorter and shorter, I became more confused about the nature of my hair. My usually ruler-straight hair had suddenly become wavy and would refuse to obey my comb. Finally, after many disastrous styles, I settled on a nice, short pixie cut.

"Your haircut makes you look more Asian," my friend Alex said.

"Your hair looks darker now," my mother said, scowling.

Despite the color, I had always assumed I had Asian hair. That is, thick, relentlessly straight hair which, according to my mother, white women are incapable of cutting without screwing up somehow.

"Mexicans cut Oriental hair better than white women," said my mother. "Their hair is more like ours."

But the hair in the mirror — short and slightly wavy with strange cowlicks and frizzy bits at the edges — looked nothing like my mother's glossy black strands, or even my sister's coarse dark-brown tresses. I had assumed that my hair had a Korean texture and an Irish color, but the confused mess straining beneath a layer of pomade was nothing but stringy, "fine" Caucasian hair. I also came to the realization that my hair was never red, that my mother simply saw it as red because it wasn't black. To this day, if I am standing in sunlight, my mother will insist, "It really is red!" as if to guard against anyone seeing it as merely brown.

When I was in high school, I traveled with my mother to Korea for the first time. My light-colored hair drew constant stares and called attention to me amidst all the black hair. Whenever I stood close beside my cousins for a photograph, my hair would seem to flare up and grow redder, just as theirs would drop to an even deeper black. I was too shy to use the public bathhouses because I feared I would draw even more stares in there, so I took sponge baths outside, hidden between the side of the kitchen and the courtyard wall.

While we were in Korea, my mother and I drove with some relatives to Inchon to attend a cousin's wedding. On the way there, my mother commented that there was a U.S. military base nearby, and if I wanted, we could go on base and eat a steak dinner. I was momentarily tempted until I realized we would be the only two people allowed on base. We both had our American military identification and privilege cards with us, but none of our extended family members would be admitted past the gates.

Just then, we passed a jeep full of American GIs on the freeway. As we drove past the jeep, I looked over with some curiosity at the soldiers inside. They glanced over at me, then did a double take as we pulled out of view.

A moment later, my mother laughed and said, "They're back!" They had sped up and were driving alongside us, hounding our car and staring at me. From the backseat, my mother yelled, "It's your hair! It's your hair! They saw your red hair in the front seat with all this black Korean hair around it! I bet they're happy to see another American!"

Shy and embarrassed by their aggressiveness, I covered my face with my hands and bent forward to hide my head behind the car door. From the corner of my eye, I glimpsed the soldiers' faces pressed against the windows of the jeep, waiting for me to lift my head so they could see my face. The Korean driver next to me smiled and waved and winked at the soldiers, pretending that they were looking at him. My mother jabbed me in the side to try to get me to look at the soldiers.

"They just want to see another American! Go ahead and look at them!"

Stubbornly, I kept my head down, hoping they would take the hint and drop back. Instead, they persisted. Time slowed, and I found myself unable to lift my head, unwilling to give in to their stares. On the streets in Chung-ju, it had been fun to return the stares of Koreans who did double takes, glancing from my hair to my eyes to my mother then back to me. Somehow this was worse.

I felt crowded in my seat, caught between my mother's manicured pokes and the soldiers' grim masculinity pressing through the space between the cars. From my quick glances, I had seen that they were large men, barrel-chested with muscles pushing through their uniforms. The scene clashed with my images of my grandfather in his clean, pressed uniform in the amber portrait and of color snapshots of my father in his own military uniform standing in the shadow of a C-130, holding my two-year-old hand as I stared wide-eyed at the camera. Turning from fear to anger, I thought to myself, "Why should they be happy to see another American? They see nothing but Americans when they're on the military base."

Did they know that I was mixed? Did they think I was just another tourist? Did they know I was only 16 years old? Were they staring, as my mother suggested, simply because they hadn't seen an American in a long time, or because they hadn't seen an American woman? The longer they stared, the more paranoid and angry I became. Inexplicably, I suddenly recalled being teased in junior high that I looked just like the Vietnamese prostitute in Full Metal Jacket, a comparison I have yet to fully understand. Stereotypes of war brides and war babies and even stereotypes of loose and liberated American women ran through my head at a hysterical pitch. It didn't make any sense, but in that moment, these random thoughts surfaced as I tried to understand the scene. What exactly were the soldiers hoping to see beneath my "red" hair?

After finally ditching the soldiers and even after returning to the States, I felt nothing but loathing for the color of my hair. What was once magically and exotically Irish became simply white, with all the attendant marks of power and privilege. My hair had become the thing that seemed to stand between me and Korean-ness; what was once a passageway had turned into solid wall. There have been many times when I was deeply tempted to dye my hair black as if, by virtue of my hair color, I would be left with this constant ambivalence, as if I could begin to blend in with my Korean cousins. I have also considered getting a temporary dye job, just to see how different I might look. Would I look more Korean or even full Korean? When I told my mother I was thinking of dyeing my hair black, she said, "Oh no! You're so pale, you'll look Japanese!"

College proved to be no more enlightening, as I noted the increasing numbers of Asian American women with their hair highlighted auburn or bleached blond, and the equally increasing numbers of white women dyeing their hair black, sometimes wearing it in buns stuck through with a pair of chopsticks. I grew even more confused upon my second trip to Korea five years later, when I found that many of the young women there were also lightening their hair. In fact, now nobody seemed to notice my hair color at all.

What ethnicity is my hair if it behaves like Asian hair when it is long and like Caucasian hair when it is short? What color is my hair if everyone is dyeing theirs to match mine, and I dye mine to match theirs? I asked a hairdresser once what it would take to make my hair a glossy black. She described a complicated process of bleaching, dying and highlighting. And if I ever wanted to go back to my normal color, she said, I'd have to live with a bi-colored head or shave it off and start over. Even so, the texture and the roots would always betray me.

I Want to Live My Life

BY TRINH MAI

I want to live my life with courage and flair — said Maya Angelou
And thank God she did too.

I was drowning in a body of water
that could fill a cup

thinking I could let go
for the first time I was ready

Your World

By Dolly Veale

What kinda world you wanna see?
Need be asked
Before what you wanna be.
Will it be
Where a few can make it
While most don't have sh*t?
A world
Without hesitation
At mass incarceration
Of even children.
Inequality from bottom to top
The answer to every problem
Is more cops
Where will it stop?
Or will it be
A better world tomorrow
No more today's misery and sorrow
That's all around?
Where you won't live in fright
As exploitation no longer abound
And your dreams can take flight.
Such a future
Is up to you.

Memories of
Mrs. Menesses

BY EMILY PORCINCULA LAWSIN

At St. Edward's Elementary School in the early 1970s, there were two first-grade classes. Miss Cross, a skinny woman with long strawberry blonde hair, was my teacher. She taught us how to read "Dick and Jane" stories, how to print straight sentences, how to mold pots out of clay, and even how to play "Duck, Duck, Goose," a game where one is dubbed a goose and must chase whoever has dubbed them. I never really liked that game; my classmates always hit me hard on the head to slow me down so I wouldn't catch up to them. I never knew why we played it. Maybe it was supposed to teach us how to become the hunter instead of the hunted. Miss Cross kept a tally of who won on the front chalkboard.

One day, my class met in the other first-grade classroom, right next door, to prepare for the upcoming Christmas pageant. We walked into the room, and I looked around for pictures of Dick and Jane chasing Spot, like the ones Miss Cross had. I was surprised that they were absent from the bulletin boards. In the back of the classroom, where Miss Cross would've placed our reading circles and clay tables, hung traditional Filipino Christmas parols—delicate green, red, and white stars as large as globes of the world—made from cellophane, tissue paper, and curved bamboo. Their cut-out designs sparkled with glitter just like the ornaments that my parents displayed at home. Then when I sat down, I looked to the front of the room and the numbers one through 10 were spelled out on the chalkboard in English, Spanish, and even Tagalog! I wondered why this classroom was so familiarly comfortable, yet so different from ours next door. Then I met the person who had transformed a dark classroom in southeast Seattle to a world of opportunity: Mrs. Menesses.

Mrs. Menesses stood tall, with long, wavy black hair and big brown eyes, just like my eldest sister. She spoke loud and forcefully and had a big smile. She made all of us introduce ourselves and tell where our parents were from. Later she made us read the numbers on the chalkboard. I was the only one who could read and pronounce them correctly! For the first time, I felt proud to be the only Filipina student in the classroom. Then when it was time to rehearse for the annual Christmas play, she led us in a round of songs. No hits on the head or running around in circles.

When we finished our joint lesson, I felt sad to leave. I wanted to change classes and have Mrs. Menesses for my teacher. It was my first contact with multicultural education, and I couldn't even stay in the class. It was then that I knew I wanted to become a teacher. I wanted to provide a classroom atmosphere that was just as culturally and intellectually stimulating. Oh, sure, I did the typical Asian dutiful daughter routine and enrolled in pre-engineering courses in college. I even interned as a civil engineer one summer, all to please my father, whose own education was disrupted by World War II. However, when I discovered that most of the engineering jobs in the Pacific Northwest were tied to torpedoes, missiles, B-1 bombers, Trident nuclear submarines, or hazardous waste, I had a serious change of heart, or should I say, I let my heart take over my head. My mother and father, both survivors of the WWII atrocities in the Philippines, eventually understood.

Since then, I have been blessed with many fine teachers and mentors. They have shown me that, like Mrs. Menesses, I can also bring the community into the classroom and vice versa. My experiences as a former student, tutor, and teaching assistant gave me a strong foundation in helping students learn our collective and individual history. Now, as an Asian American Studies instructor, I enjoy assisting students with their assignments and witnessing the evolution of their thought patterns and creativity. Every semester, I get a new group of students from different backgrounds and neighborhoods from all over the country. When they walk into the classroom on the first day of classes, many of them are surprised to see a Filipina professor at the chalkboard. Those enrolled in my English courses often confess that, with the spelling of my last name, they had automatically assumed I would be white. I enjoy surprising them like that, because it engages us in a discussion of the importance of names in relation to identity, stereotypes, and family history. Not to mention the fact that it introduces them to hierarchy and the state, when I reveal how my Visayan great-grandfather changed our last name from "Lau" to "Lawsin" to avoid racism and over-taxation in the Philippines.

In turn, the students share their own family stories. I also share many educational props daily: eye-catching movement posters, mounted historical photographs, path-breaking books, Filipino American music, oral history performances, field trips to surrounding ethnic enclaves, and even an end-of-the-semester potluck of food items that are mentioned in the readings. My colleagues may think it's a hassle to lug such items to class, clear across campus, but I think that it's worth it. It is an exciting challenge for me, just as exciting as walking into Mrs. Menesses' classroom all over again.

I Used to Be ...

BY KELLY EMIKO IWANABE

I used to be
  A thousand paper squares,
    Ordinary and plain,
      Gold, silver, red, and purple.
        Now I am
          A thousand folded cranes,
            Floating through the air.
              Bringing hope and happiness

Para Sa Isangmahal

By Anida Esguerra

destruction.
i had forgotten. i have forgotten.
suddenly cut off from the revolutionary
energy of my college years,
temporarily leasing a world i had created

then quickly ushered out into the world
i was suppose to inherit
i have been lost for 2 years now
mindlessly employed to commercialize
my vision for THEM
entrapped to frolic with the privileged few
who self-proclaim their "progressive" political correctness
through bullshit rhetoric

self-absorbed in a kind of noisy silence
sensationLESS
i let THEM mess with me
taking a detour from my thoughts
and taking refuge in my baby's love
forgetting that inside my voice was dying
becoming a part of the invisible minority
and adding to their collection of geisha girls
and denying that i had fallen
and so i hid
and so i denied.
and so i died.
destruction.survival.

survival.destruction.
i had forgotten
only now to be reminded by distant . . . pinoy poets
all of you . . . isangmahal
your words punched through my soul
slowly shattering the reality i was living
reminding me again that
i was once a part of a collective spirit
forged together by a turbulent force

we called the MONSOON.
   i/we had strength
   i/we had voices
   i/we had love

survival
remembering fragments of our anthem
that we wrote in cataclysmic blood
   "invisible minority
   historically silenced
   those who give a shit
   fuck the power
   and kiss my ass motherfucker!"

   survival.
   being reminded again
   to remember by pledge
   and my allegiance to our anthem
to find myself again
through creative self expression
to believe in something stronger
   to be a part of something more
to kick, scream, and shout,
   to announce and denounce
to make myself
to make we-self
heard again

survival.
to speak the truth
to be true
to self
to i

i am i
and i am we
i be
i be

   to discover myself
to find my voice again
   to remember to NEVER FORGET
   to believe, to believe
   to love, to love
   isangmahal. . .

isangmahal . . .

And
You reminded me to pass it around
Ikalat muna . . .
And that's what it became for me
A message of survival from distant pinoy poetry
Remembering that the spirit survives
That the spirit lives on
    In all of you
    And in we . . . and in me.

Sharing Ambivalence

BY MARI FULI TOM

I t was to be a sleepover party, and those of us who were already there lounged around the couches reading comics. Our hostess had obtained some new *doujinshis,* Japanese fan comics, about Samurai Troopers. The other two girls were eagerly trying to interpret the pictures while the hostess worked on cleaning the living room, in between peeking in on the fan comics and doing some basic translation. I'd seen most of the fan comics before and was not too impressed. So I was sitting on the couch, playing with her two stuffed white tigers. They were Fiesta toys, very well-formed stuffed animals. I tended to like tigers in general, but the particular significance in this case was that there was a white tiger in the Japanese animation *Yoroiden Samurai Troopers.*

Heavy knocking interrupted the simple serenity, and I was about to get up when the hostess said, "I'll get it."

The other two girls nodded and continued to read their *doujinshis.* There were some excited screams as our hostess greeted the other two girls whom we had been expecting. Well, in truth, the enthusiasm was directed at her best friend, who had come up from Fountain Valley. The two girls came in, and one set a bunch of comics on top of the radio.

"Hello, Minna," she said. "I brought some *Yuu Yuu Hakusho doujinshis.* There's more in the car."

The two girls who had been reading Trooper *doujinshis* squealed with delight. Unfortunately, being a serious sort of person and a tomboy by nature, I was incapable of such high-pitched sounds, so I could only join their excitement by smiling. I burrowed my face into one of the stuffed white tigers, once again following a long tradition of finding comfort in inanimate objects.

The other girl put a box of stuff down and started yelling at me in Cantonese, "Wah! So lazy. Just sit on the couch and don't even help to carry things in."

I laughed at this because the phrases were so familiar, so much a part of the culture itself. I got up from my place on the couch and gently set the tigers aside.

"Okay, okay. Gee, Yin, so mean!" I said in English.

We were among white girls, and I never spoke Cantonese in such situations. But Yin often missed being able to speak Cantonese, having come over from Singapore just a year ago, and insisted on using the language with me. She said that I should practice my Canto, and in truth, I would've felt more comfortable speaking Canto with her than with my Hong Kong friend whom I had known since elementary school. Unlike those who became fixated on their "native language," Yin was fluent in English, Mandarin, French, and Japanese as well as Cantonese. Thus, when she wanted to speak Canto with me, I knew it truly was because she missed the sound of the language itself. But everyone else was white, and at best, they spoke Japanese, not Cantonese, so I refrained from replying to Yin's familiar phrases. I didn't even say *"ho ah"* or *"uhn"* instead of *"okay."*

After everything was moved inside from the car, the group fractioned off in its normal way. The two girls who had been reading Trooper comics were now riffling through the Yuu Yuu comics. Our hostess was catching up on times with her best friend. And eventually, just because neither of us were doing anything else, Yin and I started talking.

"How is it?" Yin asked in Canto.

I shrugged. "It's okay. Still swinging."

"Mee-ree-ah!" she said sternly. I loved the way she said my name with that odd accent of hers. I don't know why. Maybe it's because she didn't call me Miri-chan like the others. Chan was a friendly Japanese suffix for women. The white girls all called me Miri-chan, but they'd never asked if it bothered me. It did. It annoyed the hell out of me.

"What?" I said innocently.

"Oh, boy. I can see the halo," Yin teased in English. She was referring to the e-mail habit of making smiley faces with halos. "But what's this? Your halo looks a little tarnished."

I smiled. "Oops. How strange. I shine it everyday." Then I turned to being a little more serious and asked, "What about you?" She, too, was a moody person.

"Still alive," she said. "Pendulum hasn't been oscillating too badly. Just swinging in the gray area. But not walking the line, so that's a good thing."

I nodded. I didn't know if it was a racist thing or what, but I loved the way I could talk to Yin. We never talked about our problems directly, but we both knew that the other was emotionally strained so we tended to keep tabs on each other. Maybe it wasn't the fact that she was Chinese. Maybe it was because she had the same kind of parental pressure to do well in academics, and it was just coincidence that both of us were Chinese. But that kind of mental stress was something that our other friends didn't understand. Sympathy was not understanding. One had to be there to know.

Later in the evening, everyone turned to watching last week's episode of *X-Files* on a videotape that had been brought up from Southern California. I didn't follow it religiously so didn't really care. Our hostess's best friend was e-mailing. And Yin was organizing her belongings because she had already seen the episode.

"Hey, Miriya," Yin said. "Do you want to listen to *Ambivalence?* I brought it up with me."

"Hm? What's that?" I asked, going over to where she was with a tiger under each arm. Although I felt older than most of the people present because I was one year above them in school, they tended to treat me like a child since I was so short. White people had a habit of doing that. I was always considered "cute" just because I was "small" when, in truth, the two matters were unrelated. It didn't help that I didn't like being cute so I resented it when they said, "Kawaii Miri-chan." But despite objecting to being cute, I did play into the role of being a kid. It made them more comfortable. So I brought the two white tigers with me wherever I went.

"It's from *Ai no Kusabi*," Yin explained as she pulled out a CD and put it into her

Discman. "Sorry, no Kaneto-sama or Seki-san. This is just music, no voices. But the music's kind of cool. Kind of dark. Here." She offered me one of the earplugs of her earphones.

I knew nothing about this series, *Ai no Kusabi*. I only knew that one of the characters named Iason was played by Shiozawa Kaneto, one of my favorite voice actors because of his deep, deep voice, and that the other main character was Riki, played by Seki-san, who was another favorite because of his versatility as a voice actor.

But this wasn't about a Japanese series; it was a social issue. This whole sleepover was a social event, one that my parents didn't know about. Yin had kept the other earplug of her Discman and had put it in her left ear. She was offering me the right one. It seemed like such a normal thing to do, to share a Discman to listen to music, but I'd never done it before. I was flattered by her offer. At first, I had thought that she was going to give me the whole Discman to listen to the CD, but this was even better than that. I accepted the earplug and put it in my right ear. We listened to the CD together while Yin continued to unpack. I was inwardly beaming from the experience, and it helped that the CD really was good.

"Hey, Miriya, I need to go over to the sink okay?" Yin said.

I had no idea how much time had passed since I had started listening to the CD and reveling in my own thoughts. I nodded to Yin's request. We got up carefully and walked over to the kitchen. Yin was the tallest full-blooded Chinese girl I had ever known. She was 5'11", taller than even the two tall white girls by an inch or two when she slouched. I was merely 5 feet tall, maybe 5'1" with my shoes on. The height difference between us strained the wire of the earphones. I kept expecting to have my earplug yanked from my ear, breaking that bond that had been formed between us. I felt the earplug shift, but miraculously enough, it didn't come out. I was relieved. I thought about this, how we hadn't been separated, while Yin washed out some Tupperware that had contained her lunch for the long drive up here to the Bay Area.

"Okay, let's move to the couch now," Yin said. "*Babylon 5* was recorded after *X-Files*, and I haven't seen it yet."

"That's fine," I said. We moved carefully once again, and it wasn't until we were finally seated that I became convinced that the earplug wouldn't be tugged from either of our ears. I didn't follow *Babylon 5* at all, so I simply concentrated on listening to the CD while playing with the two stuffed, white tigers or looking at the various anime paraphernalia that was strewn on the floor.

My eyes lingered on a particularly nice picture of Touma, the blue-haired boy of Samurai Troopers. In his character file, it had said that he lacked normal sociability. I had always thought that this phrase was the result of a problem in translation, but now I began to understand what it meant. I reflected on my unusual pleasure at being able to share a set of earphones and thought, this is what is meant by "lacking normal sociability."

The CD ended with a song in Japanese. I could only understand the English words like "calling," "silent," and "night after night." As the singer progressed through the song, I grew to love it. He was a good singer, one who could control the pitch of his voice very well. I didn't understand the Japanese words, but I understood the tone of his voice. His voice was pained, and the words were dragged forth from the depth of a soul in despair. Although his scream of sorrow was beautiful and melodious, the "aaaah" still conveyed a sense of a torn existence.

I poked Yin when they were fast-forwarding through a commercial break and asked, "Hey, Yin, who sings this?"

"Oh, it's just a random singer. Not Kaneto-sama or Seki-san. But it's still a nice song anyway," Yin said.

"Yeah, it is," I agreed whole-heartedly. "What's it called?'

"Eternal," Yin said. A CD with good music and an excellent song with an appropriate song name. I knew I had to get the CD, to commemorate this experience.

"What's the CD called again?" I asked.

"Ambivalence."

Transplanted Korean

BY JENNIFER KIM

I went to the blood bank
and asked for some Korean Blood.

What type they asked.
I said, unleaded,
give me premium.

They hooked me up.
I watched as my American blood
left one arm and the Korean blood
pumped into the other.

This is good, I thought,
this is going to make me
feel more Korean, having the best,
highest octane
Korean Blood.

So I signed the credit receipt,
wiped up the extra drops of blood
and zoomed out of there.

I went to a gathering of Koreans.
Hey, I've got Korean blood, I said,
Give me that drum, or is it chang gu?

They stared at me as I
beat the rhythm.

It appeared that I had no
rhythm in either culture
because no one joined me.

Hey, I said, I·can't make
music alone.
No one responded.

Listen, I've got the
same blood as you now.
We are the same.

No one gave a shit and
they continued to speak
their language.

I think I heard,
Why doesn't she speak Korean?
She was born here.

And that was that.

2

Circles

Family

Silent Love

By Socheata Sun

I remember playing outside with the rest
of the children as a little girl. I remember
going to the liquor store across the street
on Banning Boulevard every Monday to
buy lemon heads and cherry clams. And I
remember my father telling me, "When
you get a boyfriend, make sure he takes
care of you just like I would." He would
smile after that and go cook me spaghetti
with big meatballs. I used to run around
in my little Barbie underwear and dance
like a ballerina. My father would say,
"You're such a clown." And I would give
my father a bear hug because I knew he
loved me. We used to watch *Nightmare*
on Elm Street together at night, and
when a scary part came on, I would go
under the covers and hide; a little mouse
hiding from a cat. In the evening, he
used to brush my hair and talk to me
about growing up. The special part was
when he would tell me he loved me.

Now that I'm older, we don't

communicate too much. He once in a

while gives me advice about my future

and my boyfriend; but other than that

he's become such a silent person. When

I come from school, the house still smells

great from his cooking. But I don't run

around and dance in my Barbie

underwear, he has stopped brushing my

hair and we don't say "I love you" to each

other anymore. We still watch movies

together, but in the evenings he's always

gone, and I don't know where he goes. I

know my father loves me, but I wish

there were a way for him to say it to me.

So I will say: I love you, Daddy, with all

my heart and soul. I'm just worried

because you're such a silent person now,

and it's a mystery to me.

Don't Forget the Whiskey

BY FRANCES LEE HALL

My vegetarian friend lovingly calls me a carnivore. She preaches about the horrors of red meat whenever we go out. "I won't eat anything with eyes," she says. But it's no use; I can't tell you what I'd do for a piece of roast beef.

When the smell of roast beef invades my senses, my father's image appears before my eyes. His smile, his matter-of-factness, his cooking come back to me.

Every Christmas, my father made a roast for our family. He'd meticulously check all the supermarket ads to see who had the best deal. All the ads would be laid out on the sofa, marked up with red pens. "See," he'd nudge me, "Cala isn't bad, but Safeway — much better!"

Preparing the roast was like a sacred ritual to him, and I watched, hoping to learn his secrets. He'd turn the raw hunk of meat over in his hands like a newborn baby, massaging it with salt and oil. Then came the marinade: dark Chinese soy sauce, oyster sauce, corn oil, a dash of cornstarch, and tons of garlic and ginger. He never measured anything. And the secret ingredient: whiskey. JB Whiskey. Two capfuls and the marinade would suddenly come alive, the aroma filling the house.

"To make it better," he told me, while throwing in another capful. "Don't ever forget it." The roast marinated all day, the chunks of garlic and ginger glistening on top. I couldn't wait to eat it!

Family members would arrive, and finally, the prime rib would be roasted to perfection, coming out a golden sizzling brown. My Dad would ask me to mash the potatoes, which meant the meal was almost ready. I mashed, and he carved the meat. Watching him, I secretly planned which pieces to put on my plate. He looked at me and slipped me an end piece, filled with the most flavor, of course, because of the marinade. Mmmm, it was so juicy and tender; I'd lick my fingers to get every last drop. And my Dad joined me with a little piece of his own.

Well, sooner or later, it comes time for me to make my own roast. I'm trying to impress my boyfriend's family, so I figure, hey — I'll just make a roast! My boyfriend's family is huge. Four big brothers, all with healthy appetites. His mother is checking me out for the first time, up close and personal, this woman dating her precious oldest boy. And just for fun, can his two aunts from Hong Kong come over since they're in town this week?

Ay-Yi-Yi! My apartment is a mess. I don't have enough dishes and chairs. I hope I've got enough soy sauce. Oh God — I don't even know how long to cook the roast. I can just see this family gnawing on burnt pieces of what was supposed to be prime rib, trying to be polite, and his two aunts wondering, "How come she didn't make Chinese food?"

Well, the boyfriend has no idea how to cook, and I'm not about to ask his mother. I call my Dad.

"So, Dad, how long do you cook a four-rib roast?"

"Mmm, four ribs? Uhh — that's a lot of meat."

"I know, but I've got a lot of people to feed."

"You know, sometimes it's better to cook two smaller roasts, then it takes less time to cook."

"Well, next time I'll remember. So how long?"

"I'd say about an hour and a half to three-quarters of an hour at 350. You have to check it every so often, you know."

"I know."

"Baste it. Don't let it dry out."

"Okay."

"Did you marinate it?"

"Yes, I used your recipe."

"Beautiful," he says, and we hang up.

Five minutes later the phone rings. "Did you remember to use whiskey?"

"Yes, I made sure I used whiskey. Thanks. Gotta go." We hang up.

Two minutes later the phone rings again. "What kind did you use?"

That dinner seems a million years ago. But it happened just before my father died. His life came to an end after a short and exhausting bout with cancer. I still can't believe he's gone.

I crave roast beef. But, I can't make it — I won't.

I knew his first birthday without him was coming up. I thought maybe, just maybe, if I didn't turn the calendar page to reveal May 1, everything would be OK. I'd be OK, he'd be OK, everything would be A-OK. Kind of like what the doctors said.

The day arrived, and the world was fine, great even. Everybody rolled through the day without a care, no big deal, like everything was just grand and hunky-dory. And I wanted to kill everybody for feeling so good on a day when I felt like I was dead.

Like a lost child, I wander up and down the aisles of a noisy supermarket. The fluorescent lights flicker above me. The creaking shopping cart makes my skin crawl. The meat department with rows and rows of red, raw flesh is almost sickening.

I overhear an older man speaking Chinese to his wife next to me. I think they're talking about chicken, but I can only make out a few words. The dialect is familiar. I just want to listen. The wife walks away, and he sees me lamenting over the beef. Smiling, he says, "You want a roast? You should go to Safeway. They're on sale."

For a second I feel something warm and soothing flow through my blood. It envelops my body like a flannel blanket, hugging my sides and holding my head. I smell whiskey! And then it's gone.

Tree

BY AIMEE PHAN

She would always tell them the same bedtime story every night about how she had met and married their father. She would sit on the floor in between the girls' beds and speak in a hushed whisper so they would have to lean in close to hear the familiar words they knew practically by heart.

She was a young schoolgirl in Vietnam. He was an American soldier who offered to marry her and bring her to America to escape the war. He had saved her life, and for that, she was always thankful. He had given her two beautiful daughters, and for that, she was always appreciative.

Sometimes, if it wasn't too late, she would go into detail of what it was like to live in Vietnam during the war. The inescapable echoes of gunfire and scraping bicycles that lingered in her ears. The pungent fragrance of rotten vegetables and sweat. The muggy, dusty air that often made it difficult to breathe and see. When the girls closed their eyes and listened to their mother's descriptions, they pictured the images they had seen on a *60 Minutes* Vietnam War retrospective, black and white visions that belonged in a movie and not real life. The vibrant shades of color just didn't apply to that world.

The girls loved this story when they were too young, imagining their father to be a modern Prince Charming sweeping the damsel in distress off her feet and into the happy kingdom of America. And their mother would silently allow them to believe that. She didn't think the girls were old enough to know the whole story yet. They were too young and they couldn't understand. She wondered if they would ever be old enough to understand.

So she left certain details out. She would conveniently forget to tell the girls that it had been an arranged marriage by a resourceful and manipulative aunt who had found an innocent soldier to fool. She would forget to tell them that she was already pregnant with her oldest, Sophie, when she first arrived in the States. She would forget to tell them how she didn't speak for the first six months here because she didn't know the language yet, and she was convinced that she was the first Asian woman that the people of Bozeman, Montana, had ever seen. She would forget to tell them that she forgot about her home country because it wasn't fashionable in Bozeman to talk about Vietnam, because it would inevitably include memories of the war. She would forget to tell them that she had once wanted to be a poet, that she had even been published in the newspaper in her hometown. But here, she was just a Vietnamese war bride, cowering behind the shoulder of her tough, fat American husband.

As the girls got older and became more enchanted with the Disney fairy tales they would see on TV, they stopped asking their mother to come to their room when it was time for bed. Their mother's story had become old and redundant. Secretly, their mother was glad. She had grown tired of telling it.

She hadn't meant to call her daughter's apartment that evening. She had been cleaning some closets and had come across some of Tree's old writing journals. She'd called just to find out if she still wanted them. Hanh remembered how Tree used to cherish her journals when she was younger.

But she wasn't there. Her husband Jack had answered the phone.

He told her that he came home on Monday to find her and all her clothes gone. He already tried calling her friends, and they hadn't heard from her either. That or they weren't telling. When he called her office, they told him she'd taken an indefinite leave of absence. The last time they talked was on Monday morning just before she was supposed to leave to pick up his dry cleaning.

"I've been wearing the same suit all week," he complained.

Hanh bit her lip fiercely before she could start screaming. It was Friday night, so she had been missing for four days. "When the hell were you going to tell me about this?"

When he didn't answer her, she slammed the phone down in anger.

She called Sophie despite the fact that it was almost midnight. She was probably up anyway because of the baby. Sophie answered the phone after the fifth ring. After hearing what her mother had to say, she was completely awake.

"Well, where is she now?"

"I was hoping she would be there with you. She always comes to you first."

"No, she's not here," Sophie said. "I can't believe she hasn't called me. Where the hell is she? What the hell is she thinking?"

Hanh told her everything she found out from Jack.

"Are you sure he's telling you everything?"

"Sophie!"

"Ma, there must be a reason for Tree to just up and leave him like this. I want to know what he did to her." Sophie and Jack had never liked each other, the only source of conflict between Hanh's daughters.

Hanh shook her head. "That doesn't matter right now. I just want to find your sister."

"Well, I can call some of her friends from high school. I know I have their numbers around here somewhere. . . . "

"Sophie, I want you to call me when you hear from her. Even if she says not to, please."

Hanh hung up the phone and reached over and turned off the lamp. She looked over at her husband who had been asleep the entire time. He could always sleep through anything. She watched his chest heave up and down with every deep snore he exhaled. She considered waking him but after realizing how he would overreact, she decided it could wait until the morning.

Realizing she wasn't going to get any sleep tonight, Hanh slipped from bed and crept out of the room. Her warm feet quickly darted across the cold wooden floor as she reached the end of the hallway and Tree's old bedroom. She closed the door behind her and glanced around the room briefly. She had transformed it into a guest room after Tree had left for college, but she still considered it her daughter's room.

Even though all the lights were off, the moon had imposed its presence into the room, shining brightly enough so she could see everything. Her eyes wandered around the room, trying to concentrate on something, anything. She finally focused on a framed photo of her daughters on the nightstand. It was her favorite picture of them, the one taken on Christmas day after Sophie's announcement that she was pregnant. Everyone had been so excited that day, especially Tree.

Hanh softly rubbed the pad of her index finger onto the glass of the picture frame. It was funny how she never thought of how different Sophie and Tree looked from each other unless she was looking at them in a picture. But they did look different, completely. If you didn't know them, you would never even suspect that they were sisters. But if you spent a few minutes with them, saw their intimacy, the kind of closeness that would make anyone feel like an outsider, then you would understand.

That had been a concern when the girls were younger, how different they looked. Specifically Tree. Although Jason never admitted anything out loud about it, Hanh had been worried for her youngest. While Sophie had her father's curly brown hair and hazel eyes, Tree had taken after her mother with her straight black hair and dark eyes. Hanh knew from her first few months in Montana that the people looked at her suspiciously, especially since the war had just ended and soldiers were only now returning to their homes in America. But the people of Bozeman looked at Jason as if he had brought the war back into their sleepy little town in the form of his five-foot-tall, non-English-speaking, pregnant wife.

Although at first hurt by the cold treatment she received from the neighbors, the other women in town and even her own in-laws, Hanh fought fiercely to be accepted. She spent the rest of her pregnancy with Sophie trying to master the English language. She learned how to cook American hamburgers and make pot roast. She killed her neighbors and in-laws with politeness and generosity until they could no longer ignore her. She was determined to make them comfortable with her presence and eventually they conceded. At least, it appeared that way on the surface. And while her English was almost grammatically perfect by the time Tree was born, she still couldn't get rid of her Vietnamese accent, no matter how hard she tried to imitate the voices she listened to on television.

But Tree faced a different kind of ignorance. Children didn't understand the subtlety of passive prejudice. If they thought you were in any way different, they would tell you directly and make you pay for it. And while Tree had always been very stubborn and self-righteous, Hanh could only hope that courage was strong enough to protect Tree from the children in the schoolyard who were already armed with the inbred bigotry of their parents.

If Hanh had known what Tree was going to go through as the only Asian-looking girl in her town, maybe she wouldn't have agreed to bless her youngest daughter with such a peculiar name. Sometimes Hanh wondered if it was her daughter's namesake that caused Tree more trouble than her mixed heritage.

"Why'd you and Daddy have to give me such a dumb name?" she once asked. They were in Hanh's station wagon, driving home from Tree's first day at kindergarten.

"I thought you liked your name." Hanh looked at her as she stopped at a streetlight.

Tree bit her lip and crinkled her eyebrows. "I thought I did, but now I'm not sure. Some kids at school said my name wasn't real. It's not a real name you give to a person."

"I think what they mean is that it's not a typical name to give to a person," Hanh said. "But you're not typical, Tree. That's why we gave you such a special name."

Tree picked at a scab on her knee. "I'm named after Gramma in Vietnam, right?"

Hanh nodded as she made a right turn onto their street.

"Does she spell it like me?"

"No, honey, she spells it in the Vietnamese language."

"But if her name's the same as mine, how come I don't spell it that way too?"

Hanh didn't answer right away. She really didn't know how to explain it to her. She remembered when she and Jason were naming Tree. When Hanh was first pregnant with Sophie, they'd had a heated argument over what to name her. Jason took advantage of Hanh's poor English to manipulate a compromise: They would name the first kid after his mother, Sophia, and they would name the second kid, if there was a second kid, after Hanh's mother. But now Jason said he was having thoughts over this.

"We made that deal five years ago, baby, things are different now," was his pathetic excuse. "Plus, I didn't know your mother's name. If I knew that was your mother's name, I never would have agreed to it."

"You were the one that came up with the deal!" Hanh reminded him. "And what's wrong with my mother's name, anyway? We named Sophie after your Mom. Fair's fair."

"First of all, I can't even pronounce the name, and second, it's spelled all wrong. She won't be able to remember that. I won't remember it."

"Thuy Anh," Hanh said very slowly. "Say it with me, Thuy Anh."

He didn't even try. He never did. He just gave her that slit-eyed, thin-lipped look he always gave her when he pretended he couldn't understand her.

They eventually came to a compromise: Tree. It sounded like part of her mother's name, but it would be spelled in a way that every Ugly American could understand.

"It's spelled differently because it's special," Hanh told her daughter, going back to her old argument. "Just like you're special."

But Tree looked out the car window and didn't seem to hear her. That was the first of many times Hanh would be trying to say something to her and Tree wouldn't be listening. Not exactly ignoring, just not really interested in paying attention. Somehow, that seemed to hurt more, the seeming indifference.

Hanh spotted Tree's Taurus coming up their driveway from the window. She met her daughter at the front door.

"What are you still doing up?" Tree asked.

But Hanh just stared at her daughter, not answering, astonished at how tired and disheveled Tree looked. Her dark eyes were blank and expressionless with heavy bags under them. Her normally shiny hair looked listless and dry, gathered in a low ponytail.

Tree saw the shock and pity in her mother's face and immediately wondered if coming here was the right thing. "You talked to Jack." She looked away when her mother nodded.

"Sophie and I have been up all night worrying about you." Hanh tried to brush a strand of brown hair out of her daughter's face, but Tree gently pushed her hand away. "Are you all right?"

"No, not really," she sighed. "Is Dad awake?" She walked past her mother through the doorway and into the living room.

"No," Hanh replied coolly, slamming the front door shut. The house shuddered in shock. "He doesn't know yet. Do you want me to wake him up?"

Tree was silent for a few seconds, contemplating this. "No, forget it. I think I've kept enough people up tonight."

As soon as they entered the living room, Tree leapt for the couch, sprawling her body across it as if ready to fall asleep right there. She shielded her eyes with her forearm, her face grimacing in pain, as if the mere effort of breathing was too difficult. Hanh wanted to comfort Tree, to gather her in her arms and gently squeeze the story out of her. But she knew Tree would never allow that.

Hanh went into the kitchen to make them some tea. She heard some muffled whisperings in the living room. When Hanh pushed the kitchen door slightly open, she saw Tree still curled up on the couch but now with the telephone.

"I'm sorry I didn't tell you earlier. . . . " Hanh could hear Tree whisper. "Please don't use that voice on me, that's all I need right now. . . . I've just had a lot on my mind. . . . I'm calling from Mom and Dad's. . . . No, you have your hands full with the baby, I'll just stay here. . . . We'll talk more tomorrow. . . . I'll tell you everything later, after some rest. . . . No, this is it. . . . I don't care what Dad says, he's not gonna talk me out of it. . . . It's over."

Hanh let the kitchen door softly swing shut and bit her tongue slightly, refusing to allow the bile and resentment to build inside her. She told herself it was irrational and childish to be jealous of Sophie, but it was hard. Hanh wanted Tree to confide in her. They were both awake, she was making tea, the stage was set for a great mother-daughter husband-bashing moment. It only seemed right that Tree should want to share with her. But it wasn't that way. Hanh couldn't make her talk to her if she didn't want to. Just like Jason.

Even though Tree looked like her on the outside, she had Jason's stubborn silence. No matter how much Hanh would nag, pout and threaten, they could clam up for hours. It frustrated her like nothing else, how easy it was for them to shut her out. She wondered if they ever knew how much it hurt.

She remembered one incident when Tree was in the second grade. The principal's office had called asking her to come pick up her daughter immediately. She had been in a fight with a third grader. The teacher on recess duty had seen a group of children crowding around the tetherball court. When the teacher broke through the crowd, she found Tree sitting on a boy's chest with her tiny hands gripped around his throat. The teacher had to literally pry Tree's fingers off the boy's neck and then drag her to the principal's office, twisting and howling.

But when Hanh came to take her home, Tree didn't say a word. Nothing in her defense. She just went upstairs to her room while Hanh sat downstairs trying to come up with a strategy to make her daughter talk. Hanh was sure that she would tell all to Sophie, but Tree wouldn't even confide in her sister. Sophie tried to reassure her mother that it would be okay, eventually Tree would confess everything.

She should have known all it took was for her father to come home. Tree had been waiting at the front window around the time Jason usually returned from work. Once she saw his car pull into the garage, she threw herself in his arms and sobbed the entire story. Jason told Hanh what had happened later that night. The boy had asked Tree what country she was from. When she told him America, he asked what country her parents were from. After finding out that her mother was from Vietnam, he told her that his uncle died because of her people. That a lot of Americans had died trying to fight for the Vietnamese because they were too weak to do it by themselves. That she was a slant-eyed, yellow-skinned weakling who couldn't fight for herself. So she tried to prove him wrong.

Hanh turned away from him so he couldn't see her. "Why couldn't she tell me this?"

Jason's hand went to her shoulder, but it didn't feel comforting. "She was scared that it would hurt your feelings. She loves you. Can't you understand that?"

Hanh didn't answer him. She kept her back to him and wished there were a window on her side of the bedroom that she could stare out of.

The principal called the next day and told them that Tree was suspended from school and could return on Monday. Hanh was relieved that she wasn't expelled. Jason was furious, though, and before he left for work, gave Tree a five-dollar bill and told her to have a wonderful day off from school.

"You're just encouraging her," Hanh told him as he was getting into his blue Chevrolet. "By giving her money, she's going to want to beat up every little boy who happens to insult her."

"I don't want our daughter to ever feel like she shouldn't stand up for herself," Jason replied as he pulled on his seat belt. "I'm proud of what she did yesterday. And so should you be."

She watched as he started his car. "I want to talk about this some more."

He shook his head, smiling. "Baby, I'm already late for work. We'll talk tonight, I promise."

Her eyes burned as she watched him back the car out of the garage and drive away. She used to like it when he called her Baby.

Hanh needed to go to the supermarket, and although Tree was reluctant at first, she quickly changed her mind when her mother reminded her she had five dollars to spend.

"Can I get anything I want?"

"We'll see, Tree." Once they entered the store, Tree immediately took off for the candy aisle, while Hanh made her rounds for vegetables and fruits.

When she was finished with her grocery list, Hanh headed to the candy aisle to find Tree. Her eyes narrowed when she saw Tree at the end of the aisle holding the hand of a stranger.

"Tree!" she called out, pushing the cart faster down the aisle. "What are you doing?"

They turned to her, her daughter and the stranger, an older Asian man, still holding hands.

When she reached them, she pulled Tree over to her side and glared at the old man. After getting a better look at him, she realized he seemed harmless enough, but she was still suspicious. Tree wasn't usually so friendly with strangers.

Tree tugged on her mother's hand insistently. "Mommy, is he one of our relatives?"

"Of course not! Why would you think that?"

" 'Cause he looks just like us."

The old man reached over and took Hanh's hands into his. "Good morning," he said formally in Vietnamese, although he couldn't contain the eagerness in his voice. "You must excuse me, I recognized your daughter as Vietnamese immediately and I was so excited to see a familiar face after all these weeks of living in this town. . . . "

Hanh hadn't heard Vietnamese for so long that she thought she had forgotten it. The old man introduced himself as Bac An and talked to her as if they were old friends. She marveled at how the Vietnamese words and phrases seemed to burst so easily out of her, having been dormant inside her for so many years.

While they were talking, Tree continued to jump up and down, tugging on her mother's hand and whispering questions for her to ask their new friend. She watched her mother carefully, noticing how her face had suddenly taken on this glow she had never seen before.

"Why don't I know Vietnamese, Mommy?"

Hanh pretended she didn't hear that question. She didn't want to tell her it was because Jason had convinced her that it would be better for the girls if they concentrated only on English so they wouldn't develop her unfortunate accent.

"It'll just confuse them," Jason had said. "They're Americans. Let them have their own language."

Now, Hanh wished she had fought him a little more on that. She always let him push her around.

He always thought he was right, just because he had lived here longer. "America's different, baby, we're fighting a different kind of war here."

Bac An and his wife had recently moved to Bozeman. They used to live in Boston but relocated to be closer to their daughter and her new husband. After a few minutes, Bac An invited them to come to their house for dinner.

"I'm sure my wife would love to meet you. Has she tried *pho* yet?" Bac An asked, smiling down at Tree.

"Do you want to try some Vietnamese food at Bac An's house?" Hanh interpreted.

Tree nodded. "Is it good? Have you tried it?"

Hanh could almost smell the beef broth, rice noodles and cilantro of her favorite Vietnamese dish. Her last bowl of *pho* was more than 10 years ago, back in Vietnam. "It's delicious Tree, you'll love it."

"*Pho,*" Tree repeated, trying the new word out. "Can Daddy and Sophie come too?"

Bac An looked to Hanh for a translation.

"She wants to know if her father and sister can join us later tonight."

"Of course they're welcome," he replied warmly. "What's your husband's name? What village is he from?"

"He's an American, actually, his name is Jason McKinnon."

Mother and daughter both watched as the man's face slowly changed from accepting familiarity to cold awkwardness.

"I see," Bac An replied stiffly, straightening up. He glared at Tree briefly as if just recognizing the whiteness inside her. "I'm sorry, but maybe tonight is not a good night for your family to come over. My wife and I — "

"I understand," Hanh said, deliberately ignoring a cardinal Vietnamese rule to never interrupt your elders. "There's no need to explain."

She grabbed Tree's hand and started to walk away. "Say good-bye to Bac An, honey."

"What happened?" Tree asked as they waited in line at the cash register. "What did I do? Why did he look all mean at me just now?"

"Don't mind him, Tree." Hanh knelt beside her daughter, pulling her coat up tighter around her. "He looked at you all mean because he's a mean man. He probably looks at everyone that way. You didn't do anything wrong."

"But isn't he our relative?"

"No, he's not. A relative would never do that." Hanh stood back up.

"I guess we're not going to have *pho*, huh?"

Hanh looked down at her daughter. She looked so disappointed and confused. For a brief moment, Tree had a relative, another person who looked like her, someone who could understand. And now, she didn't.

"How about this," she said, coming up with an idea. "I'll make *pho* for us. We don't need him, we can do it ourselves."

Tree gave her mother a doubtful look. "Do you know how?"

"No," she admitted, "but I'm sure there's a recipe somewhere. Do you want to help me find out? You, me and Sophie can make it our new project."

Tree beamed in response as she helped her mother put the items onto the conveyor belt.

Hanh promptly lifted the kettle as soon as it started to wail and poured the scalding water into two cups, watching as the tea leaves engulfed it, transformed it into a rich brown liquid.

Hanh brought the tea out into the living room and saw that Tree was asleep, clutching the cordless phone in one hand and a pillow in the other. She carefully set the simmering beverages on the table, walked over to the piano bench and lifted the seat. She retrieved the throw blanket she kept in there for chilly nights when she didn't feel like sleeping upstairs with Jason. Hanh took the phone out of her hands, pulled off Tree's sneakers and gently placed the blanket on top of her.

Hanh placed her cheek next to her daughter's and held it there for a few seconds. It was something her mother used to do to her.

Tree's eyes fluttered open.

"Do you want to go upstairs? I could make up your room."

Tree shook her head. "I'm fine."

Hanh smoothed Tree's hair away from her face, and she smiled in response. "I talked to Jack tonight."

Tree's smile faded and she looked away.

Undeterred, Hanh leaned forward and brought her lips close to Tree's ear. "I don't like him that much, Thuy Anh."

Hanh stood up and turned off the lamp next to them. "Good night."

"Mom?" Tree said, as Hanh started up the stairs. "Did Dad . . . did you ever think it wasn't worth it? Giving in all the time? Like you just woke up one day and realized he didn't deserve all you were doing for him?"

Hanh swallowed. "Do you want to have this conversation now?"

There was a long silence. "No . . . never mind . . . tomorrow."

"All right honey, good night."

Jason was still deep in sleep as she'd left him. Hanh slipped into bed next to him and after staring at him for a moment, grabbed his shoulder and shook him hard. He quickly bolted upright, his bedhead hair flapping as he looked around wildly. When his red eyes focused on Hanh, he took a deep breath and relaxed.

"What's wrong?" he asked groggily as he scratched his stomach and yawned.

"Tree is here," Hanh said clearly looking him in the eye. "She is downstairs on the couch sleeping. She left Jack. I know you like Jack, but you're not going to change her mind about this. I'm not going to let you."

Jason blinked a couple more times and stared at his wife. His face held on to the same confusion and perplexity she had grown to know and hate and love for so many years. He looked at her as if she was a foreigner, speaking another language.

"Huh?"

"Never mind," Hanh said in English, snuggling under the covers. "Go back to sleep."

Several minutes passed until Hanh could feel the sleep wrap around her easily, perhaps because this time, there was no snoring next to her to disturb it.

Circles

BY KLARA YEIJIN KIM

*** the bells chimed over the old doorway late last fall ... ***

i gingerly entered the korean grocery store. in plain sight there were the familiar apples and pears that contrasted with various types of gum, chocolate, and artificially fruit flavored sweets on the candy counter. i breathed in the heavy ginseng smell emitted from upstairs, where i could hear a dog barking.

as i walked in circles, i scanned the aisles for rice candy. i saw the store owner from the corner of my eye. he was a warm-looking old man who intrigued me with the wisps of still-black hair on his head and the deliberate motions of his hands. i grew hypnotized as he whistled a tune i couldn't recognize. the old man swept the floor in a circular motion that drew the dust and autumn leaves toward him.

"ahn yong ha se yo."

the old man greeted me in his native tongue, the one that i tried to speak at home in vain, as he swept the floor of his small shop.

i bowed my head slightly forward out of respect and awkwardly responded with my heavily accented but gentle response.

the old man beamed at me, happy to hear a young stranger speak his own language. he then directed what i considered gibberish at me.

not again. in my mind i rolled my eyes.

EXPLANATION OF CIRCUMSTANCES
OR
A SMALL POINT TO PONDER IN SPECULATION ABOUT THIS SHORT STORY

when i was little, my parents taught me to speak english and korean. as i grew older and started attending pre-school, my knowledge of korean words deteriorated at an alarming rate. by the time i reached first grade my vocabulary had dwindled down to almost nothing other than my name.

at first that's what my parents wanted for me. pause. they taught me english so that i wouldn't speak with an accent like other second generation asian kids. so i would fit in and be like everybody else. then they started to doubt themselves. they would peer at me closely to see if i was anything like them. to see if i knew who i was and if i was in touch with my heritage.

it is a sad and unfortunate fact that i am yet another example of asian assimilation into american culture. when i talk to people in my neighborhood, i can hear them talking about me in korean, thinking that i'm trying to be something i'm not and that i couldn't possibly know what they're saying. but i do know. i'm not as ignorant of my culture as most people might think. i may wear street-sweeping jeans, joke loudly with my friends on the El — to the annoyance of those around us — and occasionally watch Dawson's Creek to make fun of the characters' ineffectual relationships, but does that say anything about who i really am?

(you are now free to resume analyzing this meandering composition)

i remember being halfway through my circle as i said it. "i don't speak korean." i hoped a nervous smile would save me.

momentary pause

the old man's expression transformed. it changed from a look of familiarity to that of a man who viewed me as an american foreigner, a stranger. i turned from an insider to an outsider in that one moment. the tension between us couldn't have been blown apart by guided missiles aimed at hydrogen bombs in a pool of nitroglycerin.

i wanted to explain. i wanted to say that even though he and i couldn't speak the same language, we were still connected by our roots. he was a distant cousin of mine. i wanted him to know that language wasn't the only source of communication. i remember wanting so badly for him to understand.

something died inside of me that day.

he wasn't listening. it didn't matter.

extended pause

he wouldn't have been able to understand anyway. the situation we were stuck in wasn't his fault or mine.

language is important. without it, i strongly doubt that the human race would have plodded on as doggedly as it has. language can be manipulated to express so many things if one carries it out properly. there have been fleeting emotions i've wanted to share with others but couldn't put into words, thus causing a breach in understanding with people i know.

sigh

i reached the end of my circle and paid the old man's daughter for a pack of gum. i left just in time to catch a scornful glance from the store owner as i walked out the door.

*** the cold breeze that had swept through me
swayed with the bittersweet tones of the wind chimes ***

REALIZATION: circles are made every day. the curving paths lead you to where you began your journey. that way, you and others may begin again. perhaps something will change the second time around.

Order, Order:
What Really Matters

In Memory of Susana Remerata Blackwell, Veronica Laureta Johnson, & Phoebe Dizon

BY EMILY PORCINCULA LAWSIN

My kuya Bing, always the first to ring the coconut wire,
called me the other night, chomping his gum,
saying in his don't-you-know-*tsismoso* tone,

"Hoy girl, have you heard the scoops?
This crazy white man murdered his estranged wife today!
Right up in King County Superior Court!
          Yup, you know she was a Filipina.
It's all over the news here: KING-5, KOMO-4, KIRO —
(oh, you know they're not CBS anymore girl, lost their affiliate, uh-huh)
— anyway, even got it all over the radio and on the
cover of the *Times* and prob'ly the P-I tomorrow morn. Uh-huh.
          What? What happened?
Oh, ok, well check dis:
according to the po-lice,
ten minutes into closing arguments of their divorce proceedings,
homegirl's supposed-to-be-soon-to-be ex-husband
took a nine-millimeter semiautomatic gun from his briefcase,
          yes, girl, from his brief-case,
strode down the hallway where she sat,
and blew her,
her unborn fetus,
and two other Pinays
away —
right in the lobby of the King County Courthouse, girl!
          Yeah, she was pregnant. Eight months, uh-huh.
Baby died right along with her, mm-hmm. It's a shame.
He shot her like a madman —
once in her head,
missed her heart, and then
once in her stomach. Point blank range.
Then, to top it all off,
her two friends, who earlier had testified in her behalf,
huddled on the bench next to her, tried to come to her aid.

Dis fool wasted no time and silenced them too.
You know he is puti,"
                                my brother said, as if color here really mattered.
The next day, my birthday of all days,
my 71-year-old father taps the coconut wire,
after reading a *Seattle Times* report, and greets me with static:

"Well, you know, de paper says that he did not want a dee-borce,
he wanted it annulled so she could be deport-ed.
But she *claimed*
dat he had abused her,
beat her, you know,
dat he choked her when dey missed a ferry in de P.I,
one other time knocked her head in de sink,
beat her during only her first week here in de states,
that's why she left him then, wanted a dee-borce,
because he beat her,
but
we don't know if dat's
really true,
if he had *really* been beating her."

I shook the phone's receiver like ketchup from a bottle,
glared at it as if its voice had come from some outer space mustard
patch.
My gums dropping, falling.
"You been in the ship's boiler room too long, Pop.
Already lost your hearing
and now your mind," I mutter.

"Ha? What? I can't hear you. This gud damn phone, too much static!
Mommy, get me de other phone! Please, I said please!
Well, like I said,
we just don't know por sure.
What did you do for your birthday anyway?"
                                Papa said,
                        as if that *really* mattered.

Momma grabbed the coconut wire from her strange husband,
her mouth chewing rice and bagoong:

"Happy Birthday, anak. Oh, my baby's getting so big now."
"Mom, I'm — "
"Yes, yes, yes — you know, they interbiewed me on T.V. today."

THIS
is what eating with knives, forks, and shrimp paste makes you do:
Shake, shake. More ketchup from the bottle, please.

"What
did
you
say,
Mom?"

"Well, all those cameras come to the Community, you know, and we
have dat senior citizen dancing Tuesdays at Thursdays. No dancing-
dancing today, too many cameras — well de old pogies did do a
number — but anyway, dey just ask us what we think about de case.
You know Mimi, your Auntie Dolly's daughter, represent her as her
lawyer. Five minutes and she would almost got killed too, but she stay
inside de courtroom. Thanks be to God. You know, your Papa knew
her other friend dat died — "

"What
did
you
say on T.V,
Mom!"

"Oh, well, I just say dat it's really a shame. Dat Pilipina women are very
loyal to their husbands. Dat even if de baby was by a Black, he still
shouldn't have killed her — "

"By a what? You did not say that on television — "

"Well, dat's what dey say, dat baby was not his. Now de paper says it
was a Pinoy gangmember's dat molest her. We just don't know."

As if any of that *really* mattered.
"How could you say — "

"Well, dey ask me, so.
You know, anak, it's embarr-assing. Really.
What you call dat:
Dom-es-tic, Dom-es-tic, Dom-es-tic Vi-o-lence?
First there's Tessie, now dis.
They're calling her a 'mail-order bride, mail-order bride,' "

Momma murmured, herself a war bride from generations passed.
Had she forgotten the tsismis circles that once hounded her
and her friends?

How the province folk taunted her, called her and her sisters
"hanggang pier lamang,"
a "G.I. Joe's bride," married "up to the pier only"?

Still, Mom munched loudly on some mustard greens,
knives scratching her plate, saying,

"It's really embarr-assing. It's embarr-assing to us Pilipinos here.
By da way, how was your birthday?"

"Too
late,
Mom."
"Ano?"

"It's too late to be 'gud damn embarr-assed!' Ya'll should be pissed off!"
                    PISSED OFF, PISSED OFF.
Click. Deserted. At the pier. Ketchup from the bottle. Shake, break.
Gavel, pound.
            Order, *order.*
Order in and out
of the court. Please.
                        POW!
            Silence?
                    As if anything else *really* matters.

                                    — *1995, Los Angeles, California*

Cross Country

By Natasha Singh

"Ma, just check here," I said, pushing the school form beneath her nose. Ma was sitting at the dining room table, picking from a bowl of *dal mot*. She munched loudly.

"What's this?" she asked, reaching for her glasses.

"No! No!" I yelped, pushing her glasses further out of her reach. "Just check here!" Ma grabbed her glasses and slid them on. She read the form in silence.

Please check the appropriate box for your child
   ( ) Downhill Skiing
   ( ) Cross Country Skiing for Beginners

Ma said to me, "Reena, bring me a pen."

I raced to the kitchen and returned with a pen. "Check the first one, okay Ma?" I peeped over her shoulder and then snuck a look down her blouse. Ma always stuffed bits of paper and Kleenex down there and even had some paper sometimes sticking out of her petticoat. When I looked up, she had finally picked up the pen.

Ma hunched over the paper, then carefully placed a small tick beside the second choice marked *Cross Country Skiing for Beginners*.

"Ma, I think you checked the wrong box. You have to check the first one."

Ma squinted at the form again. "No. I checked the right one."

"But Maaaaaaaa! Everyone else is going downhill skiing and I wanna go, too. Ma, please, I have to go. I'm gonna be the only one in the whole school who's in cross country skiing. Maaaa, please!"

Ma took off her glasses and put them carefully away in her case. She began to wave one hand in front of her mouth. "Get me some *pani*, this *dal mot* is hot!" I went into the kitchen and reached up on my tiptoes to get her a glass. I put it under the tap and then walked back to where she sat, careful not to spill even a single drop.

"Ma . . ."

Ma took a sip and then said, "Reena, you're only nine. I don't want you coming home with broken arms and knees. Oh, no, no, no. I don't want you involved in this skiing business. Already they want you doing these crazy things. You're still too small. *Chee!* Shame on your school! Have they no idea how dangerous these things are?" Ma was getting excited. I could see her munching rapidly, the *dal mot* being crushed between her teeth. "Acrobatics, acroshmatics, one day they want you in this, the next day in something else. *Hai Ram!*"

I scowled as Ma dipped her fingers back into the *dal mot*. "Crazy *angrezis*," she muttered. "Sliding on snow with sticks." She shook her head and munched even louder.

As it turned out I wasn't the only one in the whole school in cross country for beginners. It was worse. "Okay, cross country skiers, I want you to come up to my desk to pick up your forms to give to the secretary. The school has plenty of cross country skis. As for the rest of you who are going downhill, you know that you have to provide your own skis."

Mrs. Couture sat waiting at the front of the room, and our small group lined up at her desk. First there was Dennis, whom nobody liked because he was weird, then there was Snot-nosed Susan whom everybody made fun of because she wore the same clothes to school almost every day, and finally there was Russell, who was a dummy. At least that's what Mrs. Couture said every time he left the room. And then there was me. I tried to explain this to Ma the very first day I came home from skiing.

She was in the kitchen, and Papa was sitting at the dining room table looking through the *TV Guide*. I took off my snow boots and stood on my tiptoes to hang my jacket in the closet. If it weren't hung, Papa would not be pleased. I took off my mittens and placed them in the drawer and then came up behind Ma, who was kneading dough to make *roti*.

"Ma, I have to join downhill, okay?" Papa looked up. Ma's bangles jingled as she made the dough into round balls.

"Reena, I already told you . . ."

Papa cleared his throat. "What's this?" he asked Ma.

"She wants to go down big hills on sticks and kill herself. I told her no. Besides, the school gives them cross country skis for free, so it's easy for us. Last time they wanted us to buy you skates. Cost 100 dollars. . . . Where do they think we get the money?" Ma began to mutter, and Papa spoke up.

"Her skis are at school? Thank God." I looked over at him. He was now underlining his favorite shows to watch in red. His grey head was bent over the table. After some moments, he looked up from the table, glanced at me, and frowned. "Reena, you don't know how much money it costs to do all these things. You have to think not only of yourself but of others." I glared at Papa. He was always coming up with sayings. He called them proverbs. I waited. "As the sages say, Reena, life is 99 percent perspiration and one percent inspiration. Just focus on your studies and forget everything else. You're in school to learn and work hard, not to do all this other foolishness. We all have to work hard, you know, especially me and your Ma."

"Perspiration!" Ma laughed. "This one here," she said, pointing to me, "doesn't do any of the work I was doing at her age."

I glared at both of them. They didn't know how embarrassing it was to have skis with "Jasper Elementary School" written on them. Only people who didn't have their own brand new ski jackets and nice new boots had to use those ugly old skis.

Ma sprinkled flour onto the balls and then began to roll one into a flat circle. I watched carefully. Whenever I tried, mine came out looking funny, and often Ma would re-roll them into perfect circles again.

Papa yawned and I looked over at him. He was now looking past Ma out the window.

"Do you remember when we first came here?" he asked suddenly.

Ma looked up, troubled. She then looked down at me and said, "Yes, when we came, Reena, it was just like this. No one told me it would be this cold." She flipped the *roti* and I watched it quickly fill with hot air and swell. I reached out to poke a hole in it, but Ma pushed my hand away. "But you," she said, pointing at me, "you're used to this. Me, I still hate it." Ma laughed suddenly, and I frowned. I didn't know if she was laughing at herself or me. Yet as long as she was laughing, I thought I would try again.

"You never let me do what they get to do. Last year you said I couldn't go camping and last month I wasn't allowed to go on the field trip. I just want to do what everyone else is . . ."

Ma moved over to where her *roti* was baking on the *tava* and flipped it over. "Hah, if all the kids jumped off a bridge, you would be running to follow." I filled Ma's spot and began to tear off tiny bits of dough to roll into little balls. "Reena, how do I know what they're going to do, wanting to take you into a forest to stay in a little plastic house. For what, I ask you? These *angrezis* here. They want you to stay in strange places without your parents. We don't know what they'll do. Now if they wanted you to come to a party at the school, we wouldn't say no. At least people are there to watch and . . ."

"Ma, we always have people come with us, the teachers and . . ."

Ma shook her head. "These *angrezis*, they all divorce, kids leave their homes at 18. They don't know how to love their children properly. They're mostly all rascals. I tell you. When I was 18, I was still at home, happy, living with my parents, and if I was still in India, I would be living with them."

Papa looked up sharply. I bet I knew why. Once Ma told me that she had never wanted to come here or to even marry at all. She said that I would have been a different girl if I had been born in India. He said to Ma, "Why do you put that foolishness into her head?" He looked angry.

I made a face as I rolled out the dough with a rolling pin. "Everyone makes fun of me because I don't get to do the same th—."

"Who makes fun of you?" Papa asked.

I tried and tried to get the *roti* in the same round shape, but it came out looking like a baby cloud instead. "This rolling pin is broken."

Ma laughed. Papa repeated, "Who makes fun of you?"

"All the kids."

Papa cleared his throat and then sighed. "As the sages have always said, only monkeys fight one another." I frowned again. Papa was always talking about monkeys and sages. Yesterday when I was sitting in the sink in the bathroom, brushing my teeth, he told me, "Get out of the sink, only monkeys sit there."

Ma piped in, "Call them red farmers' potatoes."

"Maaaa . . ." She and Papa began to talk about money again. Ma didn't know that it hadn't worked. I called Nikki Reddmen a farmer's potato once, and she had laughed at me. During dinner, I told Ma she had to eat the baby cloud-shaped *roti,* but she gave it to me instead.

Midway into the week, our teacher, Mrs. Couture, made an announcement. "Okay, class." This was always her signal for big news. We waited impatiently. "We're having a day of shared skiing. Mr. Meesh can't teach cross country today or the day after. He's sick, so cross country skiers get to downhill ski for the day." I spied Susan, who was looking very happy. *Downhill skiing! I would get to go like everyone else!* We're just going to call your parents for their permission. So eat your lunches, and get ready to board the bus. Those of you who can't go can join Mr. Garcia's fourth grade class. She looked pointedly at our small group. I quickly bent my head, pretending to be reading. I knew Ma would say no. I went up to Mrs. Couture after the bell rang for lunch.

"Um, Mrs. Couture . . ."

"Yes, what is it, Reena?" Mrs. Couture pushed up her glasses, which always slid down her nose. We called her Owl Face behind her back.

"Um, my parents aren't home right now, so you can't call them," I lied.

"Oh." Mrs. Couture's eyes looked like bug eyes from behind her glasses. I stared at them. I bet she was an alien. "Well, tell me where your mother works, and I'll call her there. Oh, wait a minute, doesn't she waitress at the A & W?" I shook my head. Mrs. Couture took off her glasses and rubbed her eyes. "Oh, maybe I'm thinking of that Mexican woman."

I frowned. Ma didn't waitress! She cleaned people's rooms. She told me she had tried waitressing once when I was a baby, but her mean boss wanted her to touch meat, and there was no way she was gong to have meat hands—ever. "No, my Mom doesn't want meat hands, Mrs. Couture," I said. She just stared at me with her bug eyes. "Well, um, anyways, my Mom and Dad are gone for the day."

Mrs. Couture put her glasses back on so her eyes looked even bigger as she said, "Oh, well in that case, I'm sure it will be all right for you to go, won't it?"

"Yes, Mrs. Couture. My Mom really wants me to do everything." I nodded my head up and down.

We all crowded onto the bus. Even the other grade four class was there. All the popular kids sat in the back, and the ones that nobody liked sat in front with the teachers. I pretended not to see Susan, Russell and Dennis, who had all taken seats close to one another with the teachers. *Babies,* I thought. I made my way down the aisle, wishing someone would smile at me so I could sit beside them. But no one smiled or even moved over. I took a seat as close to the back as I dared, just so I could hear what they were saying. Pressing my face against the glass, I peeped out. I could see all the skis on the side of the bus. So many! I wished I didn't have to get rentals. All I wanted was to have new skis like everyone else. I frowned as I looked up and saw Nikki Reddmen coming my way. She waved to the kids in the back. "Where's my seat?" she yelled. They giggled and someone pointed to where I was sitting. She looked my way and before she could make a face, I looked down at my shoes.

"Reena, can you move your stuff?"

I pulled my mittens towards me. I wished I had brought my reader with me. Nikki jumped onto the seat, and my mitten fell to the ground. I reached over to pick it up, noticing her ski boots. I tucked my feet as far under the seat as I could, so that she wouldn't see my regular snow boots, which meant for sure that I would have to get rentals. The bus pulled away from the curb. We were on our way! Ma would never have to know.

"Reena!" Nikki's bubble-gum breath was close to my ear.

"Yeah."

"You want some gum?"

I nodded.

"Up your rubber bum!" she giggled. I hated that old joke. She turned towards the kids in the back. I opened my lunch bag. Ma had packed me a *roti* and some dried *channa*. She had also packed lots of mango pickles. Mostly, I ate lunch at home. It was only during skiing week that I had to eat a packed lunch. Usually Ma would always have something hot when I came home, and I would eat and watch *The Flintstones* with her. I wondered what she was doing now. Had Mrs. Couture tried calling her? I tore off a piece of my *roti* and put it into my mouth. With a spoon, I ate the *channa*. I was looking out the window. The bus was going higher and higher. Soon we would reach the mountain! Beside me, I heard Nikki sniff loudly.

"What's that you're eating?"

"Food," I said, scowling. She never minded her own beeswax, plus she was a show-off. Out of the corner of my eye, I saw that she was holding her nose. Ma should have packed me a sandwich, I thought, my face burning.

When the bus parked at the bottom of the hill, everyone jumped out, each kid running off with his or her very own skis. Only Dennis, Susan, Russell and I were left. "What are we going to do now?" asked Susan. I didn't know either. Looking around, I was amazed. I could see people skiing down those big hills way up high. Suddenly, Mrs. Couture appeared.

"There you are! I was worried you cross country skiers had gone off by yourselves. After you get your rentals, go to Mr. Brown. He'll be waiting outside for you. Now, follow me." I ran after her, and soon we were in the rental place. We had to wait in a long line, and I kept on looking at the clock. We had only a few hours up here, and everything was taking so long. We had to print our names and the name of our school on pink forms. Finally a man said, "Who's next?"

"Me," said Susan.

"Hey, you're butting. I was first!" I yelled. Susan ignored me and sat down on the bench. "Snot nose," I said.

"Brownie." From where I stood, I could reach over and pull her hair. I yanked it.

"Ouch."

Another man called out, "Who's next?" This time, I ran forward. I had to sit near Susan and wait while he looked for our boot sizes. I hated waiting. Ma always made me wait whenever we went shopping. I always had to stand quietly beside her while she spoke to Mr. Roychuck, the grocer. He was bald and spit when he talked. Ma always told him to give her a better deal on her groceries. "We have marked prices," he would say.

"Mr. Roychuck, this is too much money, give me this for $5 and I'll take it."

"Look," he would say, "I don't care if you buy it or not."

"Okay, you don't want me to buy anything from your store, then I won't come back.

C'mon, Reena." Ma would always grab my hand and act like we were going to leave the store.

"Okay. Hey," he would yell to the cashier. "Take $3 off her bill." He would point at Ma and shake his head. And the cashier would always roll her eyes. Why did Ma always ask to pay less money? No one else's ma did that. At least that's what Nikki Reddmen told me. She said her mother said Ma was acting like this was a backward place, and if she wanted to cheat people, she should go back to where she came from. Was Ma cheating Mr. Roychuck? If she felt bad about it, she never showed me. She was always happy when we left the store. She even said it was Mr. Roychuck who was a rascal.

"C'mon kid, how do these boots feel?" I looked down at the man who had his hands around my feet. "Fine." I would soon get my skis and get to go down that big hill!

"Hey, what are you doing in this group? I thought you were in the cross country group." I turned around, and there was Owen from the other class, who looked like he was a superman skier in his shiny blue coat. We were both standing outside. I had finally got my skis and boots on, but the ski people had to help us. On Owen's zipper was a ski pass with his face on it. I pulled my scarf down over my zipper so that he wouldn't see my day pass. "Nope. I'm a downhill skier, too," I said, nodding my head up and down. Owen looked at me doubtfully. And he glanced down at his skis, and then at mine.

"My skis are brand new, you know. My Dad just bought 'em for me. They're for racing," he said, matter-of-factly. I stared down at mine. How I wished I could have sleek new red skis like his. Even my boots were rentals! I wished the snow would cover them up. "Have you guys done those killer moguls yet?" he asked.

"Yup, we did 'em on the first day." Owen looked impressed. I drew a kitten face in the snow with my ski pole and then looked up, beyond his shoulder. There were people skiing down the hill so fast! We never went that fast in cross country. We just got to ski down a tiny hill for babies.

"Wow," Owen continued. "Mr. Jaco said we couldn't go down moguls on the first day. They're so easy, I don't know why they make such a big deal out of it. Did you guys get to go down Black Diamond, too?"

"Huh?"

"Black Diamond — the hardest hill, you know."

"Um. No, but I think we're gonna do that maybe tomorrow," I said, still staring around me. There were people in bright-colored jackets everywhere. I wished I had brought my sunglasses. Even Owen was wearing sunglasses around his neck, but his were fatter than any I'd ever seen.

"Why are your glasses so fat?" I giggled.

Owen looked down and then back at me. "They're goggles, you dummy," he frowned. "Where are yours? Mrs. Couture says we can't ski without wearing them, especially if it's snowing hard."

"I forgot 'em at home."

Owen looked around. "Have you seen Sean? We're supposed to go up the T-bar together."

"No." I was wishing Owen would leave. Mr. Brown was going to come soon, and

Owen would find out that I wasn't in downhill, and then he'd call me a big fat liar.

"Hey, Owen!" Owen looked up and then over towards a line of people. They were all waiting to get on a funny thing that moved up the hill. Two people sat on it together, and it moved slowly.

"Hey, look!" Owen said, pointing excitedly. "It's Sean, and there's Robin and Nikki." His face fell. "Awww, Sean's going up with someone else." He looked over at me. "C'mon."

"Where are we going?"

"I need someone to sit on the T-bar with me."

I frowned and then looked around. I could see Mr. Brown talking to Dennis and Russell. Snot-nosed Susan was there, too. She pointed in my direction. Mr. Brown put his hands to his mouth, as though he was going to call my name.

"Hurry!" I said to Owen, and moved as fast as I could on my skis toward the short line of people. *Downhill skiing is not so hard,* I thought, *Move your skis forward, and that's it.* I watched the people in front of us getting on. It looked really easy. It was our turn. A lady held out what Owen called the T-bar.

"We can't sit on this!"

"C'mon, hurry," Owen said.

The lady pushed the bar under my bum and away we went. My skis were going all over the place!

"Hey! Get your skis off my skis!" Owen yelled.

"I can't help it — I think I'm gonna fall off!"

"Just hold onto the bar, you dummy, and keep your skis together." I clenched my thighs together, and my skis stayed straight. Every time they veered towards Owen's, he growled.

I stared straight ahead. I noticed we were going further and further up. I strained my neck to find out where it ended. Were we going to get to the top of the mountain?! Ma would not like this at all. She didn't like hills.

Once she took me tobogganing. She let me go down the hill again and again. When it was getting dark and most of the kids were gone, Ma was nowhere in sight. "Ma!" I had called. "Ma!" I waited and waited. It was dark, and I was the only one left on the hill. I finally saw her. She was walking down the hill from behind all those trees. "Ma, where were you?" I shouted. She didn't say anything. She just grabbed my hand, and we walked home. I could tell that she had been crying.

When we got home, Papa said, "Where were you? I was worried sick." Ma sat down in the chair and cried. Papa turned to me and screamed. "What happened?" I shrugged, so he told me to eat some toast and go watch TV, but I heard Ma telling him how she had gotten lost up there in the hills and thought she'd never find her way home again. She said that if she hadn't held onto the bushes, she would have fallen and broken her neck. "My god," Papa had shouted. Ma said she would never go again.

"But Nikki's Mom climbs that hill all the time, and her neck isn't broken," I had said. So now when I ask to go tobogganing, no one will take me.

"Hey, quit moving so much!" Owen yelled. "Gosh, you'd think you'd never been on a T-bar before. Last time some dumb guy fell off and pulled everyone down with him, so you'd better watch it."

I tried to sit very still. I didn't want to fall off. Imagine pulling everyone off behind me! I tried to picture what it would be like and my stomach felt funny.

"Okay, it's gonna be our turn," Owen said suddenly.

I froze. I didn't know how to get off this thing! What if I let go and fell underneath? Maybe everyone would just ski over me! Owen lifted himself off the T-bar and skied away. I held on tight.

"Hey, little girl, you have to get off!" a voice yelled.

I was suddenly staring at a lady and man in ski patrol jackets. The T-bar stopped moving. I could see a man sitting in a booth looking at me. He shook his head. I turned around to look and could see people straining their heads in my direction.

I got up.

"See, that's all you have to do," the woman in the ski patrol jacket encouraged me.

I scowled. It looked so easy, but I could have been dragged off or something! The T-bar began moving again.

I skied towards where I saw a shiny blue jacket. Owen was standing with Sean, Nikki and Robin. Nikki was showing off. She thought she was the best at everything. "Reena, what did you do to make the whole T-bar stop?" she asked.

"Uh, I think the machine broke or something." I shook my head in annoyance.

I looked all around me. I was in awe. So many skiers whizzing past. Below us was a long and bumpy hill. I could even see the spot where I had stood talking to Owen! Everyone looked little. Beside that spot was a lineup for yellow chairs that moved in the sky! But Mrs. Couture had told us we weren't supposed to go up on that. And even further below, I could see the parking lot where our yellow bus had dropped us off!

"We're really high up!" I said. Owen frowned. Robin and Nikki giggled. "This hill is nothing, wait till you get higher." I didn't say anything. *I bet Susan wouldn't know how to go down this hill at all!*

"C'mon, guys, let's go for a run," Owen said. Robin pushed off on her skis. Nikki glanced down at my skis and then eyed my zipper.

"Only a day pass?" she said. I stared jealously at her ski pass and then looked down.

"I lost my ski pass, so I had to get a day pass for today." She looked at me doubtfully and my face burned. I made a face as she skied away. *Those dummies*, I thought. *I'll show them.* I could see the back of Owen's jacket as he moved from side to side. Robin and Nikki skied behind him. Placing my skis close together, I pushed off.

I picked up speed. This was easy! I was moving faster and faster. I could see Owen's shiny jacket as I was catching up to him. I passed Nikki, then Robin, and finally even Owen! *I bet they are jealous now,* I thought. I was faster than a speeding bullet, faster than Mighty Mouse. I was passing everyone! Gosh I didn't know it would be this easy. I was the champion skier, a famous flying princess, the best skier in the whole world and . . .

I was going too fast. I passed several people who seemed to be barely moving at all. I passed the spot where I had stood to put on my skis. I passed the place where I had lined up to go up the T-bar. Gosh, I even passed Snot-nosed Susan, Russell and Dennis, who were all looking at me with their mouths open. I heard Mr. Brown yell "Slow down!" Then I passed the crowds of people lining up for the yellow chair. They, too, were staring at me while I sped past. I even passed the cars in the parking lot. Finally I felt my skis slowing down, but it was too late. I fell, and that's how they found me. Mr. Brown came skiing towards me with Dennis, Russell and Snot-nosed Susan.

"Look, her ski tip is on her nose!" squealed Susan. I looked up at them and began to cry. It was true. My ski tip had bumped my face and was resting on my nose, which was now bleeding.

"Reena, I told you to wait for me," Mr. Brown said, "and this is what happens when you haven't learned how to parallel ski or even stop, for that matter! My goodness, you could have really hurt yourself!" By this time, a crowd had gathered.

It was the ski patrol people from the T-bar. One of them said. "That girl. We saw her earlier. I think you'd better take her into emergency, just in case."

Emergency! I had never been to emergency before! That only happened on TV. Mr. Brown pulled the ski tip away from my nose, and I began to cry harder. Then he picked up my other ski, which lay somewhere in the snow beside me. The ski patrol man picked me up. I saw that Susan was making a face. I bet she wanted to be picked up too, that copycat. Then I saw that Owen and Nikki were standing only a few yards up. "What happened?" they yelled. Quickly I closed my eyes and dropped my head. Maybe they'd think I was dead or something! "Hey Reena!" they yelled. I pretended I couldn't hear them.

"Hey kid, your friends are calling you," the ski patrol guy said. I scowled. How did he know I wasn't dead?

I sat in the emergency room. It was boring. No one was even there except for an old man reading a book. Mrs. Couture came in. She had a toilet paper roll in her hand. Looking at me, she tore off some and rolled two tiny cones, which she handed to me. "Stick one of these in each nostril," she said, looking real mean.

I stared down at the Kleenex. In each nostril? I bet she was an alien for sure. "It's okay," I said in my most grownup voice. "I think my nose is fine."

Mrs. Couture sighed. "Just do as you're told, Reena." I didn't move. And suddenly she came towards me, took the cones out of my hands and plunged each one into my nose. I almost started to cry.

"Goodness, now I'm going to have to call your mother about this as soon as we get back to school. If only you listened like everyone else, you wouldn't be in this mess. Next time, you—" Just then, Mr. Brown came in and said it was time for us to leave for the day.

"We're leaving already?" I asked. Most of my time had been spent in the line to get rentals, and now we were going home. It was no fair. Mrs. Couture grabbed one hand and led me outside, where the bus was waiting. I climbed in behind her. Everyone was mostly seated. I followed Mrs. Couture down the aisle, and everyone stared up at me, giggling. I caught my reflection in the big mirror at the back. I had two large tufts of Kleenex sticking out of my nose. I felt my stomach turn over, and my eyes begin to sting. I took my seat beside Mrs. Couture.

Behind me, I could hear Nikki's voice and Owen's, too. "Did you see what happened to Reena? She's a cross country skier."

"She told me she was downhill," I heard Owen say.

"Well, she's a liar," Nikki said shrilly. "Anyways, I saw them all this morning. Her group didn't even know how to put their own skis and boots on by themselves." I stopped listening and stared out the window, my face getting hotter and hotter. Mrs. Couture patted my mitten, and I pulled it away, refusing to speak to her all the way home.

When the bus dropped me off, I walked slowly back to my house. I opened the door quietly and saw Ma standing by the kitchen table. "Beti, I was getting worried about you. All this snow. How was your cross country today?" I jumped. Mrs. Couture hadn't called yet. I didn't say anything. "Look, I made you a heart-shaped *roti*, hot and buttered. A baby, just like you. Here."

Ma was standing there in front of me, her hand holding out the *roti*. I glanced at her and then at the *roti*. For the first time, I hated Ma. This was all her fault, I thought. If she hadn't made me join cross country, this would never have happened. If she let me do what everyone else got to do, then no one would make fun of me. If she could pack me sandwiches instead of *roti*, then . . . I felt tears in my eyes and looked away from her so she wouldn't see.

Ma laughed. "Why are you so grumpy today? Don't you even want the baby *roti* I made especially for y—." Just then, the phone rang. Before Ma could say anything to me, I opened the door and stepped back out. It began to snow harder, and I almost couldn't see anything. I moved farther away from the house, wondering if I should go back inside. I turned around, and in between the flakes I thought I could see Ma peering anxiously out the window. It began to snow even harder, and I could no longer see her, nor she me — a wall of whiteness stretched out between us.

Tired

By Maiana Minahal

Not demon nor god
　　　　just my tired father
　　　　　who snaps off the useless bulb
　　　　　　burning above me.
　　　　　　　Home from another night shift
　　　　　　　at the machine shop,
　　　　　　　　grimy at midnight,
　　　　　　　　he finds me
　　　　　　　　　half asleep,
　　　　　　　　　　face down in a book, tired
　　　　　　　　　　from trying to cram
　　　　　　　　　　too much in one night.
　　　　　　　　　　Too young, he thinks,
　　　　　　　　　　to work so hard.
　　　　　　　　　　But he wants me to work hard,
　　　　　　　　　　and ace this American country.
　　　　　　　　　　His footsteps fade away
　　　　　　　　　as I try to shake off sleep
　　　　　　　　　to tell him,
　　　　　　　　　no American dream drives me,
　　　　　　　　but fear,
　　　　　　　fear of failing to conquer words
　　　　　　I don't
　　　　　understand.

Watermelon-Heads

BY JOYCE S. LIU

When I was a kid, I got the idea ingrained in me that my father wanted a boy. Unfortunately, my mother bore him two little girls instead, me and Winne. Nevertheless, my father never stopped wanting, or even trying, to have a boy. This thought first occurred to me when I was about five and Winne three. We were in our little North Hollywood apartment one evening when Dad began taking pictures of the four of us after dinner. Dad wanted Winne to take her shirt off. I remember him pleading, "Here Wei-pee, you be a boy like me." Horrified, she cried and protested, tormented that she couldn't be a girl like Mommy and me. I said nothing. But my father was too charismatic and succeeded in getting his desire. He tickled her into shrieking hysterically and wiped away her tears. In the pictures, you can see that her eyes are still red and swollen, but she's beaming like crazy, her black eyes shining with laughter and gleaming with forgotten tears. She is reclining on the rocking chair, her soft, round body poised in a coy and rather seductive manner for a three-year-old. She is naked from the waist up; a pair of tiny, red cotton shorts clings to her bottom for dear life.

That was just the beginning. There were many other instances that seemed to shape and support my theory that Dad always wanted a boy. When we needed new shoes for school, he went out and bought us soccer cleats.

"Dad, they're ugly!" we protested in horror.

"What do you mean? They're great!" He looked at them with uninhibited admiration, secretly coveting a pair for himself.

They were horrible, all heavy and black with those awful spikes on the bottom. No way. They would not go with my sky blue cotton knickers and knee-hi tube socks at all. I would never hear the end of it from my friends at school.

There was also the period of time when Dad was the official haircutter in the family. (I was eventually forced to take over his position and learn all of his coiffing techniques and stratagems, when I came of age. But that belongs in another story.) I think my father must have really wanted a boy then. He kept our hair very short, in the shape of your typically uneven bowl cut. My mother called us *shigua toa,* or watermelon-heads. Winne and I really looked like boys then, especially me with my blotchy skin and boyish grin.

On many weekends the neighbors would see us raking leaves off the lawn or hosing down Dad's beige Dodge Dart and nod with approval.

"What fine boys you've got there, Mr. Liu," they'd say to him as they walked past our house with their dogs on their leashes.

"Thank you," Dad replied proudly, not bothering to correct their error.

These incidents left me vaguely uneasy. Amorphous questions concerning my identity were only beginning to take shape in my little mind. But deep down I was definitely a girl! One day, my mother brought home a pair of new panties for me. I was delighted because they were a special pair, with pretty pink and yellow flowers woven into rows of white lace sewn horizontally across the bottom. The material made me itchy, but I didn't mind. It was the only pair of underpants I had that wasn't 100% pure cotton and didn't have any holes in it.

"Now don't go to school and show everyone," my mother warned me the next morning as she dressed me.

"Of course I won't," I promised. But of course I did. When it was recess time, I shoved Kyoko, my best friend in Mrs. Abichandani's class, into the nearest empty stall in the girl's restroom and flipped up my skirt.

"See how pretty my underwear is," I pointed to her with huge satisfaction.

"Yes," she agreed. "And mine, too," revealing her lacy, frilly bottom.

I also remember playing with Gina who lived in our apartment complex in North Hollywood. We were the same age, but she didn't go to Rio Vista Elementary School. Instead, she attended a Catholic school down the street. One afternoon, she came over to play and said she had a new game to show me. We ended up lying on our backs in the hallway with our crotches exposed. I remember how the green, short-haired carpet felt rough and dirty beneath my young skin while we pretended to moan and kiss our invisible male lovers, touching ourselves sensually, reenacting the tender caresses and passionate kisses men and women shared on TV. I believe now that I innocently discovered my sexuality when I was five, although I didn't know it was sex then. To me, I was just playing with my friend Gina who lived upstairs from us. And it was comforting.

As the years progressed I struggled with my gender identity more and more consciously. I knew I was a girl, but I wanted so desperately to be a boy for my father. I wanted him to be proud of me and respect me and, above all, love me. So I did what I thought were boyish things. I made fun of the girls in school who wore dresses all the time and couldn't kick a ball in the air for their life. I burped and farted a lot. I even picked my nose vigorously and wiped the boogers on the wall next to my bed at night. Eventually so much mucous had collected and dried on the wall that my mother had to come and scrape it off with one of those single-edged spackling tools.

When I took a special science course designed for gifted children in the sixth grade, I learned about genetics and x and y chromosomes. A zygote with two x chromosomes indicates the female sex, while a zygote with an x and a y means male. I learned that women carried only x chromosomes in their eggs while a man's sperm carried an x or y chromosome, and that it was the man's sperm which determined the sex of a baby.

"Aha," I thought triumphantly, "it was all Dad's fault." I no longer had to blame myself for not being a boy. Trembling with excitement and a twinge of fear, I went home and informed him of the truth that evening during dinner. He was unimpressed and half-heartedly denied any sort of participation in the whole matter.

My anticipated triumph was denied me. Once again, I failed to gain recognition from my father. I began to feel invisible and slipped more and more frequently into depressive bouts of blame and self-deprecation. My adolescent's eyes recast myself as a mere offspring whose duties consisted of bringing home straight A's and washing the dinner dishes three times a week. The household code was "Do your duty for the good of the house and family." Why share your thoughts and emotions when you can share your labor? Dad never said anything to me as long as I did the dishes and brought home the A's. He rarely acknowledged my accomplishments, believing that they just came with my role as the dutiful daughter. But as soon as I slipped — like breaking a rice bowl or bringing home a B — the entire house would rumble with his rage.

I both dreaded and anticipated Parents' Night at school. I knew I was in good standing with my teachers, but what if there was something I had overlooked? Our house sat right across the street from Charnock Road Elementary School, so it was convenient for my parents to walk over there after dinner. I would crouch near my parents' bedroom window, which faced the side entrance of the school, and eagerly wait for my parents to return, watching all the other parents come and go as they learned about the progress of their children. It seemed like forever before my eyes noticed two familiar figures slowly crossing the dark street.

"Well?" I asked, sucking in my breath when they came inside. "What happened?"

"Mrs. Mullen said you and Hana are the two smartest kids in class."

"Is that good?" I asked doubtfully. I didn't know if I should be proud of that statement or try harder to outdo Hana so that I would be *the* smartest kid in class. I was insanely driven to be Number One in everything I did. Dad insisted. I became an overachiever *extraordinaire* and, to everyone's surprise and chagrin, spectacularly burned out by the time I was 15, a year after my parents divorced.

When my mother moved out of the house, my number of duties increased and I became the child-Mom in a house where my paternal grandparents, my father, Winne and my older cousin Young resided. Although my grandmother was the eldest female in the house, she had suffered two strokes within a week of each other the year before. *Nai-nai's* soul was trapped within a body that had essentially betrayed her; she could neither speak nor control her body's functions and movements. As a result, she wasn't much help at all.

Trying to juggle three jobs on top of maintaining a family, Dad decided that we three kids would take turns cooking dinner during the week. We almost always made the same meals. We ate little english muffin pizzas Monday nights, bacon fried rice on Tuesdays, spaghetti on Wednesdays, BLT sandwiches on Thursdays and Kraft's macaroni and cheese with ground beef on Fridays. Guess who cooked what which night? Sometimes I would get a little daring and make a vat of the Nissin instant wonton soup and add tofu and vegetables to it. *Yieh-yieh* cooked for himself and *Nai-nai* since neither of them could digest the spaghetti sauce or the Kraft cheese stuff. Dad cooked on the weekends. This routine went on for about a year. Then Dad remarried, and we kids no longer had to cook weeknights.

Perhaps I read too many fairy tales when I was a little girl, because *Hai-yen Lee* turned out to be the breathing incarnation of the wicked stepmother. She was the sister of one of my father's best friends in Taiwan, and I remember every bit of the journey we took there in order for him to find a new wife. My stepmother's Chinese name translates into *yearning for the sea.* Upon Dad's request, I chose an English name for her. *Irene.* A name that seemed beautiful, yet frosty, to me. And that's the way she was — cold, yet beautiful. Years later, I would joke with my friends that the name Irene was a truncated version of Irate Yet Serene.

Irene had so many faces layered on top of one another that only the most discerning eye could detect her true scheming self. My lonely heart was often duped by her saccharine smiles, and I fell prey to her many manipulations. She hated the life she had married into and complained bitterly about her poor fate. And yet she was the one who brought the bad luck with her when she entered into our family. We had a tiny orchard in our backyard that produced an abundance of juicy plums and sweet apricots every other summer. The year Irene moved in, a heavy weight fell over the house, and the Liu family luck changed. That no tree would ever bear another luscious piece of fruit again gave testament to Irene's bad karma.

Life in the Liu family became burdened with a heaviness that I could not quite understand or control. We grew so accustomed to the thick tension and stony silences that they became paradigms of normality. Yet internally each of us was suffering. Winne became more withdrawn and angry; only spiteful words ever rolled out of her mouth. She and Irene hated each other and would often engage in heated arguments. Cousin Young became more absorbed in his studies and eventually found peace in being a Jehovah's Witness. My grandparents lived out their lives quietly, dreaming of better pasts. Though their eyes would follow us around the house, they rarely communicated with us — only when they wanted a cup of hot tea or the TV channel changed to a Chinese station.

My father took everything in with his masked eyes and went to work every day without a word. Only when things were really bad between Irene and another member of the family would he speak. Amazingly enough, he encouraged us to resist Irene. He knew that she wanted all of us out of that house. He knew that she wanted her own procreated nuclear family, not to live in a house that was already occupied. And yet he refused, or so I thought, to give us up.

"Do not budge, or you will lose the war," he said to us.

But I was sick of fighting, for it served no purpose. Fighting only left everyone miserable. What was the point? I had to get away.

I first discovered freedom when I was in high school and learned to forge notes in my parents' handwriting in order to ditch class. My friends and I would ride the RTD bus over to Venice Beach and hang out for the entire day. We'd swim in the polluted water when it was warm and lie around on the sand — reading, listening to our Walkmans, eating chili and cheese hot dogs with the works for only a dollar. I cherished those moments of truancy with my friends and would often go to Venice by myself on the weekends. The locals came to recognize me and thought I was homeless, for I always wore an old shirt and torn jeans and carried around with me my favorite brown blanket from my childhood.

"Hey, you found a place to live yet?" they'd ask.

I'd smile and reply yes or no depending on my mood. I made up names for myself, and different ages and where I was from and what I was doing, and people believed me. They saw a young, raunchy girl and accepted her. I had nothing to prove to anyone.

During my moments of refuge at Venice, I began to make sense of my unhappy life. I came to remember and discover things about my parents and especially about myself. I began to distinguish between those things that were expected of me and those things I could realistically do and be responsible for, realizing somewhere in the midst of much psychological emotional trauma that I was indeed a good person with a lot of potential for growth and wisdom.

Eventually my father did have a son. Oliver was born when I was 17 and preparing to go to college. There was much rejoicing at his birth, and we still celebrate the joy of little Oliver's life. But beyond this small, precious gift there is only more hardship and sorrow for my father and his second wife. Strangely enough, I no longer feel responsible for their pathetic lives; I am no longer connected to my family in such a metaphysically destructive way. The first time I returned home from college, my step-mother greeted me by declaring that I was no longer a member of the household, that I was, instead, a mere guest in her house.

My proud and injured heart left the house at 3580 Bentley Avenue four weeks later and has not returned since. Even today, the stain of her words cannot be wiped away from my heart.

I used to hide in the mirror when I was younger. There was no place else for me to go. My parents were too strict. In my reflection I would see another Joyce — one that smiled knowingly at me and spoke of blissfully rich and promising days to come. She and I would chat the night away or carry on staring contests until our eyes got too droopy to focus. Occasionally I would lean my face against the surface of the mirror, trying to synchronize my breath with that of the other Joyce. I even tried catching her breath, believing that if I did so, we would switch places and I would become her. All I ever captured was disappointment when I realized that I was still in my bedroom. I suppose I watched Lewis Carroll's *Alice in Wonderland* on TV one too many times.

My reflection has been one of my closest friends, from the first moment I discovered her in my mother's bedroom mirror through my years in high school and even throughout college. These days the only mirror in the house measures one-and-a-half by three feet and stands about six feet off the ground. It gets hard to stand close to it, because the bathroom sink gets in the way. But I don't mind. I don't need it as much anymore. Plus, I feel less vain this way.

Words for Angela Carter, Dead at 52

BY PADMINI MONGIA

I, an old woman,
with wrinkled female dugs
thick milk in my eyes
years of extra flesh loose on my arms
and smells that have ripened over ninety years,
speak

In my youth I wore flowers,
champak around my wrists and neck,
fragrant tight buds
two-hour creamy before wilting.
No, I am not that tainted flower my moment past.
My scent is stronger now.
Odors of ninety years
wind around me like gloom.

Oh
    I am a mad woman
    I lived in a shoe.
    I killed all my children
    I knew what to do.
Come, smell the blood:
Is it not heavy like a summer bloom?
Layered thick slow.
Shall I thread it as a garland
weave it into a dream
wrap it around as a cloak?

Better dead young,
before your own odors choke.

champak: jasmine

From War to Welfare

BY FAM LINH SAECHAO

Whenever I hear people talking about welfare reform in the news, it's always someone who has never been poor. That's why I need to tell my side of the story. My family came to this country as refugees from a war we did not create. Both my grandfather and my father were killed by land mines in Laos, and like most Laotians living here in the United States, the rest of our family had to leave because of our loyalty to the U.S. government during the Vietnam War. We didn't come to the United States to get welfare. We came because we had no choice.

When my grandfather and father were killed, we didn't get any veterans' benefits like the families of U.S. soldiers. Yet they gave up their lives just the same. The only thing that was offered to us was to come to the United States.

I was six when we landed in Oregon. I didn't really understand what was going on. My family struggled just to be together. Mom was stressed out because she couldn't speak English, and my brothers and sisters were really small. The only way for us to live was to get on welfare. Mom wanted to get a job, but the kind of training available to her was only for low-paying jobs like cleaning rooms at cheap hotels. The pay was low, and there was no health insurance for her or for us kids. She thought it would be better to stay on AFDC so that if we got sick we could at least see the doctor. Also, if she worked, there would be no one at home to take care of us.

Later we moved from Portland, Oregon, to Richmond, California, so that we could be near our other family members who had survived the war — three uncles, three aunties, and 11 cousins. We helped each other by combining three families to live in one house. We had 16 people in the house. We didn't have a car, so the nice people at the First Baptist Church of Richmond (with a congregation of 1,000 lu Mien people) drove us around.

At the beginning of the month we would have enough to eat, but when the middle of the month came around there would hardly be any food. We would eat old vegetables and meat chopped up so small we could hardly taste it. We wore clothes donated to us from the Salvation Army or Goodwill. Now I think back and realize that those clothes were pretty raggedy, but we were so thrilled to get "new clothes."

Today my Mom has a job making jewelry, candles and incense. She has a good wage and good benefits like health insurance, and we get to eat every day. My brothers, sisters and I are now old enough to watch out for each other. But we wouldn't have made it if AFDC had not been available to us when we were struggling. I want people to know that being on welfare is like when you are almost drowning in the ocean and someone throws you a life preserver. It's not a good way to live, but it helped us survive.

Here is another side of my family story. I have a Grandma who is now 69 years old. She has been trying to learn how to read, but she has a really hard time. In Laos, she never went to school. The Iu Mien language was not a written language. She needs to be able to pass the citizenship tests or she will not be able to get SSI. SSI is not much money, but those checks are my Grandma's life preservers. We help her whenever we can. When I listen to the older people in my community talk about losing their checks, they talk about asking the U.S. government to ship them back to Thailand so they can die near Laos, or they talk about suicide. They feel like they no longer have a life preserver to hang onto.

Before my Grandpa died, he used to talk about a place where there is a lot of happiness and everyone has enough to eat and a house to live in. I think my grandpa was talking about the United States, but I'm not sure. To me, he is talking about what a democracy should be.

Democracy to me means that the government cares about us and represents us. But now I'm confused. It looks like the elected government officials care more about rich people who give money to their campaigns, but those people don't make up most of our society. People like me and my family make up most of this country, yet we don't have a voice. We don't get to tell our side of the story. My hope is that these politicians hear my story. I hope that they listen with their hearts, and understand that a life preserver is often the only thing that separates life and death.

Friends Before Family

By Satomi Fujikawa

"*O*baachan, *Obaachan!* I want that one!" *Obaachan* means grandmother in Japanese. With a wide grin, my Grandma picked out a new purse in my favorite color, hot pink, and handed me the money to pay for it. I rushed to the cashier, grasping the purse as if it were already mine.

"You like it, Asako?" she asked as I walked out of the store, showing off my new purse.

I always felt like *Obaachan* favored me the most. She taught me how to ride a bicycle and how to play rock-paper-scissors, and she always listened when I played the piano. Even when she was losing her hearing, she told me how much better I was getting.

Years later, I hardly had time for her, although she was once my best friend. I was too busy studying for exams, going shopping with my friends, or trying to catch the attention of the guys in my high school. She was just another family member, and I began to think my friends were more important.

When my sisters and I found out that *Obaachan* had cancer and might die soon, I was shocked. "*Obaachan?* No, it can't be." A month later, my parents decided to put her into a hospital across the Bay in San Francisco, where the doctors could look after her more closely. My sisters and I went to see her every week to find out how she was doing. We went partly because my parents forced us to, but another part of me felt guilty for not having spent more time with her when she was well.

"Asako," my mother called after me as I grabbed my coat from the kitchen chair on the way out. "Don't forget that we're going to San Francisco when you come back."

"Okay, Mommy."

I wouldn't pass up a chance to go see Grandma. Every visit was important and reminded me of how much I missed having her around the house.

At lunch period, I found my friend Julie waiting for me by my locker. She had some good news to brighten my mood after I received only a satisfactory grade on an essay I'd thought was my best yet. "We're all going ice skating after school."

"Really?" I loved ice skating. "I want to go, but I can't."

"Why not?" Julie asked, hoping to persuade me. "You have to come. Guess who's going to be there."

"Don't tell me. I don't want to know if I can't go." I bit my lip, and then I gave in. "Who's going to be there? Just tell me."

"Greg. And his friends. They told us they're going to be there." Julie looked right at me. "You *have* to go, or he won't notice you."

I dropped my books inside the locker. Greg was going to be at the skating rink! "No," I whispered. I couldn't miss going to see *Obaachan*. "I can't go."

"Can't you just ask your parents to take you tomorrow?"

I tried to convince myself that I needed to go skating. "I'll talk to them."

My mind was spinning from thinking over and over about what I should do. In one of my classes, the teacher called on me to give an answer, but I was so intent on deciding what to do that I didn't hear her until my friend poked me. By the time I figured out what the teacher was asking me, the whole class was laughing at me.

Finally I got home. Walking through the kitchen door, I made up my mind. Going to San Francisco was important, but friends were important, too. And I hardly ever got to see Greg. I just couldn't miss this chance.

"Mom, can I go ice skating?"

Mom looked up from the flowers she was arranging. "When?"

"Now. Julie can take me there."

"You don't want to go see *Obaachan?*" I knew she was going to say that.

"But this is important."

She was silent for a few seconds. Then she spoke. "Okay, if you can get a ride home. I'll just have to tell *Obaachan* you couldn't come."

"Thanks, Mom!"

If she had said no, I would have had an excuse not to go ice skating. Now I felt guilty. When the telephone rang, I jumped out of my chair. "I'll get it." I was still debating about whether I should go or not.

"Hello, Asako?" It was Julie. "So you can go?" she asked hopefully.

"Yeah. My Mom said I can go," I replied uneasily.

"Great! When do you want me to pick you up — in 10 minutes?"

I hesitated. Then, when I was about to agree that she should pick me up in 10 minutes, I stopped myself. "Not today. I'm not going."

"Why not?" she shrieked. "Your Mom said you could!"

"I just need to see my Grandma today. I'm sorry."

"Oh, all right. But you're going to miss Greg."

"He can wait. Besides, he doesn't even know me."

I breathed deeply. I had passed up a chance to go ice skating and to talk to Greg.

On the way to San Francisco, I was plagued with doubts. Should I have gone with Julie? But when I arrived at the hospital room, I knew I belonged there. I knelt next to the bed and stared at the motionless body on the mattress.

"She died about an hour ago," my sister said. She had heard from our Dad, who had heard from the nurse.

A tear started forming in my eye. While I was trying to decide whether to come to the hospital or not, *Obaachan* had passed away. To know that I wasn't there to say goodbye made me cry. I stepped outside the door and leaned against the wall. She had been such a big influence in my life. Without her, I don't know where I'd be right now. She had done so much for me, and now I couldn't even pay her back.

When I returned home, I called Julie to see what had happened at the skating rink. She told me that it was fun but not as great as it would have been with me there. I told her that my Grandma had died, and she comforted me as much as she could.

I was tired that night. As soon as I hung up the phone, I went to sleep. When I got up the next morning and went downstairs for breakfast, I was surprised to see Julie in the kitchen, talking to someone. When I looked more closely, I saw who was with her — Greg. *What is he doing here?*

"Hey, Asako," Julie said as she came up to me and hugged me. I was too shocked to speak.

I couldn't stop staring at Greg. "What . . . what are you doing here?"

Greg stood up and came over to me. "I heard you couldn't come ice skating yesterday because your Grandma died. I'm sorry about that. I made Julie bring me here to see if you are okay. I know I felt really bad when my Grandma died."

"I was really surprised. She looked fine the last time I visited her." I wiped away a tear.

Julie nodded. She pulled out a chair for me. "We just wanted to see if you are okay. I'm sorry I tried to make you come skating with me. I mean, your family's more important than ice skating anyway."

"It's okay, I'm fine."

I looked down at my tattered clothes and remembered my half-combed hair. But then I realized that they cared enough about me to come over. Sometimes, friends seem like all you have in life. But it's important to remember that family should come first. Whoever is truly your friend should know that and support you through both sad and happy times.

Kuv Txiv (My Dad)

BY MEE CHA

What can I say about old folks or your parents? They're annoying, they always want you to follow their rules, and they're just here to ruin your life, right? Well, not all the time. For example, Who put clothes on your back? Your parents. And who put food in your belly? Your parents. See, so parents are not that bad.

You go through life spending very few minutes with your parents. As far as you know, you never seemed to have shared a memory with them, but there is a time, maybe just once, that you spent with them and remembered it. It could have been a picnic, a family's day out (or in), or just spending Christmas with them. As for me, my Dad spent his time doing other things and spending time with my other family members, and not really with me. So, I can be a pain in the butt sometimes for being jealous, but I do remember something, and it was when I almost lost him (my Dad).

It has been 40 days since it happened. The symptoms were pretty visible. My Dad was taking in breaths as if he could not breathe, and he was sweating. It was in the early morning, nearly 7 a.m. I was getting ready for school, and so was the rest of the family. My Dad could not take it a minute longer.

"Call for an ambulance," he demanded.

"Yes," I answered rushing to the phone.

"Everyone go to school. Mee will stay. I don't want any of you guys getting all worried. It's not much," my Dad explained.

I dialed the number 9-1-1.

It seemed to have taken forever for the operator to pick up, and when she finally did I had to wait a billion times before I could reach someone important. I gave the lady my name, my address and my phone number. I described the symptoms, and she told me to wait for the ambulance and check on my father's breathing. The phone call then ended.

I rushed to my Dad's room and checked on him like the lady told me to.

"Come on, what's taking so long?" I whispered to myself running outside to check for the ambulance. My sisters had already gone to school with my cousins. When the firemen arrived, I ran to them, showing them the way to my sick father. They rushed in after me and saw my father.

"How is he doing?" the first fireman asked.

Translating for my father, I reply, "He says he's having a hard time breathing, and his chest hurts."

The first fireman checked my father. "Blood pressure? Okay. Temperature? Fine." He informed everyone there. "Well, he doesn't seem to have anything wrong with him," the first fireman said. "So, we'll be leaving now."

What? I thought. "Ho-hold on. Are you sure?" I asked.

"Yeah!" the first fireman shot at me. "What do you want?"

Whoa, I thought. What is he doing giving me an attitude. Isn't he supposed to be here to help me, not make it worse?

I asked my father what he wanted to do, and he said he wanted to go to the emergency room. I translated, "My Dad wants to go to the emergency room."

"Okay," the second fireman asked calmly. "Which one?"

"The one on 30th and J streets," I replied.

The men brought my father out and put him on a stretcher.

My head turned back and forth to listen to the men talking. They were not making any sense. They were talking so fast, it made me feel a bit dizzy.

The men rolled my Dad outside and into the ambulance. I walked and followed. I was about to climb in after my Dad when . . .

"Where do you think you are going?" the man asked me blocking my way to my father.

My head searched over his shoulder looking at my father making sure he was all right.

"Where do you think you are going?" the man asked again, even louder and blocking the door to my father even more.

What am I supposed to do? I can't reach my Dad, I thought.

"I'm going with my Dad!" I demanded with an angry face. My fists were rolled up ready to swing out if this man objected.

"All right," he said waving his finger in my face, "but you'll have to sit in the front." He pointed to the passenger seat.

What? The passenger seat? I thought. What about here with my Dad? I stood there staring at my father. Better move it or you won't be going, I told myself.

I walked to the front passenger seat and sat still. My Dad was in the back with the other ambulance man. My Dad was still having a hard time taking in breaths. We drove, but with not extra speed or any sirens on. We just rode, and it was quiet. Why are we moving so slowly? I thought. My father needs to see a doctor and now! I thought angrily.

We arrived at the ER, and they took my Dad in. I sat with him. They took his blood pressure and checked his temperature. The doctors also did a scan on him. The ER doctors checked him. They gave him medicine and drew some blood. Everything was happening so fast. I couldn't focus right anymore. I sat there — actually, I stood there — and answered all the asked questions and translated throughout the whole scene. Then the commotion died down, and it was just me and Dad, Dad and me. I sat by his bedside as he slept, and I was frightened.

Am I losing my Dad? I asked myself. So clueless and without an answer. Dad, are you all right? I asked myself. Yes, of course, you are. I answered my question. What's going on here? I asked. My Dad is going to be all right. He'll be better just like the fireman said. He was all right, right? Then why does he look so sick and weak? I lost myself there with no answer.

"Miss," someone said interrupting my thoughts. "Can I speak to you?"

"Yes, of course," I said quickly, not sure if she understood.

"Can you come with me?" she asked me.

And leave my father alone? No, I thought. What about my Dad?

"He'll be fine," the nurse said answering my question that ran through my mind.

"Okay," I mumbled and followed her through the curtains.

I filled out papers that said that the results would be sent to my father's primary doctor, and I was his translator. After this, I rushed back, scared something had happened to my Dad, but he was sound asleep as I had left him.

I sat still next to my Dad. Tears started to blur my eyes. What do I do? Are you all right, Daddy? I need to call home. Why didn't I bring my wallet? What's wrong? Is everything all right? Daddy, are you all right? I thought and thought. What will I do?

I sat next to my father, alone in the empty section they put us in, and then as I glanced at my Dad, his eyes opened slowly. With a tear in his eye, he whispered, "Mee, when I leave take care of the family."

"You're not going anywhere!" I told him.

My Dad smiled weakly and fell asleep again. I sat and waited as the hours went by. Three hours later my cousin came in.

"How's your Dad?" my cousin asked.

"He's sleeping right now," I replied.

"Your mom's outside in the lobby. Go outside. I'll be here," he told me.

I looked at my sleeping father. No, I thought. I don't want to leave him. Not without my supervision. My heart was racing. No, I thought. You leave. I want to stay.

He looked at me, and I knew my cousin needed to talk to my father alone.

I walked out of the curtains and after several wrong turns I finally reached the lobby. I saw my mother there in the empty room. No one around. She sat in the third row, slumped down and hopeless. I walked to her and put my hand on her shoulder. She turned and faced me with a weak smile. I went and sat next to her. After several minutes, I broke the silence.

"Dad's sleeping right now," I told my mother.

"What happened?" she asked.

"Nothing much. Just a few tests, scans and x-rays."

"Okay," she replied.

I sat there, what's my Dad doing right now? I shouldn't have left him. I couldn't sit. I looked at a magazine but was unable to concentrate. My mind was only on my father. Will he be all right? Is he? Thinking only about my father, a question popped out of my head. Why did my father want me here, and not anyone else in my family? I don't know. I thought with no answer coming to me. Why? Why? Why? Why did Dad choose me over everyone else? Why? Why??? I didn't know.

It has been five weeks and three days, and I've finally found the answer to my question. Why did my Dad choose me to be with him in the emergency room instead of anyone else? I now know my Dad wanted me there more than anything and anyone else. He had spent a lot of time with my family doing something special with each person, except me. I guess, he saved the best for last, because that bed in the ER could've been his deathbed, and he wanted me there, with him and not anyone else. I am happy I was there even if it was for three hours only. Sitting next to my Dad's hospital bed and just being there was an event I would not ever trade. I was there when it could have been my father's deathbed. I am happy I was there just in his presence.

I will never forget what my Dad said, "When I leave take care of the family." It haunted me at that time for only a second because I knew my Daddy wasn't going to leave. I did not really tell anyone, except my mother. I'm glad that day happened, because if it hadn't, I'd never know why he never does anything with me. He just wants to save the best for last.

Thieves

BY CORINNE LEILANI DOMINGO

This always happens during lychee season.
— The Maui News, 6/25/98

Auntie's tree is stripped again.
They took all the red-skinned mangoes,
left the unripe still hanging
from bent branches. All we can do
is salt and pickle the green leftovers,
and wait for the sale at Safeway
for $3.99 a pound.

I've seen them come at night
with their large truck bed to catch the mango falling in thumps
and bruises, their boots heavy
on glinting ladders. The first time
it happened, uncle asked them to leave, but they chased him
bumper to knee, wagging a rake in his face
until he ran back to the house.
a week later, uncle found those mangoes
at a beachside fruit stand. He could tell
by their smell: *distinct Domingo, only*
our soil can grow. But the police
didn't believe and bought a dozen
for their wives to make salsa and pie.

This season, we were prepared.
When the tree grew full, uncle marked
each mango with paint, just like
our neighbor did with her backyard
papayas that were constantly snatched.
Uncle's legs dangled out of the leaves,
his torso streaked with blue, black,
yellow and white paint — he couldn't decide
on the color. There were so many mangoes
he was up there for weeks, took his saimin
and siestas sitting on the branches, sometimes
a mango for dessert.

Our neighbor found her papayas
sold at the swap meet for a dollar.
She had a glow-in-the-dark pen special
ordered from the mainland, and when she placed
a papaya in the shade, it shone.

I found the mangoes
next to plastic leis and imitation
conch shells at the International Marketplace
in Kihei, surrounded by tourists
grabbing and shoving. The sign said
Hawaiian Art, three dollars each,
and on the mangoes were paintings
to rival murals and mosaics added to hotels
for that native feel: smiling hula girl, sun
setting in Pacific, outrigger canoe, petroglyphs
of warriors spearing mahi mahi.

Uncle didn't care that tourists
bought the entire set of ten to display
on shelves back home, or that
the salesman claimed he was the artist:
The mango will rot in a few weeks,
and the smell is something they cannot wash
away with soap and water.

Forgiveness

BY REBEKAH FARRAH QIDWAI

My mother calls me today at six in the morning here in California to tell me that she had forgiven my father at *Hajj* [Muslim pilgrimage to Mecca]. That as she prayed for the long list of people she had compiled (some of whom she didn't even know — these were professional *Hajj* schemers, spiritual moochers who do anything to get their prayers answered in Mecca), my mother spontaneously added my father's name, a name that hadn't been in her prayers since the day she tried to kill him all those years ago. In the midst of thousands of Muslims, with God as her witness, she pronounced my father forgiven. There is something in her voice today, a sort of resiliency I haven't heard in a while. Despite my crankiness, I don't question her — I don't ask, "Ma, are you sure?" or say, "Don't get your hopes up. He's never gonna change." Instead, I choose to leave out the necessary warnings that have become protocol for situations like this. I am quiet while she speaks, realizing that she is not the same person today, sounding more like the woman she was before she became a ghost.

I try to look like my mother sometimes. Or I should say: I try to look like Shano, the woman she was before she became Shehnaz, our mother, before she married the man who burned through her life like a cigarette placed against the flesh and left her with a gaping hole in her heart that nothing but pain could fill. Funny, part sweetheart, part smartass, Shano.

I put Shano together myself from a variety of sources. I resurrect her using stories I've heard, old photographs and observations I've made of my mother during rare moments, like when she is on the phone with an old friend and laughing so hard I can see all the shiny fillings in her mouth. I try to wear my hair like her, tightly pulled back with my big ears sticking out. Or I'll buy clothes that match things she owned when she was younger, clothes I see in old photos or else are described to me herself in the few times she slips around the corner of her memory and tells me a story.

Like the plaid skirt I own. Looks just like the one she wore in a picture taken of her in Pakistan, 1974, a year after Zuby, my sister, was born and a month before they stepped on that plane for America. She's wearing a long brown plaid skirt, the kind that makes her look so, so tall, until she is the height I imagined her to be when I was younger (even though she's really just 5'4", the same height as I am today). You can tell she doesn't want the picture taken — she looks irritated and it's obvious that Zuby, who has on enough *kohl* [black eyeliner] to look like one of those *shadhi* [wedding] dolls they sell at Mina Bazaar [a market in Karachi, Pakistan] is about to cry. Shano has her hand out, as if she's saying, half-joking, half-serious, "Come on *bhai* [brother], not now." It has to be a brother who took the photo, though when I ask her which one, she holds up her hands and says, "Who knows?"

since all of her brothers, like most Pakistani men, played around with camera-shameras.

Her clothes aren't fancy or anything. Shano's family was pretty poor, so she and her sisters had to sew their own outfits, of which she owned only four that she had to wash and wear on a rotating basis. She's not like the other aunties here in America, who laughingly tell stories of calling servants *"bandhirs"* [monkeys] and playing jokes on rich old grandfathers at family vacations to Murree [a resort town in Pakistan]. No, Shano's family was "poor, but respectable." Her father was a civil engineer who was never able to find steady work after the family moved to Pakistan during the bloody partition of 1947. The irony is never lost on me whenever I hear about this. A newly born nation ravaged by war and starving for infrastructure could not employ a planner, a civil engineer. I wonder if that is the real reason my grandfather couldn't work for all those years. In my dreams, I imagine that he is desolate, unable to work with a land unfamiliar to him, a land carved like flesh by men hundreds of miles away, men who never had to witness rivers filled with blood and mountain-sized heaps of arms, legs, breasts.

They were an average family, hard-working with just enough *dheen* [Arabic term literally meaning "religion"]. During those lean years even religion was practically measured by the spoonful. Shano was the fourth of five children, two girls, three boys. With her buck teeth and not-so-fair skin, she was not considered pretty, especially next to her sister Zeenath, Pakistan's own Marilyn Monroe (or so the family thought). Shano was never thought of as beautiful, and some rude relatives even called her ugly, but everyone agreed: Shano was the nicest and definitely had the biggest heart. It's hard for me to see my mother that way. The woman I know yelled at me whenever I cried during sad movies or even sadder stories when I was younger, lecturing me that life was filled with pain, so there was no use crying over things in the past. But when she tells me the same sad stories now, and sees tears come to my eyes, she smiles, sometimes touches my cheek and says, "You are just like me." I live for those moments, when she remembers a self long forgotten and recognizes it in me.

Only recently has she decided that we look alike. When I was younger, the aunties-that-be announced that I was a mix between my mother and father, checking my features off of a genetic inventory list. During the last visit to Pakistan, when all the relatives started calling me "*choti* Shano" [little Shano], she finally agreed to the unthinkable: Her daughter, whom everyone thought of as pretty, looked just like her. My mother is subtle with praise and smiles, showing only the thinnest sliver of approval, as barely perceptible as the first silvery showings of a crescent moon. But whenever anyone remarks on the likeness of our features, she takes it as a compliment and beams so happily it looks as if the skies parted themselves just to pour sunlight on her proud face.

I look at her now and am surprised at how beautiful she is, amazed that I never thought it when I was younger.

I know that I never thought she was ugly. Starting from when I was five or six years old, Mom would tell me stories of how she grew up, always hearing that she was ugly. Oh, how the tears would run down my face, and in my small way, I would try to tell her how pretty she was to me. I remember asking why people thought that, and though she's quite fair-skinned, Mom would tell me that she was considered dark there and therefore ugly.

"You have to remember," she would say, "this was just a few years after independence and everyone still wanted to be like the British. Everyone still wanted to be white."

Although I am young, I nod my head gravely because we both know: This is how my father is.

But then, there are incidences I dread to remember, that creep through my body with a feeling of ice water in my veins. These are the memories I am ashamed to admit, of a time when I was embarrassed by my mother. A period of a few years during which I cringed when I was around her, when I thought everything about her was too foreign, too racial, too un-American. I tried to hide school conferences from her, terrified to think of her going to my school, but she'd always find out, digging through my school bag like it was a dirty secret. It was unbearable to imagine my teacher with a name like Anderson or Christianson meeting my crazed mother with her tea-stained teeth, too-apologetic English and sad eyes. Eyes with such dark hypnotic circles below them, which I was convinced would betray our foreignness and family problems during the 15 minutes she talked with my teacher. I'd go along with her, showing her my neatly organized desk with its color-coordinated folders and notebooks, in hopes of distracting her and making sure she didn't embarrass me too much.

I never wanted to bring my friends over because I was terrified that they'd see the same thing the kids in school saw in our orange geography books that always smelled like rotten milk and rubber. Their edges rubbed down smooth from age practically to velvet. I knew what was in that book, the same text we used in social studies for three years in a row. Pages 74-76. My face would burn red with a throbbing sense of being found out if the teacher assigned that section. Pages that still haunt me to this day.

A slim chapter on the Indian subcontinent, three pages on the history, the people, the climate, the customs. Smiling brown children playing with a large animal in equally brown mud, with only their glowing white teeth to distinguish them from the filth they are in. Men with colored turbans and dirt streaked faces on camels crossing through a field (this one is labelled "Main Street"). The last picture clings to me like a ghost, its shimmery, translucent skin slips its way into my dreams with the sound of rushing water. It is a photo of a village woman, with light brown streaks in her hair that match the indescribable color of her eyes. She is squatting (on her "haunches," as anthropologists would no doubt say), while flies buzz around her dirty *dupatta* [head scarf]. Her face is not smiling as she stares straight into the camera, a few feet beyond the brown mound piled in front of her. The caption of the photo reads, "Rural woman making dung patties."

The teacher could not simply leave the photo alone; she had to inform the class that she had, in fact, been to India and that "the natives" had such a "charming" way of doing things.

"Poor devils seem to do everything in a backward way," the teacher said, but she was "fond" of them nonetheless. "In fact," she said, "housewives in India make *chapattis* [flat breads] the same way as those dung patties, flattening them between their hands."

Her blue eyes scanned the room until they focused upon my brown ones. And then she did The Unforgivable: "Fatima," she said to me, "does your Mom make *chapattis* like that too?"

I didn't even know what a *chapatti* was (in Pakistan we call them *rotis*), but I was certain that it had to be some dirty, humiliating thing. My heart nearly stopped beating at that moment, and before the class broke into laughter, I had already created a black hole in my mind, large enough and dark enough to swallow both me and my Mom.

Everyday after that, a copy of that picture was taped to my desk, by the same kids who, years earlier, beat me up and called me a "sandnigger" [derogatory term for "Arab"] or "wog" [colonial-era derogatory term used for South Asians], though how that derogatory term managed to find its way from Britain to that small Minnesota suburb I'll never know.

Each day, the same word was written on the picture with accusing blood red letters: MOM. I tore those pictures off the desk, pretending not to be embarrassed, even though I could feel my own skin darkening so much until I prayed I was as dark as a shadow, unnoticeable to their taunting blue eyes. I took home each copy of that photo and stared at them at night, examining them to see if they might be my mother after all.

It was years later until I was finally able to look my mother in the eye and even longer before I could actually entertain the thought that she might be beautiful. When the mother of a friend of mine, a Brazilian woman, told me she thought my mother was pretty, I thought she was joking. Or pitying me. By that time, I had grown so distant from my mother, hating her almost as much as I hated myself, that I did everything in my power to defy her, to be nothing like her. I chose a night when my cousins slept over, to push that defiance to a new level.

The four of us were about to go to sleep in one room when my mother came downstairs and pursed her lips in disapproval. She told Yusuf, the only boy cousin, to sleep in the other room. My other cousins looked disappointed, but said nothing. I was devastated, and a bit paranoid, wondering if my mother had seen through the flimsy one-day crush I had developed on him. Something came over me, I don't know what. Maybe I was drunk with cruelty after teasing my cousin Amina, who, at the same age as me, 12, was so weak and fragile we all tormented her. Or maybe my mother is right, and I was possessed that night by a *djinn,* some evil spirit planting itself in my mouth. After protesting the decision, I muttered to my mother, "God, it's not like we're going to have sex with him." The look on her face was a mixture of shock and something else, something I now recognize as a broken heart. The response came so quickly, I barely had time to realize what I had said. She slapped my face six times. Six quick, consecutive slaps, the kind they show in Hindi movies after a lover has been betrayed. She dragged me upstairs and beat me, so much that I'm not sure who was more hysterical, me or her. Afterwards, she calmly told me that if I ever even thought about anything that dirty she would either send me to Pakistan or a mental hospital; in both cases, with no return in sight. To this day, I sometimes have nightmares when I spend the night with a boyfriend, imagining that his high-pitched snores are actually the sirens of ambulances coming to take me away.

Those are years I still feel so bad about, so much that I view everything in life through a rosy tint of guilt. If I ever apologize for it, she pretends not to remember, gently brushing it off by saying, "Kids don't know what they say sometimes." I wonder where I learned to be so cruel at such a young age, why I chose to take it out on my mother. I close my eyes and try to remember what taught us both to share humiliation like a blanket on cold winter nights. The memories flash through my body with each beat of my heart, and even though I'm thousands of miles away and the only thing connecting me to the Minnesota of my childhood is the thin blue line of the horizon, the ghosts still find me and I remember.

My mother's hand, shaking as she puts on a gold ring, getting ready for an Islamic Center or Pakistani function. (In my mind's eye, her hand looks so old, covered in folds of wrinkles, veins and liver spots. The small details always get blurred when I remember, the only things I can change to make the horror a little less real.) The room is so silent as my sister and I slip on our homemade *shalwaar-kameez* [Pakistani clothing consisting of a long dresslike shirt and loose pants] suits, matching, of course, made from materials bought at Joann Fabric Store in Sunray mall (I've long forgotten the street that mall is on or even the city it's in — the only landmarks and points of reference in Minnesota are malls). While Mom sewed the suits the day before, Zuby and I would both stand by her sewing machine, eagerly modelling the style or design we wanted. Zuby wanted a square neck and *churidar* pyjama [a certain style of pants], while I wanted my *kameez* to have maroon piping along its seams. Those were the only times we ever really felt pretty, so I guess we both talked a little too loudly and repeated ourselves unnecessarily. Mom would yell at us to move out of the light, or tell us that we were eating her head [an Urdu phrase for something like "bothering"]. We probably drove her crazy, but those suits always came out perfect, and I usually kept mine on the rest of the night, too excited to take it off for the function the next day.

But by the next evening, we all hold our collective dysfunctional-family breaths while Dad storms in the kitchen. As if breathing out loud would have been too much, forcing the walls of our old yellow house to fall down. We don't want to make a sound, do anything to trigger Dad's temper, even though we all know there are some bombs you can't stop from destroying everything. Without words, the three of us negotiate who will be the mediator, who will travel from this side of the house that is the world of women, to his part, the kingdom of man. As the youngest, and therefore the sweetest looking, I am picked to be the delegate (although Zuby, as the good older sister, goes along with me anyway), chosen to travel through the hallways to where he stands, in the middle of his jungle, waiting.

I ask, in the smallest voice I can find, "Dad, are you gonna' start getting ready soon?" And the line he has been rehearsing all night and we have been dreading all day comes out, laced in honey.

"Get ready for what, *behta* [my child]?" as if we haven't played this game a thousand nights before.

I mumble some Auntie's name or other, before I take a gasp of breath, to brace myself, for the barrage of insults that will follow. It looks almost like a cartoon: my six-year-old, fifty-pound body practically blown away by the force of his yell, but instead of the standard "roar" in the little bubble caption above, a mix of English and Urdu words appear, containing a bilingual assortment of the word, "whore."

He makes up excuses, that we didn't tell him earlier, and that this is just a plot by "your mother" (which is spit out like a curse) to turn everyone against him. He gives us the same speech we hear over and over again while growing up: "I hate Pakistani people. I hate the way they smell, the way they look. Look at you, look how dirty you both look. Hey, Zuby, did you wash your face today? I work 18 goddamn hours a goddamn day just so that the three of you can all sit pretty like princesses, like you're not actually the ugly trash from Lalukaith [a Karachi slum] that nobody wants. What does your mother say about me? That I go to whorehouses? Your mother is a whore!"

At this point, he would feel a little bad for yelling at us, only six and 10 years old, and would invariably come back the next day with some cheap stuffed animals his secretary/mistress, Kathy, had picked out. Despite my mother's training, which taught me to respect any elder, I would glare at him, or at least try to. Didn't he know anything about me to realize that any toy I owned would later become haunted by ghosts or *djinns* (I'm not sure I can explain the difference between them, the two exist side by side in my mind, English and Urdu)? Didn't he know that my world was filled with Barbie dolls with butcher's knives and stuffed animals who turned their heads backwards at night?

The worst thing about those parties was that Dad would eventually stop terrorizing us and go, although not before making sure we were at least a humiliating full hour late. He would later sit and tell jokes, laughing with all of the other uncles, having a good time. Zuby and I did our best to ignore him then, conveniently dodging him when tea was served, pretending not to hear his stupid comments about the *kofta* [Pakastani dish of meatballs in a stew] as we stood together in the makeshift buffet line of the auntie's kitchen. I think he knew how much we hated him, and it scared him. Our hatred was quiet and calm, as clear as the blue of kids' evil eyes at school. I think Dad knew that his was a fleeting reign of terror, that one day the buildings would topple and the roads would be repaved as we moved on with our lives. He hid this fear well, though I do remember one night seeing the frozen look of horror on his face.

Zuby was 12, so I must have been eight. He had taunted Zuby and, in defense, she said something "smart" back (*desis* [Indians, in diaspora lingo] always associate "smartness" with disrespect in children). He raised his hand to hit her, but was stopped dead by Mom.

She had the calmest look on her face, as if the simplest answer had just occurred to her. She hissed at him in English (his language, the language he loved), each syllable punctuated with perfectly controlled rage, "Don't you ever hit my children, or I swear to God I will kill you myself."

I was so startled by the strength of her words that it took me a moment to notice the butcher's knife she held to his chest. He must have been so scared, must have seen the determination and honesty in her eyes. He honored her words and despite all of the promises he broke to her, all of the sleepless nights he made her spend waiting for him to come home from some white woman's house, despite all of these things, he never laid a hand on us.

When I look back, I don't remember the stillness, the fear my sister and I felt as we watched our parents. When I remember them now, they seem almost unreal to me, practically re-enacting a Hindi movie scene. That moment is forever frozen in my mind, as my parents are framed in a sunlight from the kitchen window that is so saturated I can almost taste its color. My mother could have been Perveen Babi [a famous Hindi film actress from the 1970s and 1980s] holding a knife to some *dushman* [villain] like Amjit Khan [a well-known Hindi actor], who had betrayed and ravaged her family. The appropriate fighting-scene disco music plays in the background while my father and mother practically dance together in this nightmare like two ghosts.

My mother calls me in California later that afternoon to ask me if I've been doing *namaz* [obligatory prayers in Islam]. After I guiltily reply, "No," casting my eyes down as if she can see me through the telephone wire, she scolds me. Continues to remind me, over the phone, in graphic detail, how God will punish her on Doomsday for not making her children good Muslims. As she says this, we sift through years of pain and disappointment so easily, the memories slippery with tears on our fingertips. Those memories follow no chronological order, but they follow each other like the painted dashes that divide roads, that divide continents. They mingle with each other, get confused together as they collect like a pool of tears in the reservoir of flesh above my clavicle.

If I close my eyes, I can almost see the images and thoughts flash behind her closed eyelids, the histories relived and faces remembered. In these cases, I wear guilt like a comfortable old sweater, slipping into it with a mixture of relief and resignation. It feels heavy with the weight of my mother's broken heart. For so much of my life I felt so humiliated, so small, so far from God, that now all I can hope is that my mother, whose face is so beautiful that God must have breathed the same breath into it as that which created the heavens, that this woman prays for me and forgives me as well as my father.

As she talks to me on the phone, I want to say something. I want to scream, *Ma, don't you know that we are the same? That the same hands that flutter about your face and neck are the ones before me now, the ones I use to wipe away tears? I will stand by you on Doomsday, I will tell God, that despite the horrors we lived through, you did make us good Muslims. You planted hope in our hearts and taught us how to love God. I want to tell her, How could I not be religious when the only way I have to explain how much I love you is by thanking God and the universe for giving you to me?*

These are the things I feel in the middle of the night, as I grab my face, my hair — her face, her hair — to stop the ripping of my heart. But instead, I remain quiet on the line and hope that the weight of my silence can communicate the words my heart screams.

Memoir

BY BARBARA J. PULMANO REYES

1984, Fremont, California

Mama, you are delirious in your last days. You don't know your husband from your dead brothers from your son, your daughters from your nieces or the neighbors. You are delirious in your last days, still hanging on to this world and at the same time floating with the seraphim and cherubim, already at God's side.

But I am here, and you are there, in that country you forgot you had ever left. I'm here, on the other side of the Pacific Ocean, and it's purple mascara and new wave dancing that is all the rage. I'm here, dressed like the chicks in Bananarama and wishing I were blonde, with my mouth full of orthodontia and my head full of dreams of being a rock star.

I'm here and you're there, delirious in your last days, and Manang Carmen, your faithful maid servant, begs you not to come back and haunt her. She's terrified of ghosts, she reminds you as she rubs your bony feet, and in your hazy dementia, you don't know what to say.

I don't believe in ghosts anymore. I can't remember how to believe. It's tough being a hot-shot American preteen because I swore I would forget all those things that hurt. You left me here, Mama, after you got sick. How I hated you for getting sick, for never laughing anymore, for never listening to my stories. You would just sit there, wondering how many angels could dance on the head of a pin, and I hated that. I hated thinking about you becoming a ghost, and I hated those angels for taking you away from me. I hated you for going back to the P.I.; they said they wanted you to die in your homeland. I thought we were already home.

I don't believe in ghosts anymore because I am in America now, and I'm doing things The American Way. There are no ghosts in suburban shopping malls and at slumber parties, nothing supernatural about flirting with cute white boys with braces and learning how to French kiss.

But you are delirious in your last days, calling for Abee and BJ — that's Anna and me, your first two grandchildren whom you raised as your own children — to come to your bedside. In your mind, Abee is still rubbing her snot on the walls and BJ is falling down the stairs again, because you are delirious, and you don't remember that 11 years have passed since then, and that a great ocean separates you from us. And there's this disease eating away your brain.

And there is something else too, but I don't want to think about it because I can't even look at pictures of you without seeing that ghost I can't afford to believe in anymore. You left me, and I am tired of always hurting. I am tired of sadness. You left me, and I can never feel pretty anymore. You left me, and now there's no one to ask me, "How was your day?"

and no one to hug me the way I like being hugged, huge and warm like pillows and soft things.

But in your last days, you are thin as a rail, and so weak that you can't even check to see if Abee and BJ are hiding under the bed. You swear you can hear them giggling, but you're not sure if it's them or God's mischievous angels, playing a game of hide-and-seek with your mind. You are weak, and you need so much — oxygen, medicines, and you can't eat or go to the bathroom by yourself. Papa stays steadfast by your side. His many years of saving lives, and even he cannot stop your brain from eating itself up. He cannot stop you from suffering. What good is being an M.D., he thinks, if he cannot save the one he loves most in this world? He only prays that you will not pass on having completely forgotten the name of this man who spent his lifetime by your side.

But I don't think about these things because I am in junior high, and I don't like this heaviness. It's already too much, being a sassy, smartass 12-year-old Pilipina in suburbia. Everybody's forgotten me, and now you have, too. So I'm gonna forget you. You left us, and now Daddy can get away with being an asshole. You left us, and now nothing can stop him from hitting me. You left us, and now my Mommy seems to have gone, too. Nobody sees me cry in the girls' bathroom at school. I am a tough girl.

But in your delirium, Abee and BJ are happy little girls in matching spring dresses. Sobee the dog sits at my feet, the love birds chirp in their cage, and Tito Romy, Mommy's youngest brother, hasn't gone bald yet. He's still skinny, and he plays Beatles songs on the guitar, and we laugh and eat papaya together, and we believe that he's really our big brother, and that he could protect us from anything, even Daddy.

In your delirium, Abee and BJ don't have to watch each other's asses because Daddy is unemployed again, and he's pissed at the system, and he hates this country more than anything in the world. In your delirium, Abee and BJ don't lose sleep over seeing their mother, your daughter, on the verge of mental collapse, wishing you were here to hold it all together the way you always did.

I come home from a junior high dance in my striped purple and black miniskirt. I have been smooching with a boy named Percy, and I feel naughty. Mommy looks like she has been crying rivers and oceans. She looks at me like I am to blame. Mama passed away today, they say. No no no I don't want to hear them say it. Mama passed away. Mama is dead. Next thing I know, Mommy is on a plane to the P.I., and I feel like I'm the one who just died.

You left me Mama, and now you're never coming back.

November 2, 1993, Manila, Philippines
It is All Souls' Day now, and even after all my Catholic education, up 'til recently, I still only believed in Halloween as nothing but dances and parties and dark as death costumes like all my cool friends who smoked clove cigarettes and wore nothing but black. But today, whole families spend the day in the cemetery, drinking San Miguel beer and talking with their departed loved ones, bringing mountains of food and fresh flowers, rosaries and statues of the Santo Niño.

Mama, almost nine years have passed since that junior high dance, and sometimes I don't want to forgive myself for getting through high school and most of college without thinking of you at all. Not even remotely. I had to be tough because Daddy got used to kicking the shit outta me over the years. I learned to be hard; I had to close the door.

It wasn't until I sent my rebellious self, to the P.I. that I finally walked through the door you had always left open for me. All Souls' Day 1993; I am 22 years old now. I pass through the high iron gates and beneath the grotesque, emaciated Jesus statue with spidery long limbs of weathered stone, dying in the arms of his Virgin mother, so quiet and saddened. For the first time in my life, I am terrified that I am surrounded by ghosts older than I could possibly understand. All Souls' Day 1993, and I am talking to your headstone even though no words come out of my mouth. I stare hard at your name engraved in marble. Praxedes Adviento Pulmano. You are the mother of my mother. You will always be that amazing woman, so loving and wise. I remember you. You are the one I almost shut out completely.

Papa says to me, *My darling, this is where I belong. When my time has come, you lay me next to your Mama.* I want to cry and weep and sob and moan, but I'm still stubborn as hell, and I'm overwhelmed with revelations. I can't speak. Nothing I could say right now could make up for years of betraying my memories.

I've spent six months in the country of my birth feeling like a damn foreigner, and as ghosts around me start to rise from the earth, I wish to God that I were a believer. I wish that I could see you, watching me kneeling here, in my Doc Martens and torn up Levis. I wish that I could see your eyes as your benevolence flows into me, through me. I know you are here, beside me, all around me. Are you touching my hands, Mama? My face? Have you always been with me, all this time, as my guardian angel? Can it be that it is you who has kept me together all this time?

I touch your cold headstone, read the obituary on paper yellowed by time, feel the hot Philippine rain on my face. Real things. Six months in the country of my birth, this place in which you came full circle, Mama, and it's finally real to me. I compose poetry in my mind; words I never had a chance to say to you. How can I thank you for holding me up, continuing to exist when I had already convinced myself that you were gone forever?

This is my tribute to you, Mama, for making me everything that I am, for not abandoning me when I had already abandoned you. I remember you. I will never, ever forget.

CHAPTER 3

The Flat Truth

How Do I Look?

The Flat Truth

BY LYNN LU

My first job in high school was selling lingerie at a large, Midwestern department store. (Being a respectable, family-values kind of store, they called my department "Intimate Apparel.") I loved my job — it was easy, and it paid well. Every weekend I was content to hang, rehang and ring up assorted functional foundation garments, satiny self-indulgences and the odd garter belt (always a gift). Customers ranged from power-suited professional women and breast-feeding mothers to old ladies and the occasional male in search of an "intimate" present (garter belts do nicely). People who shopped in my department sometimes knew exactly what they wanted; more often they were grateful for some discreet assistance. But it was ironic that they had to ask me for help, since I happen to be flat. Completely and utterly flat. Flat as a badly told joke.

Of course, being mammarily challenged is not in itself a problem. For many young Asian women, a lack of huge breasts is merely one insult in a world where a beautiful woman must also have blonde hair, blue eyes and an epicanthic fold. Moreover, plenty of flat-chested women live perfectly normal lives with no psychological scars or traumatic adolescent memories. I just do not happen to be one of them. Unlike those women, I internalized the message in magazines, TV and the movies: that women are judged not by merit but by beauty, and that beauty generally refers to "what men find attractive," and that "what men find attractive" are big boobs. There is, of course, a male equivalent of the "bigger is better" school of thought, perhaps with more damaging consequences for society (war, the castration complex, ridiculous architecture), but for men the physical part involved usually remains hidden from public view (outside the locker room, anyway), rather than being so readily visible and quickly assessed.

Even my mother — who did her best to raise two Chinese American daughters in a white-bread town with a shred of our self-esteem and positive body image intact — must admit that small breasts are not highly valued in our culture. Today, my mother views President Clinton's dalliance with Monica Lewinsky as inevitable. Normally modest and polite, she just shrugs, "She has big tits."

Thankfully, Hooters restaurants did not appear in my town until years after I had passed through puberty, but big breasts have always played a prominent role in my concept of what is normal and, therefore, loveable. Since I spent most of my adolescent years making extraordinary attempts to be as normal as possible, and the rest of the time trying to make boys fall in love with me, my supremely abnormal breasts were a source of constant embarrassment. I didn't bother to dream "I cured cancer in my Maidenform bra" like the old ads said, I just wanted to be able to wear a Maidenform bra. Instead, I had to settle for a dusty-beige piece of stretch-polyester that looked like a surgical bandage for a cat.

Perhaps if I had not spent every weekend surrounded by racks full of colorful, luxuriously silky, lacy confections in all cup sizes but mine, I wouldn't have coveted them so much or mourned my own shortcomings so dearly. Perhaps I would have been happy to go without a bra and let other women worry about styles and support and the correct fit. Then again, faced with the mortal fear of being braless in gym class or in a white T-shirt or at a slumber party where someone's sacrificial bra inevitably ended up in the freezer, I preferred to have a line of defense against being different, however small or ill-fitting it was.

Come to think of it, my mother didn't do all that much to help my self-esteem. "Don't slouch," she would carp, her iron-like fingers wrenching my shoulders backwards.

"I'm not," I would protest, drawing my shoulders back to their original, severely concave position.

"You've got to develop your chest muscles," she would insist, demonstrating an isometric exercise I knew to be useless from reading *Are You There God, It's Me Margaret.* "Look at your sister; she stands up straight." My older sister, the sole recipient of my family's entire breast quota, was blessed with two perfect, orange-shaped boobs, which my mother seemed to believe were proof of diligent exercise, not genes. Even my mother, who is herself no Bridget Bardot, did not love my flat chest.

Resigned to a lonely future, I concentrated on schoolwork and prayed for a growth spurt. Just in case I could avoid complete shame and desolation through my intellect, I studied hard. If I had no dates, at least no one could be sure whether it was because I was flat or because I was a nerd. Someday, I reasoned, I might meet a man so dazzled by my sharp wit and dancing eyes that he need never look below my neck. ("Some guys like small breasts," a boyfriend once assured me. He neglected to say whether he was one of them, or whether they're all pedophiles.)

At the same time that I was concentrating on becoming a brain surgeon, I reserved part of my brain for learning all I could about bras in preparation for the day when I, too, could have my pick of bras in fashion colors (with matching panties!) like the women who shopped in my department. I became somewhat of an expert on the intricacies of intimate apparel. I could tell the brand and style number of a bra just by looking at the cut or the fabric. I became a great judge of bra size, gently nudging women as needed toward a B cup or what I cruelly (and enviously) referred to as "horse harnesses." I advised countless women on the relative virtues of underwire, cotton lining and front closures. But all of this was secondhand knowledge; I could not testify personally about the Wonderbra or the sports bra or anything, for that matter. One in-store promotion even had me wearing a button that said, "Ask me about Bali's DDD cup." As if I would know anything about it.

What I did know was that I was conspicuously abnormal and vulnerable to other people's prejudices. One day an old woman wandered through my department and approached me.

"You Oriental girls are so pretty," she said, her tone not at all nice. She went on, accusingly, "I always worried about my husband being overseas during the war with all those Oriental girls."

I felt anything but threatening or seductive standing there in the lingerie department with a mean old lady. Even as I noticed that her aging, saggy breasts were still bigger than mine, she was clearly feeling a need to express her racist rivalry. In case I wasn't feeling enough shame about being flat, now I knew it was worse to be a slut.

During an interview for college admission with a local alum who happened to be a well-respected judge, he asked me about my extracurricular activities, which I had meticulously chronicled on my application. "I see you play tennis."

I nodded.

He looked me up and down slowly, and then asked, "Are you a gymnast?"

Squirming uncomfortably, I reminded him, "No, I play tennis."

He paused for a moment, apparently thinking about the sports flat-chested Chinese girls must excel at. "A diver?" he finally asked, leering slightly.

"No . . . I play tennis." And I want to go to college, I thought, so I never told anyone how insulting his innuendo made me feel.

Only now that I am older do I feel confident enough to talk about my insecurities and the thinly veiled insults that fueled them, now that feminists have spent decades documenting the injustices girls and women suffer everywhere, on material, psychological and emotional levels. Feminists' careful attention not only to issues of economics and politics but to culture and social conditioning have begun to chip away at our society's sexist idolatry and its hatred of that which is different. If only it were as simple as burning our bras.

The happy part of my story is that I finally found a bra that fits — in an advertisement in a magazine for Asian Americans. I have the growing consumer power of Asian American women to thank for my salvation. Finally our sheer numbers and visibility have made us an untapped niche market to be catered to, even at the risk of perpetuating stereotypes (all Asian American women have small busts, all Asian women work in lucrative careers and have disposable income, etc.). Along with the model minority's perceived desires for expensive cars and fancy wine, my own modest need has been filled, and I suppose I should feel thankful. Still, in my fear and cynical belief that marketers will soon realize there isn't as much money in targeting Asian American women as they thought — due to a high cultural value on frugality, no doubt — I have stockpiled what I hope is a lifetime supply of bras.

Of course, the sad fact remains that just because I can now buy pretty lingerie that fits, this does nothing to change our culture's fixation on breasts as the *sine qua non* of feminine beauty, or more broadly, on beauty as the sign of female worth. I have yet to see a drag queen with small breasts, and many Asian models, even in their own countries, sport implants. Whether this emphasis on big breasts is a matter of enduring and all-encompassing Western fashion or of latent biological imperatives, whether small busts will one day be preferred or some evolutionary advantage to them discovered, makes no difference; what must change is our world view that privileges one ideal over all others in determining what size of breast is best, to the lasting detriment of those who don't measure up.

I've gotten sort of used to looking like a perpetual teenager. Could it be that being flat has been a blessing in disguise, preserving me from superficiality, forcing me to develop other assets, freeing me to pursue an independent life rather than viewing a heterosexual union as the be-all and end-all of existence? Probably not, since I still covet the glamorous life of the *femme fatale*, even though I know better. At best, I've made my peace with my twin plateaus, have broken my shameful silence and can laugh about the anxieties they've caused.

But maybe someday I'll have the courage to take the next step, to go beyond acceptance to pride . . . to go topless. Or at least to show off my tiny, shiny purple bra.

The Girl Who Lost Her Face

BY SUSAN A. SUH

One Tuesday Julie noticed that she didn't recognize herself. It happened on a typical day, nothing out of the ordinary. She had come home from school after hanging out with the crew for a bit on the southwest street corner of I.S. 135. At some point after she went home for dinner, she went into the bathroom, checking herself out in the mirror above the sink, just because it was there, but also to look for any signs of pimples or other weirdness.

That's when it happened. As she stared into the mirror, a second passed and all of a sudden she realized something so big that she had no time to wonder where it came from or why she hadn't realized it before: The face staring back at her was not her own.

Not that the face wasn't hers or didn't feel attached to her body — it did — but Julie had the distinct feeling that the face in the mirror couldn't be hers.

"I don't look like that," she thought to herself. Her skin looked younger than she felt, and more sallow. Her hair was straighter than she thought, and darker. Her nose was smaller than she remembered, and flatter. But the eyes — her eyes were darker, inscrutable and smaller than her mind's eye remembered.

She had to say it out loud, it seemed so incredible. "This face isn't mine." She thought: It isn't who I am. How can my expression be so duh, so nondescript when I feel and think so much inside?

It was weird. Even though she had the distinct feeling that this face wasn't hers, she couldn't for the life of her remember what her real face looked like.

"Hey, Alison, what's up?" Julie decided to talk about it with some of her closest friends. She called Alison Nelson first, not because she was her best friend, but because she had known Julie the longest; they'd been going to the same schools and been put in the same classroom since first grade.

"Hi, Julie. I was just about to call you — you'll never guess who I just got off the phone with!" and with that, Alison started to re-enact her conversation with Mark Campbell, the flavor of the week. Even though it was obvious that Mark was out of her league — he was a year ahead of them and a "9" to Alison's "7" in good looks — Alison was known for her boldness and for her ease in making friends with just about anyone.

Julie wanted to learn what tidbits of info Alison had gotten about Mark and what kind of women he liked, so she kinda forgot about why she had called in the first place. By the time she remembered again (after finding out that he "preferred blondes" and hearing Alison joke about bleaching her brown hair), Julie didn't feel like bringing the subject up.

In fact, she didn't feel like bringing it up with her best friend and next best friend Michelle or Anna either. "It sounds weird," she thought. "What am I supposed to say, do you think I look like me lately? Do I look like someone else?" Julie wondered whether Mr. Wellman's math class had finally made her insane. That's what she concluded as her Mom called her into the kitchen because by then, everyone was waiting and the dinner was getting cold.

As she lay in bed that night — in the bed she had slept in since childhood (the top half of a bunk bed set), in the room she shared with her sister at night (and shared with the rest of the family in the day) — Julie tried to figure out why her face all of sudden looked so weird to her. She slowly went over the days of the past week in her mind, what she did, who she saw, who or what made her laugh, who or what made her pissed. She turned them around in her mind, looking for a clue, something out of the ordinary that might help explain this weird thing that happened, but nothing equally weird came to mind.

But in a flash, some divine intervention maybe, she remembered something, ordinary maybe, but maybe also related. She remembered talking about faces with a bunch of the other girls in the lunchroom the other day. At the beginning of every month, the crew from school (and not the one she hung out with from the neighborhood) — herself, Michelle Gonzales, Anna Bueno, Alison Nelson, and Wanda Lee — got together at their lunch table to look at that month's magazines together. Between Michelle's and Anna's parents, they were able to get subscriptions to their favorites: *Seventeen, Entertainment Weekly, Cosmopolitan,* and *Marie Claire.* They were all flipping through the magazines and commenting on the models and actresses: who they thought were naturally beautiful, who were fakes, and who they thought were really closer to their age.

As Julie started to drift off to that half-sleeping, half-waking state, snippets of their conversations rolled around in her brain. "She's got the biggest, bluest eyes. Do you think they're contacts?" "Do you think this shade would really make my skin look less yellow?" "She can't be only 15! She looks like 30!" "What do you think my hair would look like permed like this?" "She's the only Asian I've seen with big breasts and a big nose." "You're way more interesting-looking than her — she looks so apple pie." She remembered being slightly annoyed at Michelle for saying that last thing, even though it was meant as a compliment, but she couldn't remember exactly why.

"Julie, hurry up — you'll be late." Her Mom urged her out the door the next morning, even though her soup was only half eaten and the rice in it would blow up and take over the bowl, so that no one else would want to eat it and it would go to waste.

As she scrambled to put her papers in her bookbag, she gave her Mom a quick kiss on the cheek. Her Mom smiled the smile she always smiled, the smile that started at the corners of her eyes and became her whole face; at that time, it erased the wrinkles and tired bags she usually had on her delicate face. She had seen pictures of her Mom as a girl, had seen the likeness in her younger sister's face and in Julie's own now, and knew that her Mom had once looked very young. When had her Mom gotten to look so old? As she left, Julie wondered whether she'd look like her Mom when she got older.

At school that day, nothing eventful. No one noticed that she looked different or weird. Or at least, if they did, they didn't mention it. She did notice, though, that she felt a twinge of discomfort when Mr. Mason called Dinesh "Butch" again when it hadn't ever bothered her before. He was one of the popular teachers everybody liked because he was always saying funny things like always picking a guy in the class to call "Butch." He always made the students laugh, including the guys he'd rename. When she mentioned it to Michelle and Wanda during study hall later that day, they didn't think anything of it, since Dinesh had laughed, too. But when she asked them whether they had ever heard Mr. Mason doing it to a student with an American name, none of them could think of an example.

That night, Julie helped her Mom with the dinner dishes even though it was her sister's turn. Casually, as if it was no big deal either way, Julie asked "*Umma,* did you wish you looked different when you were younger?"

Casually stealing a glance at her daughter out of the corner of her eye, her mother replied in her native tongue, "When I was growing up and still living in my parents' home, I used to want to look like many other people. I wanted beautiful thick, shiny hair like my older sister. I wanted *go-sa-rhee sohn* — thin long fingers good for playing piano — like my best friend. I wanted big eyes like my teacher Mrs. Baxter at college.

"But by the time I left for the U.S., I cut my hair short like this around my ears — doesn't it suit me? I stopped playing piano to focus on studying, and I decided that big green eyes like Mrs. Baxter would look strange on my face, since she was from the U.S. and I was Korean."

"Oh." Julie was ready to hear the punch line now about how she should be proud of the way she looked, so wasn't expecting her Mom to continue.

"That all changed though, when I came here. It was hard working for an American company doing clerical work when I had a college degree, but it was harder because I was the only Asian woman there. So many times I heard my co-workers say 'ching chong' while I was on the phone with your auntie or ask how come my feet were so big if they were bound. And they didn't say these things to really hurt my feelings, they were just joking."

Julie remembered what happened in science class earlier that day. "But umma, this isn't about how you look and how you wanted to look, right?"

"Oh yes, it is. At first, I wanted to laugh with them, to let them know that they didn't hurt my feelings and that I was friendly. But after work, I always felt a little bit sad and tired whenever that happened. Until one day, I mentioned it to your auntie, and she got mad and said to me, 'Look how they treat us here, just because we look different from them!'

"After that, I remember I started to notice how I looked more — how short I was, how small my breasts were —"

"*Umma!*"

"What? Breast! Breast! Breast! So what? Now, let me finish my story. All of a sudden, my nose was too small. In Korea, when I was younger, I wanted to look like someone else who was Korean, but in the U.S., I wanted to look like someone else who wasn't Korean. . . . Now, I look back on that time and laugh, but I did wish that."

"But *umma*, you are short and all that."

"*Aiee-ya!* So what? Anyway, that's not the point. I was looking at myself in a broken mirror, so of course I felt bad. If one day I look at myself in a mirror and my face is fine and then the next time I look at myself in a broken mirror and my face looks funny and broken, does that mean that I am different and my face is broken? Of course not! Not when the mirror itself is broken. I should first examine the mirror and see what is the matter with it telling me that my face is broken, when it is really quite good looking."

"Oh, *umma*," Julie had to smile in spite of herself, "you are really funny."

"Yah, if I don't say it to me, who will?"

Laughing, Julie finished the last dish, put down the dishrag and gave her Mom a hug, "I will, *umma*, I will."

"And besides, how could I have such a good-looking daughter if I wasn't?"

Later that night, Julie peered into the bathroom mirror again, hoping that that weird feeling had gone away. What she saw staring back at her was a young girl's face, definitely looking younger than her 13 years, smooth skin, black hair, and a small nose. She looked like a quiet girl — until she opened her mouth to speak.

"What was up with me yesterday? What did I expect to look like?"

Her Mom must have heard her, because Julie could hear her voice through the bathroom door, "*Yah*, who are you talking to in there in the bathroom? Admiring yourself in the mirror?"

She knew that her Mom wasn't really expecting an answer, since Julie heard her walking away, so she replied more to herself than anyone else.

"No, but I'm working on it."

Big Nose

BY SHELIA MENEZES

I have a big nose
I can see it when I walk
without crossing my eyes

well you have a big nose
my sister yells her last taunt
the best one

so I scrutinize my nose
like an archaeologist
its slight skew to the left
and how
just below the bridge
between my baby browns
my bones fan out
like a delta

I train myself to
profile in pictures
but the yearbooks
catch my face straight-on
and one 8th grader
teases that girl
looks like an ape

so I follow beauty-tips
in *Sassy* and *Seventeen* magazines
highlight it with foundation
one narrow stripe down the middle
and blend
to blend
with the White girls on those glossy
pages
like the wide-eyed Asian girls
and light-skinned Black girls

who all model the same almond eyes
the same full lips
and that nose
bestowed to pretty girls
who snatch away boyfriends

maybe I should see myself
as not a pretty girl
but a funny girl
  and settle for a dorky boy
    and if I do
      maybe
        he will kiss like Luke
          the Dukes of Hazard stud but
            funny
              does not narrow my nose

                no cute nose button nose perky little nose
                no one ever
                  praises my nose

                    so I pierce it
                      decorate it with a diamond
                        and claim it
                          I watch men and women coo
                            about the mysterious sparkle
                              but the compliments never reach
                              past my piercing
                              which never heals

                                after four years
                                I take out the piercing
                                  and stare in the mirror for days
                                  confront
                                    my 22 year old body and
                                      how my skin creases
                                        where it should
                                          how my breasts curve
                                          like they should
                                            how my belly rounds
                                          as it should
                                    and how my nose
                                looks just like
                          it should
                like
        me

Whispers

BY MOLICA POV-MEAS

When I was in 5th grade, I felt normal. I was healthy and nothing seemed wrong. I ran and played like other little girls my age. But after a couple of years, things started to change. High school was coming up fast. I didn't notice then, but I was maturing. I grew taller and was breaking out with red bumps that looked like chicken pox all over my face.

In 8th grade, I looked and felt different. I didn't know why, but I felt weird. Then, people started to talk. Everywhere I walked, everywhere I turned, and every door I went into I could hear the hissing of whispers in the breeze. They said, "Why don't you be normal?" I was so confused. The same question would pop into my head, What's wrong with me? I didn't know what was wrong with me, but I knew that was why people hated me.

What was wrong with me? Was it my hair? Was is too long, too thick, or too dark? No, it wasn't my hair. Was it my eyes? Were they not light enough or were they too big? No, it wasn't my eyes, either. Maybe it was the way I dressed. Was my blue skirt too dark or too long? Was my white shirt not white enough? No, no, that was not the reason. It couldn't have been, there were hundreds of girls dressed like me.

More people started to talk. I couldn't take it anymore. Then finally, someone asked me, "Why don't you talk normal?" I was shocked. That was the reason, the way I talked? Did people understand me? I wasn't speaking a different language. Did I talk too fast or too slow? I wondered, how do normal people talk? I said the same things they did, and I also got better grades in English than most of them.

Then I realized it was not the things I said, it was my voice. I sounded like a baby! Some people said it was cute. But as I got older, people said it was irritating. That hurt. I wished there were something else besides my voice that was wrong with me, something I could change. My voice unfortunately was not one I could change. I was born with this voice.

So, loud and clear I will speak with this voice. This voice will express me as a human being, as a person, and as a young woman. It will tell you the people and things I treasure most and it will tell you what I believe in. I treasure my family and friends. I believe in love, goodness, respect and honesty. I value heritage and life.

Absolution

By Jennifer Ahn

Their eyes would widen slightly. Their teeth would bite their lower lips. Then there would always be a slight pause.

"Uteka itamani cusa!"

"How did you get so big?" they would ask in Korean.

Everyone wanted a reply to this question. Sometimes they would avoid my eyes and simply address my mother. She had no real reply for them. Neither had I. But it was a question that I shamefully asked myself again and again.

I was a very skinny kid. Skinny and tall. My body was something that I was proud of. It was what enabled me to out-race the boys in my class. I could ride my bike, play softball, and take ballet classes because of it. Adults would all marvel at my height. They all lavished me with compliments and nudged me to stand up even straighter and taller. My body and I were on great terms. It was good to me, and I was good to it. We were a team. Together there wasn't anything we couldn't do. Or so I thought.

It was something I didn't notice myself. Everyone commented on how big I had gotten in such a short period of time. So after examining my body, I came to the same conclusion as everyone else: At 12 years old, I was fat. Not big — that was just a nicer way of saying fat. This is not something I realized could happen. I had seen fat white people, fat black people, fat every people. But fat Korean people? I had almost never seen that. It was an oddity, a strange occurrence, a freak show. Now I was taking my place in the center ring.

Puberty came calling early. I had developed breasts at the age of seven. My period had come at age 10. I was so naive when I menstruated for the first time that I thought I had somehow soiled myself unknowingly. Along with these wonderful little milestones came a voracious appetite. I could eat and eat and eat and then eat a little more. And I certainly did not eat a healthy diet. While the other kids ate sandwiches and fruit packed by their mothers for lunch, I stacked my Reese's Peanut Butter Cups up like Legos. All seven of them. Every day.

Food was my best friend and my mortal enemy. As much as I despised food for making me fat, I could not part ways with it. Food would always be my cross to bear. And try as I might, there was no way I could escape it. There was the Colombian diner with fried yellow rice and sausages as fat as the thighs of toddlers. Despite her constant admonitions about my weight, my mother packed the kitchen with Oreos, cheesecake, and chocolate ice cream. Perhaps it was a test to see if I could resist. I failed miserably every time.

So I took it upon myself to try to lose the weight. I shunned the cookies for healthier substitutes, like salad with low-fat dressing. The whole milk was now skim. Butter was out, and margarine was in. I also decided to exercise. I diligently rode the exercise bike that I had begged for at Christmas. I dutifully twisted my hips and pumped my arms to Jane's blonde image on my TV. But the weight was not coming off. It was a blow to my ego every time I saw the scale creep up and my largest pair of jeans becoming as snug as stretch pants. This was obviously not working.

In all my issues of *Seventeen, Teen,* and *Sassy,* there were articles warning of the dangers of eating disorders. Ominous sounding names like anorexia nervosa and bulimia. There were girls who could starve themselves down to 70 pounds, and others who could eat massive quantities of food and then simply throw it up. To most people, it was a sad testimonial about the pressure that young girls feel to have a perfect skinny body. To me, it sounded like my salvation.

Bulimia was the way to go, it seemed. Imagine eating all the food you wanted and never gaining weight because you could simply throw it back up. It was ingenious in its simplicity. The first time I tried to make myself throw up, I was filled with giddiness and fear. I was meticulous as I wiped the rim of the toilet clean and washed my hands. I was washing my hands even though I expected to have vomit on them soon. I wasn't prepared for the strength of my reflexes when I stuck my fingers in the back of my mouth. The gagging was powerful and loud. My body was stronger than I was. I gave in and pulled my fingers out. Tears welled up in my eyes. I lay my head on the rim of the bowl as the sweat started to bead on my forehead.

"Jennifer, stop being such a baby. You don't want to be fat for the rest of your life, do you?"

I tried again. This time I felt the cool smoothness of a spoon resting in my throat. The spoon felt more reassuring and efficient than my fingers. I inched it farther and farther back into my mouth. But when the gagging started again, I chickened out and pulled out the spoon. The tears were now flowing freely. All I felt was shame — deep, deep shame. It was not shameful that I was trying to purge myself but that I was too weak to be successful.

I decided then that I would starve myself. This method was going to be more laborious, but I was determined. I gradually built up my will power. The intervals between eating became longer and longer. For periods of three to four days, the only thing that I consumed would be two small oranges. At night, I would be filled with satisfaction as I felt the hunger pangs in my belly. There was power in not giving in to the temptation of food. It was powerful. I was powerful. It was working. I was doing something right. I waited hopefully for the symptoms. I searched for the fine hair that covers the body of an anorexic. The arrival of my period brought despair because it meant that I was not losing enough weight.

I was allowed to go home for lunch instead of eating at school. This suited me fine. My house was right across the street from school, and I wouldn't have to explain not eating. I usually watched television. The commercials for after-school snacks and TV dinners looked like windows into a dream for me. I was so hungry. I had barely eaten in 10 days. The hunger pains were my badges of honor. They felt comforting to me. But I was so hungry. Maybe I could give in to temptation and have another piece of fruit.

I went into the kitchen to try to find something that would abate the hunger. There were oranges in the refrigerator. I would have only half of one. A whole one would be too fattening. As I chewed on the sweet, fleshy orange, the hunger was not subsiding. Rather the act of eating intensified my need for food and nourishment. I looked around the kitchen. There were packs of Chips Ahoy cookies and full loaves of white bread. In the fridge sat a jar of peanut butter along with a carton of whole milk that was reserved for my brother.

"Jennifer, don't do it. Don't do it. This is why you're so fat — because you have no will power. You've done so well. Have another piece of orange if you're still hungry."

But the days of hunger took over. I grabbed the cookies, the bread, and the peanut butter. I tore off hunks of the bread and used them to scoop up huge globs of peanut butter. I pushed cookies into my mouth whole instead of biting off pieces. I was eating so much food that it was breathtaking. I was literally not breathing properly because my mouth was so full. I stuck my fingers straight into the jar and shoveled in mounds of peanut butter. It felt satiny and rich in my mouth. I gulped the milk down as it dribbled out the corners of my mouth. It didn't seem like reality to me. And it wasn't. I was out of my mind. I was out of my mind because of what I put my body through. When I finally looked up, I saw the empty bag, the breaderumbs, and my sticky, dirty fingers. Then the only thing I could do was to sob.

My eating binges only brought me deeper guilt and shame. I was so disheartened after every binge. I was convinced that I would be fat forever. And fat meant ugly and unworthy of anything good. So to help myself I started taking over- the-counter diet pills. At first, I dutifully followed the recommendation of one pill. However, the hunger was not disappearing fast enough for me. I decided to up the dosage. Instead of a pill a day, I popped a pill every time I felt a moment of weakness coming. The pills were my solace. In a few minutes I could shun food. I was taking about four to five pills a day. The headaches and the sleepless nights were a small price to pay for the joy of starvation.

Despite all my efforts, I continued to gain weight. And so the vicious cycles continued on and on into my teenage years. I had no sense of self-worth. I felt fat, ugly and hopeless. Most of all, I felt terrified, terrified that this was it for me, that happiness was reserved for others — others who deserved it. And I didn't deserve happiness because I was fat. Sixteen years old and I felt like the best years of life were behind me.

It is often said that the road to recovery is neither easy nor short. In my case that cliché is certainly true. I am at complete peace with my body at 21 years of age. I eat normally and even allow myself to indulge in cake and ice cream without the slightest twinge of guilt. I try to exercise when I can because it's good for my body, not because I have to. Where once there was a painfully insecure girl, a confident woman has emerged. There was no simple solution to how I was able to end my self-destructive habits.

I wish I could say that I got better with the help of my family. It seems that if there is pressure on girls and women to be thin in this culture, the pressure is increased 10-fold if you're Asian American. In the minds of many, Asian women are petite and, most of all, skinny. That epitomizes the beautiful Asian woman. And what is most important is that Asian women be beautiful — not smart, not successful, but beautiful. Since I was not skinny, I felt extremely ugly. It didn't matter to my family that I was intelligent, articulate, talented. To them I was just fat. Since that is what everyone focused on, that was the only thing that consumed me for years. My preoccupation with my weight seeped into all other aspects of my life. Nothing that I did seemed good enough because in my mind I couldn't really accomplish anything worthwhile unless I were skinnier.

It was the help of my friends that brought me through one of the hardest periods of my short life. When you hear something over and over again, you start to internalize the message and over time, you start to believe it. I believed the negative messages I constantly received from my family, I started to believe what I was hearing from my friends. It's too easy to believe all the negative press about the state of the youth today. I was fortunate to meet intelligent friends who truly believed that I was not fat and worthless, but a beautiful young woman who had a world of potential within me. My friends encouraged me endlessly. They literally saved my life.

It pains me terribly to hear young girls and women complain that they are fat. They are fixated on nonexistent flaws. The pressure to be thin and perfect is overwhelming. I wish every young woman who believes that she is ugly could hear instead that she is lovely and gorgeous no matter what her size. There are such limitless possibilities within each and every young woman. The old adage "beauty comes from within" really is true.

Now when I see my relatives, they all comment on how pretty I've become and how much weight I lost. The reality is that I have the same face I've always had, and I only lost a little bit of weight. So when they tell me what a beautiful young woman I've become, I now know that I already was one.

Round-Eyes

BY MARILYN CHIN

I woke up one morning and my slanted eyes had turned round, which was nothing to be alarmed about. It happened to my rich cousin Amy, whose mother thought that she was too ugly to capture a rich Chinese American prince; she was gagged, sedated and abducted — then zoomed to Japan in a private airplane to a famous round-eye plastic surgeon. Well — Amy woke up with huge, round "Kathleen Turner eyes." They fixed her nose into a perky "Little Orphan Annie," and while she was deep under, they gave her new mammoth Madonna breasts for half price.

So, when I woke up with round eyes, I was not particularly surprised. But then, I thought, hey, wait a minute, my family's not rich. We don't have any money to be vain. We're the immigrants who toiled in sweatshop after sweatshop. We're the poor relations that everybody spat on. Amy's family gave us hand-me-downs and scraps that their Cairn Terriers didn't want. In the '50s, they bought my father's papers, shipped him here, and he worked as a slave cook for them in their chain of chop suey joints for the rest of his awful life.

Of course, we were supposed to be eternally grateful. I remember one steamy episode in which my father banged his head on their giant butcher block and said, "You want grateful! You want thanks! Here, kowtow, kowtow, ten thousand years kowtow!" He banged his head so hard that he opened a gash three inches wide, and the blood streaked down his face. Such histrionics continued until he died suddenly of a heart attack in 1979.

Sometimes I look in the mirror and expect to see my father's bloody face. But on this particularly succulent spring morning the birds were cheeping and the dogs were barking, and in our old, cracked bathroom mirror — you know, the kind that is so old that the beveled edges are yellowing — I saw the monster of my own making. This morning some Greater Mother Power had transformed me into a bona fide white girl with round eyes. My single-creased eyelid turned double, which forced the corners that originally slanted upward to slope downward. My eyes were now as round as orbs and appeared twice as large as before. My eyeballs that were once deep brown, almost black, had suddenly lightened into a golden amber. Even my eyelashes, which were once straight and spare, became fuller and curled up against my new double lids.

I immediately felt guilty. My conscience said, "Serves you right for hating your kind, for wanting to be white. Remember that old Chinese saying, don't wish for something too hard, you might just get it — and then what?" There were no telltale signs of expensive surgery — no gauze, no swelling, no nothing. When the good lord makes a miracle, she does it seamlessly. After surgery, Amy looked like Frankenstein for about two months. She was black and blue and had huge ghastly stitches. Three months later, she was a completely new person cut out from *Vogue*. She had totally reinvented herself — new clothes, new friends, new attitude. She even lost her Hong Kong accent. And there she was hanging out with the in-crowd — smoking and swearing up a storm like a rich white person. Like she had a piece of the American dream in her pocket. "What did you do," I asked, "pay for your face with your soul?"

The terrible truth is that I was desperately jealous of Amy's new popularity. She said once, while buffing her fake nails, "We're Americans now, we have to climb that ladder of success, keep up with the Joneses. Always *one up* ourselves." Well, that's our new motto, isn't that quaint, "improve ourselves Wongs."

Amy's family started this trickle-down effect. In the '80s, the fierce competition and struggle for status in Amy's family infected ours like the plague. Every day, after my father's death, my mother would come home from her long day's work at the factory and scowl blankly at us. My sister and I — we were never good enough, pretty enough, smart enough. My mother was the sacrificial tree, on which the next crop was supposed to flourish and bear beautiful fruit — only the present harvest was not quite ready. We were an anemic batch, or one too hard or green and small to bring a good barter at the market. My mother would scrutinize us in her sleepy sadness and sob, then fold herself up in bed and not come out again until it was already the next morning and time for her to go to work at the factory. There was no end to her misery.

My father used to say that only in America could you reinvent yourself. Morons could become presidents, fools could become princes, bandits could become CEOs, whores could become first ladies. Of course, what he was really getting at was that my uncle, the "immoral two-bit four-legged thug sodomist" became a millionaire restaurateur overnight. Somehow, the "golden mountain" dream had eluded my father. The great lorries of gold had passed him by, and all he had left in his miserable soul was rage and envy.

My father loved to bitch and mutter and spit his venom into the giant wok of chop suey — into that great noxious swill they called Suburban Chinese American food. He would spit and swear, "You, mother's c——. You, turtle's eggs. You, bag of dead girl bones." He would shovel and toss unidentified chunks of flesh and veggies into his giant sizzling wok. An unfiltered Lucky Strike dangling from his lips, rivers of sweat pouring from his greasy hair. I can still see him now, bless his dead soul, red-faced, shoveling and wokking in the great cauldron of hell, hacking and coughing up bile from his black lungs.

So on that fine, succulent spring morning in 1985, I stood in front of the mirror. After my initial shock and strange shiver of delight, I noticed that the extra epicanthic folds had made deep creases around the sockets. My eyes felt dry, I supposed because more surface was now exposed to light. Suddenly, it occurred to me that my new eyes were not beautiful. They looked like they were in a persistent state of alarm. If my cousin had had the subtle "Kathleen Turner" job at the premium price, I must have had the bargain basement "Betty Boop."

Finally, I managed to pull myself away from the mirror to go downstairs — to ask my wise sister Bessie for her opinion. She said, barely looking up from her cereal,

"Nah, don't worry about it. It's the process of assimilation. Happens to the best of us." To me my sister was God. Like my grandmother, she always had this "Buddhistic" attitude, like, "So what, you turned into a donkey, you'll get over it." She was never a team player. In fact, as a child she was always relegated to the sidelines to warm the bench. The white kids never "chose" her to play in their team sports. They used to tease her for being a four-eyed geek, and she didn't give a damn. "Dodge Ball, what kinda game is that? Who wants to be a moving target and get brain-damaged?"

She was like one of those Chinese people who could climb to the apex of a mountain and see everything. Someday, she would become a famous biologist or anthropologist and the people would pay a hundred bucks a plate to hear her talk about neo-genetic theory. And she would get back at those white folks for all those years of humiliation and bench-warming by saying something utterly inane like, "Caucasoids have more hair on their bodies because they are less evolved," and everybody would applaud, buy her book, and stand in a long line for her autograph. Afterward, they would go home and say, "I have touched the sleeve of genius."

But I was not as self-assured as Bessie. I was as shallow as everybody else. I was a teenager, for God's sake; I didn't have any depth. It was not my station in life to see beyond my petty, personal predicament. I was always falling through the cracks, always afraid of being different. In this way, I was more like Amy than Bessie. I wanted to fit in. I wanted to be conventional. I wanted the sublime, banal package they made in the mall. I wanted to be the perfect stupid blonde girl who married the perfect stupid blond boy next door. It was no secret that I wanted to be white, to be "accepted" by the in-crowd, to look as white as a magazine cover — I confess, in sixth grade, in the shameful privacy of my own bathroom, I used to tape my eyelids up with strong scotch mailing tape and pretend that I was Christie Brinkley, with big round cow eyes.

Don't worry. This is no Kafkaesque tale in which I turn into a giant cockroach and my family the philistines beat me up and kill me. I had no fear of my present transformation. We know that anything can happen during adolescence: Nipples turn into breasts, breasts turn into beards. But look, there is no mystery to this — at 15, the entire female population of the species is mired in self-hatred and every girl despises her own face and body. We all wanted to be cookie-cutter Barbies. If the dominant race had green skin and purple genitals, I would want to look like that, too. It was not until I turned 35 that I finally realized I was a beautiful Chinese woman and that my ancient features were hand-painted on the elegant Sung dynasty scrolls. But so what, my enlightenment came too late; my self-esteem was already irreversibly damaged.

Finally, on that fateful day, my sister Bessie suggested that I tell an adult. Mind you, this was the last resort. In my household, my father was already dead. My mother and grandmother were my guardians now. My mother was doing double shifts at an electronics firm, putting tiny chips into "motherboards" — she had just returned to work after three days in the hospital recovering from carpal tunnel surgery. And she was asleep, which was her favorite thing to do on Saturdays. I dared not disturb her dreams. She smiled in her sleep. I knew that it was only in her dreams that she could be happy.

So I had to tell my grandmother, the great matriarch. She was the one who raised us while my parents spent most of their lives grueling at their respective sweatshops. She was, as all Chinese grandmothers are, the self-appointed keeper of our Chinese identity. She thought that we were still sojourners, that sooner or later we would improve our Cantonese and pack up our belongings, and that the Chinese from ten thousand diasporas would fly back to China like a pack of homeward geese, back to the "middle kingdom." And there we would start over in a new Utopian village, marry yellow husbands, produce yellow children, and live in eternal golden harmony.

Indeed, my grandmother would be the one to offer me a profound explanation. She was the one who knew about the transmogrification of the soul. She used to tell us stories about all kinds of magical transformations — women turned into foxes, foxes into spirits. Don't be a jerk in this life, for you would be punished in the next by being transformed into a water-rat. She showed us pictures of a pagan Hell where the punishment always fit the crime. If you were a liar, an ox-headed hatchet man would cut off your tongue. If you were a thief, they would cut off your hands. If you were an adulterer, they would cut off your "you-know-what." What, then, would be the appropriate punishment for a girl-child who wished so hard to be accepted by white people that her beautiful slanted eyes turned round?

Right then she was asleep, snoring in her favorite armchair. See that squished gnat on her dress — that was her characteristic signature. The great matriarch did not believe in frivolity. I never approached her with the various problems of girl-children. When a pool of blood appeared mysteriously on my dress, I consulted my sister and she pulled out her textbook on the "various hormonal problems of pre-pubescent girls" and bought me a copy of *Our Bodies, Ourselves*. She said, "Damn, sorry, Sis, but you've entered the world of womanhood."

When two bullies at school beat me up and stole my lunch money, I was too ashamed to tell my grandmother. Instead, I worked an extra shift at my uncle's restaurant and peeled shrimp to pay for the missing money. This continued for three weeks — they beat me up and took my money, and I had work extra hours to pay for my own lunch. I peeled so much shrimp that my allergic fingers blew up like pink pork sausages. Finally, I told my pugilistic father. He immediately took time off from work and drove me to the hospital to get my fingers drained. They also gave me adrenaline shots. My father then went to school and grabbed my vice-principal Mr. Comely by his lapel and loudly urged in broken English that those boys be suspended. "Moogoogaipan, you want Moogoogaipan? You get Moogoogaipan."

For some reason, my father just happened to have a giant spatula in his pocket that day. He pulled it out and started slapping Mr. Comely with it, making tiny red marks the size of chop suey chunks all over his face. And there I was, a typical stupid teenager, not proud that my father was trying to defend me, but embarrassed that my geek-father would actually use a spatula as a deadly weapon. It would be a different story if he had brandished a machete or a sawed-off assault rifle. What a sight, my father waving his spatula and Mr. Comely backing up, defending himself with his gold Cross pen.

The boys were never suspended. But, suddenly, I was given a reprieve. After all, it's not divine intervention but fate that is the catalyst for change. Within the next few months, everybody sort of "poor" disappeared: My father died shortly after that episode, Mr. Comely was transferred because of his alcoholism, one bully went to prison, the other moved to Pittsburgh with his divorced mother. (And who could've predicted that I would someday end up graduating *cum laude* from Harvard Law School to become a Yuppie trial attorney for the Small Business Administration? Or that in my 30s, I would marry a Filipino activist I met at a coffee shop, a man whose radical ideas would transform my whole life? Or that I would end up devoting my life's work to defending the wives of murdered guerrillas in Luzon? Of course, this is another story.)

Well, anyway, in my terrible childhood, life was humiliation after humiliation and tiptoeing around that sleeping mother and grandmother. My grandmother had survived a series of natural and man-made disasters: the Sino-Japanese war, famine, drought, flooding, bloodthirsty warlords, the Nationalist debacles, the Communist revolution, pestilence, a long bout of the cholera epidemic. Now that she was 85 and had survived everything and reached the shores of safety, it was the ripe time for her to finally enjoy peace, her grandchildren, and napping in her favorite armchair. I was worried that she would have a heart attack upon seeing me. I climbed up her lofty lap and said, "Granny, look what happened to my eyes, they've turned round, I am sorry for having been remiss, for being a bad child. For wishing the unthinkable. For dreaming the unmentionable."

She looked at me with her complacent Buddha smile. "So, girl-child, now you're a round-eye. When you were born you were such a beautiful princess, more beautiful than Yang Kuei Fei. You had skin of jade, and slanted moon-like eyes. Our ancestors were proud to behold such a plum blossom. Now look what has happened to you, my little snake in the grass, my little damselfly, how you have changed."

Her compassionate words touched me deeply, and I began to cry from my little round eyes. The tears were especially bulbous and fat. She caressed me all night long, telling me ghost stories and fables, feeding me glazed ginger and dried plums. No mention was made of my transformation. Deep in her heart, she knew that each step backward would only mean regret — the vector only goes one direction, the homing geese must find their new nest, the ten thousand diasporas will never coagulate — there was no way back to the Middle Kingdom.

Pop Culture

By Amy Lau

Barbie never looked like me
Closest was the girl from Voltron
Even Japanese animation gave her blond hair and blue eyes
No two acre bangs of straight black hair
        Or a flat nose
        Or slanted eyes
I never had the 38-18-34
Just four inch heels
Steve Madden makes especially for me
And I never looked good in pink
        A girl's signature pop culture color
Barbie was just an All-American Girl
And Voltron got canceled
So I played with Garbage Pail Kids

4

Breaking
Silences

Sexuality

Sessions

By Nora Okja Keller

Nah, I don't hate her — I mean, she's my Mom. The only thing I hold against her is that she fed me regurgitated kimchee and rice. I was only three, you see, and had no conception of what was gross. We were flying to Hawaii for the first time, me and my Mom, to meet her new *haole* boyfriend — now my *haole* stepdad. In one arm she carried me, and in the other arm she smuggled a bottle of kimchee, a small pot of rice, chopsticks and a spoon, all wrapped in an old K-Mart sack and stuffed into a plastic Pan Am bag.

Once we settled into our seats and the flight settled into a comfortable monotony, she opened up the lunch pouch. "This is Korean sauerkraut." I'm sure she must have giggled to the screwed-up faces and surprised eyes that sought the source of the smell and found her. She took a bite of rice, a bite of kimchee, and — switching chopsticks for a spoon — spit everything back out for me. Later she explained that I wouldn't eat it without the added mother flavor, that I'd cry if she gave it to me straight. But I imagine fellow passengers, even those who had said, "Cute kid," even those who could still smile after having been assaulted by the smell of garlic and fermented cabbage, must have turned away too embarrassed to look anymore, too polite to comment on our eating habits. Even the gentleman who sat next to us in his soft blue suit, briefcase on his lap, must have hurriedly shuffled through papers and studied his documents with unwavering concentration.

Sometimes when people stare at me funny, I wonder if it's 'cause they recognize me as the weird girl on the plane, the one who would only eat spit up food.

But that's all I'd be mad at her for, not that I'm mad. I don't even hold it against her that she married Jack; she just believed his lies.

"I love you. I'll take care of you," he said to my Mom. What did she know?

"We'll live in the country. I'll buy you a pony," he said to me. What did I know?

After they got married, we moved into the Ala Wai Plaza. All I remember from that place is that I couldn't keep a pony there, or a dog or a cat, only a fish that I tried to train to come to the top of the aquarium when I tapped on the glass. I tried to pet it, my hand chasing the red and yellow tail around till water overflowed, but it got some skin disease and died. Its name was Herman Hoopster. I don't know why.

Also, I remember that a woman jumped off the roof and that my Mom wouldn't let me go out to see what was left of her,

Oh, and I remember the time I wet my pants. I was in the second grade and my favorite book was *The Little Black Pony*. That ties in 'cause one day after school I rushed to the library to borrow this book and — even though I had to pee really bad — I ran right home to read it. When I got to 12E, the door was locked. Mom used to be there all the time, but I guess she'd already started working at the restaurant by then. I didn't have a key, so I waited in front of the door thinking someone would come home any minute. I sat on my Josie and the Pussycats lunch box and twisted my legs together. I sang "I'm a Little Teapot" to get my mind off my bladder. But I ended up crying and squatting. Yellow water trickled from our welcome-mat down to that little gutter opening rainwater drains out of. Raindrops of pee must have dripped right down to the parking lot. I sat there crying, and that's how Jack found me.

"What happened here?" he said.

And I told him: "I fell in that puddle. I hurt my butt."

Jack stood me up and rubbed my butt, his hands sliding right up to my crotch. His eyes were closed. "Hmm . . . I see," he said, and he opened the door. Jack led me to my bedroom and laid out dry panties and a dress for me. The panties and the dress matched — white cotton with pink polka dots and pink lace. Jack liked lace. Whenever he bought me panties they had lace edged around them.

"Change," Jack said. He sat down on my bed.

I changed with my back facing him, but I know he watched me 'cause I felt it.

"We won't tell your Mama what you did today," he said. "As if she'd understand, anyway."

I felt his eyes, but he didn't touch me.

Then.

The first time? There was not a first time, really. Hands creeping to touch mine when Mom fell asleep at the TV, fingers wrestle-tickling me and then brushing against my chest, brushing "down there." Once he came home with groceries and asked me to scratch through his jeans for him: "My hands are full, can you . . .?" Once, when I was taking a bath, he unlocked the door with a butter knife. He came in to use the bathroom, he said, but then he couldn't pee.

Yeah, he came into my room sometimes, late at night when the crickets are real loud, the only thing you can hear above the growling of the refrigerator. Sometimes he'd watch me when I pretended to sleep — I know how to make my breaths so even and smooth, and how to make my lips smack together like people sometimes do in their sleep.

Sometimes he'd get into bed with me.

Those times I'd make him small — smaller and smaller than the palm of my hand. I'd make him so tiny that in my dreams he turned into a tiny white mouse that scurried all over my legs and up and down my arms. A little mouse that I could pick up by the tail and put into a cage.

Jack told me a joke one night. I breathed deep and even, eyes closed, but he told it to me anyway: "I had a China-girl once, but how disappointing. . . . I was horny again an hour later."

My Mom — she cried a lot and was tired and sick a lot. Jack took care of her during the days when she was off from work, massaging her feet, giving her medicine. "Let her sleep," he'd say. And he didn't like her to wear glasses or contacts 'cause of her disease called "astingementism," or something like that. Once when she did buy contacts, I saw him dump them into the bathroom sink. When she tried to ask him about it, he scolded her for being stupid and absent-minded, but she got mad. So then he just sweet-talked her.

"Now, now, hon, what exactly do you want from me?" Jack asked her, even though he knew.

"You have contak?" Mom was holding her hand out to the side of him, palm up, like she was gonna hit him. I was hoping she would.

"Contact? Contact? Oh, you mean like that allergy pill I give you, that sneezing pill?"

"No, contak, contak." Mom pointed to her eyes. "No see good."

"You mean contacts, don't you. Contacts." Jack made a real *ssss* sound. "Now you know that's a no-no, honey. Bad, bad for you."

"No, no bad," Mom said. "You have? Gib me right now, this min."

Jack made clucking and shhing-noises. "Calm down," he said. "You people have bad tempers. . . . Let me give you something to relax." Jack stroked Mom's head, her cheeks, and her forehead. "I'm your man, sugar pie," he clucked. "I take care of you, don't I?" And Mom was led away to the bedroom saying, "You right, you right." She always said that in the end.

It was hard to talk to her, anyway. 'Cause she'd be so tired most of the time her words would drool together, or she'd forget where she was and start to speak in Korean, which was forbidden in the house. Jack said that those "ching-chong" words made him nervous. Besides, he said, Mom had to learn better English for her own good.

So, no, I never did tell on him.

I have to wash my hands a lot because it got harder and harder for me to change Jack into a mouse. He'd change into animals I couldn't handle — a wolf, a giant worm, a man.

Finally, I managed to turn him into a squirrel, but only by making myself into a tree for him to hide in. When he became a squirrel, bark crept and caked over skin, and my blood would turn into sap making my body stiff and strong and very heavy. My hair became autumn leaves falling around my head, blinding me with gold, red, brown cracklings when I turned this way or that.

At first I just washed it off once in the mornings so the bark wouldn't root down for good. I'd scrub and scrub till my own skin showed itself again, pink and raw. But then I noticed I had to wash more often. One day at lunch one of my fingers — my left littlest one — sprouted a twig. I washed it off quickly. I don't think anyone noticed.

But you know something? I'm tired of taking baths.

I had a pet fish once. I named him Herman Hoopster. I don't know why. It died because I petted him to death. And I had a pet squirrel once, too. I named him Jack. I don't know why. It died. One day I made it get smaller and smaller 'til it was a small little ant crawling around way high in my branches. When I shook my leaves, the squirrel fell all the way down. If you ever wondered if animals could scream, they can.

Hey, I don't think I'll wash anymore. It's only been a day, but look at how rough and brown my skin is already. And see how dry and crackly my hair is? My toes are even getting longer and are starting to curl downwards.

Hurry, can you plant me in the country?

You don't have to take care of me anymore, my Mom can do that. She can dig around me with a spade and ivory chopsticks. She can take a sip of water from her green watering can and spit it onto my roots.

My Sexuality

By Cookie Hiponia

The rights to my sexuality have been sold to Hollywood
by writers, directors and producers who refuse to wake from
a collective wet dream.

I have been marketed as
Dorothy Lamour in *The Road to Bali*
Nancy Kwan in *The World of Suzy Wong*
Tia Carrera in *Wayne's World*.

My sexuality will no longer smile demurely.
It will not fit itself into a sarong.
It will not be contained in a long silk dress.
It will not don a kimono nor paint its lips red.
It will never say, "Me love you long time, sailor."

I take my sexuality back.
You cannot sell what you never owned.

Breaking Silences

BY GENA SANTOS

For six years I was so scared and confused, not knowing who to trust and who to turn to. I truly believed that there was only one person for me to confide in. I was the only person who could understand what I was going through. I had isolated myself from everyone else, even from my own family, because I was too ashamed and embarrassed about what I thought I had done. I thought that if I told anybody my big secret, then everyone would be disappointed in me and, crazy as it may seem, I thought that my family would want to disown me. To spare my family all of the drama I believed my secret would cause, I had decided that the best thing for me to do was to keep all of my thoughts and feelings to myself and to hide the truth from others. I went through fear, guilt, shame, anger, self-hatred, denial, and it was not until six years later that I realized that this silence was only inflicting pain on me and that I had to do something about it before I lost my sanity because of it.

When I was 11 years old, my uncle's sexual abuse started, and that was when I started blaming myself for everything that had happened to me in those few years of my life. He was my Uncle John, the one who lived with us, the one who used to take me and my brother to amusement parks, the one who used to buy us ice cream on hot summer days, the one my parents raised me to love and trust. All of a sudden he started touching me differently. I had no clue what he was doing or why he was doing it. It was something that I had never experienced before and, not knowing how to react, I let it happen without saying anything, trusting that my uncle would never do anything to hurt me.

As soon as it ended, I went straight to my room, trying to figure out what had happened to me downstairs in the family room just seconds ago. I did not think that it would ever happen again, so I just chose to pretend that nothing had happened at all. However, I could not ignore it any longer after it had happened a second time, and then again, and then again, over and over. By then, I knew that what he was doing was wrong, but I was too scared to speak up and say anything to him to make it all stop and go away. Every night it happened I can remember going upstairs to my room and breaking down, crying in front of my mirror. I would look at myself and say, "That was the last time you're gonna let it happen; next time you're gonna say 'STOP!' and then leave the room." It sounded so simple when I was telling myself all of this, but all of the times that it happened, I never could get myself to say anything to him. No matter how much emotional pain the abuse was causing me, I forced myself to take it and not make a big fuss about it.

How could I tell anybody that I let Uncle John do all of this stuff to me? At the time, I honestly believed that I was the one who was at fault in that situation because I was the one who could not speak up, I was the one who let it happen so many times, I should have had the courage to tell him to stop. I was guilty and ashamed. I thought that admitting what happened to me to anyone was like admitting that I was a bad, horrible person. I was afraid of what others, especially my family, would think about me. What I did not realize at the time was that by keeping everything silent, I was only hurting myself.

The guilt and shame I felt turned into anger and self-hatred. I was mad at myself, thinking that it was all my fault; I had done something so terrible that I could never forgive myself. Because I was keeping everything silent, I could not let anyone think that there was something wrong with me, so I had no one to turn to. I was alone and felt helpless, hiding my true self from everyone. The silence became almost too overwhelming to bear. There was even a period where I thought that the only thing that could end my pain and suffering was for me to commit suicide. As I cried myself to sleep at night, I would think about going down to the kitchen to get a knife to slit my wrists, or going to the medicine cabinet to find pills to overdose on. I wondered if anyone would care if one day they found me lifeless on the floor of my bedroom. I thought that by committing suicide I could get revenge and show my uncle what he did to me, and maybe then he would feel bad and guilty for all those times that he abused me.

Knowing that suicide was a huge decision that I should not rush into, I prayed a lot to God asking what I should do, and luckily I realized that suicide was not the right answer that I was looking for. Instead, I decided that what I had to do was simply try to forget that anything happened, deny that I ever let myself be abused by him. For a few years, I actually thought that denial would end all my problems, but I guess I was wrong. Denying the situation was just like denying myself, because all the abuse that I experienced is a part of what makes me who I am, whether I am proud of it or not. Mom was right when she used to tell me, "You can never run from the truth." I eventually found out that there would always be reminders of what happened to me in the past regarding my uncle and the abuse. I could only be in denial for so long before I had to face the truth of who I am and what I went through.

That truth finally came a little more than two years ago, when it felt like there were so many reminders of the past that I could not take hiding the truth any longer. The day I finally snapped was the day when Uncle John, who was still living with us, was the only adult home because my parents were gone on vacation for a couple of weeks and my Grandma was away in the Philippines. I was 16 years old and, not having any instructions from my parents to let my uncle know if I decided to go out, I had left the house without telling him that I was going to hang out with some of my high school friends on that warm summer night. I had left my parked car in a parking lot in front of my friend's family restaurant so that we could all drive around in one car instead of two. Around one in the morning, when I returned to my car, I found a note on my window saying, "COME HOME NOW! – Uncle John." As I was driving home, I looked in my rear view mirror and I could see my uncle's black Dodge Daytona following me all the way to our house. At that moment I knew that once I got inside, I would get another big lecture from him about me hanging out with guys, especially since I never mentioned to him that I was going out.

I was right; it was another lecture that made me feel that it was wrong that I go out with anybody of the opposite sex. This was the first time that he actually followed me home. Usually he just waited by the door for me to get home so that he could tell me who and who not to go out with. I was furious and, not being able to do what I usually do and hold my feelings in, I decided to argue and yell back at him. Normally I would not yell at a relative, but I had already lost respect for him when he violated me in the past. My brother, Richard, heard the whole conversation and started getting mad at me, telling me that I should have respect for him because he is such a good uncle who was always doing good things for us and for our cousins. That is when I lost it and had to tell him that Uncle John was not as good a person as everyone thought he was. I told him everything, from the abuse to all the effects that it had caused.

Richard was the first person that I ever told, but when I told him, I asked him to keep it silent and not to tell our parents. After I told Richard, I told a couple of my closest friends. But it was not until a year later that I told my Mom what had happened. I was able to do this only when I had finally accepted that I was abused by Uncle John and that what happened to me was not all my fault. I was not sure how she would react, or if she would even believe me, but I decided to take the chance and tell her everything. Thankfully, she believed what I told her, and she offered her support. That was a big breakthrough because out of everybody, her trust and support is what I valued the most. Having my mother on my side encouraged me to want to eventually confront Uncle John by myself so that I would not let him get away with everything that he had done to me. I felt so much relief knowing that I had friends and family by my side supporting me in trying to pull my life back together.

I finally felt like I was gaining my self-confidence back, and I could actually picture myself going to Uncle John and confronting him about the whole issue. I still had anger toward him inside of me. When I pictured myself confronting him, I saw myself threatening to expose him to the whole family, especially everyone who thought that he was such a nice and generous guy. I thought that that was the only way that I could confront him, but I held back from actually doing it because I thought about how hurt my Grandma would be if she found out what her son had done. She would probably try and deny it because it seems like he was one of my Grandma's favorite children, over my Mom. My Grandma loved Uncle John so much, and I did not want to risk hurting her.

I have not actually confronted him yet, but all of the time and thought that I have put into my decisions, along with a lot of self-growth that came along with fighting this battle, have led me to the right final decision. I think that the biggest step in breaking silence like the one that I have kept is learning to forgive and learning to let go. I have accepted the situation and have forgiven myself for everything that happened, and I have forgiven my uncle for what he did to me. I believe that if I approach him with the goal of reconciling our relationship by telling him that I have forgiven him, rather than threaten to expose him as an evil person, then I can have closure on the situation without his being angry at me for embarrassing him in front of the whole family, especially his mother, my Grandma. I will tell him that I have forgiven him, but I also have to let him know the things that I have gone through because of his actions. I just want to patch up our relationship so that I can stop worrying about the whole situation once and for all.

This eight-year challenge I have been facing is finally starting to come to an end, but only because I was able to gain enough strength to break my silence and share my story with others. Breaking silences is not something that comes easily. It takes a lot of courage, patience and perseverance. I know that it is a long, draining process, but it is well worth it to break those silences and overcome our fears. Although we may think that keeping silent is sparing others from pain, it is important to remember that we should be true to ourselves and not get caught up in the lies and facades that are associated with silences.

After writing this memoir, I was able to gain enough strength to go to my uncle and confront him about the abuse. Getting myself to knock on his door and bring up something that happened eight years ago was the hardest thing that I have ever done.

Now that I have finally accomplished that goal, I feel free. Free from the power that he had over me for all those years. Confronting him does not mean that the abuse never happened, nor does it mean that I will never think about it again. The fact that it happened will always remain, but as long as I know that I have done all that is in my power to heal the situation, I know I can finally move on with my life without any regrets about the struggle that it took me to become the strong pinay that I am now.

Silence Saved Her

By Catherine Bitney

believe.
believe what he preaches.
there is only one lifestyle.
there is only one goal.

meet.
meet the chosen one.
consummate your love.
pass on your genes.

raise.
raise your offspring.
keep the common belief.
pass on your ignorance.

teach.
teach one lifestyle.
teach one goal.
ignore your feelings.

listen.
listen to a parallel lifestyle.
one that you know well.
one that you don't live.

sit.
sit in silence.
maybe things will change.
maybe they'll never know.

Why Me?

ANONYMOUS

My mother cries out in the middle of the night, sounding like a wounded cat. The next day, I watch as her face turns green and blue from the bruises that she received from her husband. One blow after the other. At the dinner table, I listen as my parents fight over the family income. For years, all I ever did was listen and cry.

If you didn't know me, you probably would have thought that I grew up in a very loving family, one that was perfect in the eyes of society. That's what people thought when they'd come over to my house. We kids did every little thing that was asked by our parents. The house was usually clean, so no one would notice that something was wrong. And people who did come over always gave good comments to my parents. So you see, that's why whatever was behind closed doors was even harder to talk about. It was forbidden.

I grew up in a home that consisted of physical, financial, emotional and mental abuse. I had to watch as my mother got hit over and over by someone whom she defended — someone she loved. I had to listen as my mother's husband told her that she was nothing but a woman with no strength, power or will to stop him. No matter how much we tried to tell her that it wasn't her fault, she would always say that she brought it upon herself. She always had to ask before she spent money on clothes, bought food for the family, or spent time with her friends. My mother was like a walking and talking dummy that was controlled by a monster that lived in the house with us.

The control that my stepfather had was not only on my mother, but also on us kids. My sisters, brother and I did everything that we were told to do. We didn't even attempt to disobey his commands. We tried our hardest to please him because, deep down, we knew that he could hurt us in the same way he hurt our mother. I remember one incident when I was in the third grade that bruised me in more than one way.

My brother and I were fighting over our things in the bedroom. My mother told us to shut up, but we couldn't hear her because we were arguing too loudly. Then our stepfather came in with his guitar and just started hitting my brother with it. I could still hear my brother cry out in pain as the guitar hit him. The next thing I knew, our stepfather turned on me, and the guitar broke on my back. I don't remember how many times he hit us with his guitar, but every time that he did, it sounded like the drums at the Chinese New Year Festival. The next day we found out that he and my mother had been fighting. I guess he decided to take it out on us.

I also remember what happened when my sister Tammy was just learning how to crawl. It was after school, and my uncle brought my cousin and me home from school. I remember walking into the house and my grandma and Mom were eagerly telling us that my baby sister had just crawled all the way to the other side of our living room. When they told us, we could barely understand them, because it sounded as if they had just won a million-dollar lottery and couldn't wait to let the world know.

That night, they decided to let my sister crawl to her father and let him find out why the family was so happy. But when he got home, he was in a bad mood and got into a fight with my Mom because his dinner wasn't on the table. So when my sister crawled over to him, instead of picking her up, he kicked her in the face and her nose started bleeding.

So much for the excitement of celebrating my sister's new-found skills. To think, my Mom and auntie were late with dinner because they had planned something special for that night to celebrate. Now, when my sister gets sick and she doesn't tell us, we know because her nose bleeds and it gives her away.

I have so many painful memories of all these things that happened to me. Yet, my Mom won't talk about it and won't let us talk about it either. I guess it's a cultural thing. Maybe she's afraid of losing her pride, or losing face or something. I guess it's also because we're so isolated that it's hard for her to talk about it with others. By isolated, I mean she doesn't know where to go for help with these problems because of the language barriers that she has in this country.

I know that these abuses happen throughout the Mien community and in Laotian families as well. But not many of the women want to talk about it because they're all scared. People in the community add to the problem by gossiping and exaggerating. I wish that people would start talking about domestic violence, because that's the only way for them to find help or get help for their family. If more people started to open up, then that alone would give other women in the same kinds of relationships strength to speak up as well. Together, women like them would be able to fight their abusers and open up shelters in our communities.

The Cockroach

BY GRACE M. WOO

The #9 San Bruno bus isn't exactly a country club bus. The corners stink of piss and the floors are littered and worn with the careless habits of the thousands of passengers who have come and gone and come again. The #9 always seemed crowded with highly charged combinations of people: F.O.B.s, A.B.C.s, African Americans, older generation Latinos, taggers, single mothers, and white twentysomethings looking for a multicultural paradise. The #9 brought disparate people together in a tense illusion of closeness.

When one assumes that the bus will come on time, it doesn't. Emily waited more than 35 minutes before the #9 San Bruno came. When it arrived, all the anger that had been building up inside her towards the bus deities suddenly disappeared, replaced by the relief of finally being able to get home. Boarding the bus she faced the familiar crowd, the smell and the look. From the cracked sunflower seeds, empty soda cans, crumpled up brown paper bags left under seats, and spat out gum, only the graffiti really stood out. Emily knew one of the tags. It was at the front of the bus. That's supposed to be pretty gutsy.

Emily got a seat somewhere in the middle of the bus. Good timing, she thought as she plopped down into it. She thought about taking out the book she had to read for English class but didn't because it would've been uncool to run into a friend and be seen reading *Of Mice and Men*. Instead, she stared out the window, mesmerized by the flip-flop colors of the houses that the bus passed. Little pink houses, modern flats, multicolored Victorians. Her thoughts drifted. Her eyes relaxed out of focus. She awoke from her daze when she caught sight of one of the more annoying things to find on a bus — a cockroach. Another thing to remind her of her existence as a nothing high school sophomore. No license. No car. No boyfriend. Just a date with a filthy bus every day. But on second thought, this cockroach was different. It was tiny. Really tiny. Small enough to almost be cute with its chubby candycorn-shaped body and long, thin, twitching antennae.

It crawled on the air vents along side the windows, passing Emily's shoulder before tenuously crawling onto an unsuspecting seated rider. Emily watched the cockroach board onto the person in front of her. She self-consciously thought of the number of times a bug might have been crawling on her with nobody telling her. Wondering whether or not she had a moral obligation to tell the person, she shifted in her seat until the urge passed. The little cockroach scurried over the landscape of the person's sweater until it disappeared from Emily's sight. Was it okay? When the bus jerked suddenly, Emily imagined it being squashed between the person's back and the back of the seat. But Emily was surprised and happy to see it emerge and eventually find momentary safety on the smooth surface of the seat.

The cockroach moved towards the next nearest person, antennae waving as if to greet him, unaware of the surrounding danger and animosity. Emily was absorbed in the anticipation of where it would go next and what would happen next. If it were a cute little ladybug or some other socially acceptable insect, maybe Emily would have rescued it, put it in her coat pocket, and released it when she got home. But she did not raise a hand or utter a word as the little cockroach was flattened into oblivion by a man's hand.

*　　　*　　　*　　　*　　　*　　　*　　　*　　　*　　　*

A few moments after Matt got on the #9, he noticed a young Oriental girl. The thought of getting close to her immediately came to mind, but the bus was crowded. Crowded with the working class, tough, not timid about yelling "Openthebackdoor!!" In the ordinariness of the bus, the Oriental girl was different. She stood out with an attractiveness that was unassuming. Not with tight clothes or because she wore a boy's brown corduroy coat, but attractive because she was a young woman with the ripe vulnerabilities of an adolescent.

Each time the crowd in the bus shifted and settled, Matt took the opportunity to move closer. If he had found her alone, he knew he would have reached out and stroked her straight black hair and reached into her coat. Being near her made him feel powerful. The ease in which he knew he could touch her made his restraint feel even more righteous. For that moment, he was content with remaining in the background watching her as she took her seat.

He hovered in the aisle, politely offering empty seats to old men and women with young children. Because the bus would soon reach his stop and he didn't know when the girl would get off herself, Matt felt heavy with urgency. When the seat next to the Oriental girl was finally free, he felt like he could not move fast enough.

A small cockroach scurried along the seat in front and then stopped in its tracks as if to greet him. Matt did not hesitate to kill it.

*　　　*　　　*　　　*　　　*　　　*　　　*　　　*　　　*

Anna got on the #9 bus at the beginning of the line. Her stop wasn't until the end of the line. Every day she sat at the very back and saw the entire spectrum of riders get on and off the bus. Tourists headed for the San Francisco Shopping Centre, Chinese sewing ladies going home, Latinos riding the bus to the Potrero, homeless men and women going to General Hospital. Right before Van Ness Avenue turned into South Van Ness, the bus filled to an unbearable number. Most everyone was a stranger to each other so that any conversation held on the bus rang out.

Anna could not have been the only one who overheard a man talking to a Chinese American girl sitting next to him. Anna watched and listened as the man asked the girl if she were Japanese. No? Chinese. Chinese American, really? With authority, the man asserted that the Chinese were usually not so beautiful. Anna was repulsed as a part of her wondered if she herself would have had the white man's approval. She didn't know if the man was white. Maybe he was Latino or maybe *hapa*. But somehow, pointing the blame somewhere was important to her.

The man flirted with the girl, telling her that she would be really beautiful in a few years. Really beautiful, he mumbled again as his eyes moved intently from the girl's face down to her youthful breasts. He remarked further that because she was Oriental, she would remain slim and small, unlike white girls, who grew big and thick. The girl smiled nervously. Anna's heart pounded, strained with anticipation over what was happening before her. Anna wanted to raise her voice and intervene. But what would she say? The urge to speak was powerful, but the feeling of helplessness was so suffocating. Anna remained a silent accomplice to what she witnessed. It would pass, she justified to herself.

Not quite sure if she should be polite or just not talk to strangers, the girl answered the man's questions as uninterestedly as possible. To Anna, the girl's message was so obvious that anyone could see. Anna tried to convince herself that he would figure it out and stop bothering her, but he continued to look intently at the girl and make small talk while Anna remained silent, watching both of them.

The girl suddenly stood up to leave. Anna's sense of anticipation quickened. She saw the man reach out his hand. Did the girl see it? Anna held her breath, frozen by the single wish for the girl's safe passage. His groping hand brushed the girl's waist, grazing down along her thigh as she moved past him. The girl reacted quickly, swatting his hand away. The man gently called out, "G'bye," and Anna found herself exhaling the words, "Fuck you."

Flashback

By Mary-Jocelyn A. Ortega

I still remember the events of that day in precise detail, although I wish it would fade from my memory somehow. People and places appear clearly, but for the life of me, I cannot seem to recall the exact date of that horrendous day.

Julie read the composition I had written for Mrs. Fowler's AP English class about the difficulties in life. "Are you sure you want to include this part?" she asked, pointing to the middle of the page.

"It's four words; she's not gonna catch it." I was so sure of myself but it was a poor miscalculation, and it was a mistake that changed my life.

Physical education was never my favorite part of the day, especially with the desert heat of the Inland Empire [Southern California]. Fortunately, my friends were in the class with me, and they were the only consolation. We'd all signed up for weight training that quarter, though we often ended up walking around the track, an option we frequently chose over lifting barbells. That day was no different.

"Hey, Lien," my friend Tina said. She didn't have the class with us, but somehow she always had a pass to wander campus. Damned newspaper staff! "Have you seen Mrs. Fowler yet?"

Boy had I. "Yes, I had class with her earlier today." She had caught the four words I thought she'd glance over and stack above her pile of graded papers. Instead, she had set my paper aside and had spoken to me during class about what I had written.

I remember being nervous when she called me up to her desk in the front of the room, and I admit I hadn't realized what it was about until I saw my paper on her desk. Unlike everyone else's, there were no comments in red ink. There was no grade. We only spoke for a moment about the incident mentioned in my composition. When the bell rang, she sent me off to my next class wondering what would happen next. Never in my life did I expect to hear Tina say, "She's looking for you, and a cop is with her."

I felt like someone had just punched me in the stomach. I held my breath for as long as I could, and without an answer, I slowly backed away from the group of friends that had gathered around me by then. I shook my head in disbelief and fear before I started walking briskly around the track, holding back tears. Julie jogged after me.

"I'm scared, Julie," I told her. "I don't want everyone to see me with a cop, especially not here in school." I had stopped walking before finishing my sentence, and tears slowly made their way down my face. With one swift stroke, I wiped them away with the back of my hand.

"It'll be okay," she assured me before putting her arm around my shoulders and leading me back to the locker room.

I sat quietly during the short drive home, my brother's best friend at the wheel of his black Volkswagen Rabbit. As usual, I rode shotgun, and my older brother sat in the seat behind me. So many things ran through my head all afternoon that I couldn't think straight during Chemistry. Luckily, there were no labs or tests scheduled that day, or I would have surely blown up the entire science building in my obliviousness.

Quickly I turned to look at my brother. "*Da ge* [Mandarin for *older brother*] I have to tell you something." I never gave him the opportunity to interrupt. "I was sexually abused by Yiwen while he stayed with us last month. I mentioned it in a paper so briefly that I didn't think she'd notice. Now there's a cop after me."

As I had expected, he said nothing. Then again, what kind of response could one give after receiving news like that? Yiwen was like a brother to him, since they'd grown up together like most cousins in Taiwan did, and somehow, they had managed to keep this bond even after my family moved to California in 1988.

"I don't want to go home," I told my companions.

"Where do you want to go?" Sergio asked without taking his eyes off the road.

"Anywhere else."

That afternoon, Sergio would have driven me anywhere I wanted if I had given him a specific destination, but we all knew there was no point in running away. It would only add to the situation at hand, and as we pulled up into our driveway, I suddenly found it hard to breathe.

I knew the next few hours would be difficult, but I kept reminding myself that it would all pass eventually. Again, I was wrong.

Da ge and I didn't say much to each other, almost as if we were saving our breath for the inevitable confrontation with our parents. He stayed out of my way as I nervously paced the perimeter of our house, trying to figure out how I was going to break the news to the rest of the family.

Now that I look back, I don't know if I should have called my mother at work, but I did. "Tell her now while she can't see you," I told myself over and over. Knowing she cared too much about image and impressions, I knew she would not allow her co-workers to witness her breakdown, and at the time I made this choice, it seemed like a good idea.

I had dialed her number with shaking hands, my voice faltering slightly when she greeted me. I hadn't known what to say or how to say it. "Mama," I started. "I have to tell you something, but you must promise not to get angry."

"What did you do now?" she asked, ready to scold me.

"Just spit it out," I kept telling myself. My breath was heavy and I closed my eyes tightly before finally saying, "I was sexually abused by Yiwen when he visited last month." I tried to get it out as fast as I could, hoping to rid myself of the load I had carried with me the entire day.

"What's that?" she asked.

As if it wasn't hard enough to break the news, now I had to explain what I had just said. I should have expected it. After all, we'd only been in America for five years, and we all had lots to learn about the culture. "You know," I said, hoping I wouldn't have to explain, "like on television."

"What are you talking about?" I could tell from her voice that she was already irritated. "Hurry Lien, I still have a lot of work to do."

"I was molested, Mama. Last month." I paused briefly before adding with gritted teeth, "by Yiwen."

Like *da ge,* she said nothing, but I could hear her breathing hard on the other end of the line. "We'll talk about this when I get home," she finally said, her voice cold and hard, before hanging up on me. I sat down on the nearby chair and cried, as I would be doing continually throughout the remainder of that day.

The phone rang continuously, and *da ge* answered each time. "It's the police officer," he said a few times that afternoon. I gave him some lame excuse about being in the bathroom or out of the house and amazingly, he'd lie for me. Mama called back only to grunt and scold silently before hanging up on me again.

"What are you going to do?" *da ge* asked me.

I just shrugged. "I don't know," I answered amidst fresh tears. "Help me."

"I think you should take this one step at a time, Lien. You'll have to deal with Mama and the cop no matter what. Maybe you should get the easier of the two out of the way." He handed me a piece of paper and said, "That's to the police department. Call them as soon as you feel strong enough to do it."

"I'm scared, *da ge,*" I told him. "I never thought I would need to talk to a policeman before."

"It'll be okay. He sounds really nice, and I'm sure he knows what he's doing," he said reassuringly. "I'll be in the other room if you need me." He left quietly, as I made one of the scariest decisions in my life. Shortly after that, I picked up the receiver and dialed the number *da ge* had scribbled onto the Post-it in his neat printing.

I do not remember the name of the officer I spoke to, and I probably would not recognize his voice if I heard it again, but there was something about him that made me feel more at ease. He greeted me warmly and asked me how I was doing instead of getting right to the point of the report that needed to be made against Yiwen for what he had done continuously throughout his visit.

"Where is he now?" he asked.

"Back in Taiwan," I told him. "He was only here for about a month for a visit before starting school again." Yiwen was going into his first year of college by then.

He asked for information about my cousin — his full name and age. I heard a low whistle after I said, "He turned 18 earlier this year."

The officer then explained that Yiwen's name would be added to some list, and he might be denied entrance to the United States in the future because of what he had done. I asked if he would be arrested or charged with a crime, and to my relief, the police department could not do anything because he was in another country. "He'll have a record now and if he ever comes back," the officer explained. "We can take him in even for something as minor as a traffic violation."

This was the lighter side of the conversation, but I knew the dirty facts had to come out and it was just a matter of time until he'd drop the difficult questions. Instead, the police officer said, "Tell me what happened." He didn't pry as deeply as I had expected him to. So I started to tell him how my family had planned to take my cousins sightseeing in Hollywood and Beverly Hills late one afternoon. My stepfather drove home from work in a spacious van he had rented to accommodate our five guests with the normal load of the three teenagers he had been supporting for half a decade.

Excitedly, we all gathered in the driveway, but I was sent back to change my jeans because, according to my stepfather, I looked like a handful of rice tightly wrapped with banana leaves. I ran upstairs to change quickly and only one cousin didn't wait with the rest. Yiwen followed me to my room and sneaked up behind me, putting his arms around my waist before slowly slipping his hands down the front of my unbuttoned blue jeans.

I was already crying by this point, but the ordeal was far from over. I remember the police officer's soothing voice telling me, "It's all right. Take your time. I'm not in any rush here." He'd tell me to take deep breaths and pause between sobs. "Don't be ashamed. It wasn't your fault that this happened. Everything you're telling me now, I've heard before."

Whoever he was, the police officer made the most difficult task I have had to face in my life a little more bearable. "Do you want to play 20 Questions then?" he asked, realizing I would say no more. I tried to be cooperative, but my tears had a different plan in mind, coming down hard.. "I'll ask you questions and all you have to say is yes or no. Are you okay with that?"

I nodded in answer, forgetting he could not see me. "Lien?"

"Yes," I mumbled. "Thank you."

"Did he fondle your breasts? Did he suckle them? Did he perform oral sex?" It was one question after another, yet his voice remained gentle. "Did it happen more than once? Did he ask you to perform oral sex? Did he force you to have sex with him?"

Relieved from the responsibility of verbalizing the violation of my 15-year-old body, I had stopped crying and listened attentively to what the officer asked me. He had taken a great load from my shoulders, and I returned the favor by answering him with a firm voice. It was all over in a matter of moments, but he didn't let me loose just yet. He talked to me for a little longer, telling me that I was brave and reminding me that I am not to blame for what Yiwen did. And before he finally hung up, he made me laugh one more time and told me to call him if I needed anything in the future.

I got off the phone with bloodshot eyes and a bad case of hiccups, but my spirits were a little higher than I had started out with. I couldn't believe I had just gotten off the phone with the same man I tried to hide from earlier that day. *Da ge* met me in the hallway, as I walked out of my parents' bedroom where I had used the phone.

"How'd it go?" he asked me.

"Not bad, actually," I answered with a weak smile.

The house shook slightly then, as the garage door opened underneath us. I looked at *da ge* with worried eyes. I could feel my heart pounding wildly again and my words stuttered through. "They're early."

"Lien!" we heard Mama shout from downstairs. "Lien, where are you?" *Da ge* and I stood together at the top of the stairs as she made her way toward us. When she met my gaze with her cold stare, I couldn't tell if her eyes were red from anger or tears. I wrapped my hand around *da ge's* bony wrist, silently asking for his help. I loosened my grip after Mama took my other arm and pulled me into her room.

"Why are you home early?" It's the only thing I could think to say to her.

"Because I couldn't do my work," she answered sternly, her hand still tightly attached to my arm as she shook me with each word she said. "Every time I remembered what you said, I cried. My officemates kept asking me what was the matter. What was I supposed to tell them, huh?"

Unsure of what to reply, I stayed quiet for a moment. My whisper was almost inaudible when I asked, "Does *yang fu* [Mandarin for *foster/step-father*] know?" Of everyone else, I dreaded telling him most, knowing exactly how he would react.

"No, he doesn't."

I remember the rush of relief that came to me when she told me that. "Please don't tell him," I pleaded. "We can take care of this ourselves."

But she adamantly disagreed. "He has to know. He is downstairs right now wondering why I asked him to pick me up early from work so early. I haven't said anything."

I started crying again as I begged her to reconsider, but she had made up her mind already, and there was no going back on any decision Mama set her mind on.

My nightmare hit its climax when *yang fu* was informed. His bellows were surely heard by the neighbors several houses up the street. Both *da ge* and my younger sister, Yinyin, ended up in the room to witness the slow unraveling of the story I had kept hidden for weeks.

I have never cried as hard as I had that evening, as *yang fu* interrogated me with a round of questions. "How can you let him do that?" he shouted, as I pulled my legs tightly against my chest. "How did you allow him to touch you there and there?" He pointed at my breasts and crotch. Mama was in tears by then and with each answer I had, she fell into a deeper level of insanity. My siblings sat like statues, *da ge* at the foot of my parents' queen-sized bed and Yinyin on the floor beside him. Both of them were speechless from the shock.

"Why didn't you stop him? Why didn't you push him away?" *yang fu* asked again, his voice not lowering for a second.

Didn't he realize that I wasn't proud of what happened, that the torture I was inflicting upon myself was more pain than I could handle? Why did he have to add on to it? Why wasn't Mama helping me? She was crying too hard, almost as much as me.

"I couldn't," I answered.

Ever since I was a child, Yiwen and I had a good relationship. He was generous and treated me well, but I was always afraid of his violent outbursts. I remember clearly the physical bouts he had with his sister, who was my age, over the simplest of things, sometimes as minor as whether she'd admit to being a tomboy.

"It's like on television," I tried to explain.

"What are talking about?" *yang fu* said. "This is not TV!"

"It was like a flashback of when it happened to me when I was younger." My parents looked at me with confused eyes and even my siblings raised their gaze from the ecru carpeting to face me. Nobody said anything for a moment, letting the next blow sink in.

"What?" Mama finally asked.

"This isn't the first time. It happened in Taiwan, too." My voice was firm and I was regaining my strength back slowly. "Several times with different people." It wasn't a lie either.

Yinyin started to cry quietly, and *da ge* shook his head in disbelief as my parents continued to scold and yell about what the neighbors were going to think if a police car parked in front of our house, about being ashamed of facing the officer, and about how it was all my fault. It went on for a while longer.

"You'd better make sure because Yiwen is surely going to deny this ever happened," Mama said. "It's going to bring some bad tension between me and your aunt. It's your word against his."

I was too angry to care now, and I took this opportunity to raise my voice, a taboo in our household that could be met with a nice slap on the face.

"Well, he did the same thing to his sister, too!" I shouted. "She was the one who told me not to say anything." A few years later, I would come to regret having said anything, but at that point, I just wanted to get out of there.

I finally stood up from the chair after spending a good hour fighting my parents off; the same place I sat talking to the officer who told me everything would be all right. Then I realized he had said that because he doesn't know my parents.

"Are you done with me?" Before they had a chance to answer, I continued, "I'm getting out of here." I walked through the open door that separated my parents' bedroom from the hallway. I turned for a moment and called out, *"Da ge."*

As if on cue, tears came again and my knees went weak. *Da ge* rushed towards me, but he was too late. He helped me stand and led me to his room, where I sat beside him on his bed, weeping. "It wasn't my fault," I said between sobs. "You understand, don't you?"

Da ge said nothing but pulled me tightly against his thin body. Yinyin followed and sat on the other side of me before finally enveloping my shaking body in an embrace. She already knew the answer but asked anyway, "Why didn't you tell us?"

"Go away!" *da ge* shouted at my parents when they walked in shortly after Yinyin. *Yang fu* glared angrily at my brother. "Just leave her alone!"

But Mama remained unfazed by his tone and continued to approach her three huddled children, before she wrapped her arms around all of us. "I love you, Lien," she cried. "I'm sorry."

I never really stopped crying, and I skipped dinner that night. But *da ge* brought some food to his room, where I remained lying on his bed. Mama was delirious and could not decide whether she was angry or sorry for me. Most of the time, she'd come in screaming and then later on she'd apologize for losing her temper. I didn't pay much attention to what went on around me because I was preoccupied with my own thoughts, deciding between running away or committing suicide while everyone was asleep that night.

Da ge let me stay in his room, and as I cuddled close to him, I asked, "Are you angry at Yiwen?"

It took him a second to answer. "If you're not," he said, "I don't have the right to be. Mama and *yang fu* do not have the right to think up punishments. Nobody does, except you. You were the one who's been hurt, and you'll have to carry this experience for the rest of your life." He paused before adding, "I'm proud of you, Lien, because it's not an easy situation to be in. I just wish they didn't make it more difficult than it already is."

My brother squeezed me tightly, and again I started to weep, trying desperately to rid myself of the pain that weighed me down. "Thank you, *da ge*," I mumbled in muffled whispers. "Thank you for understanding."

He wiped my tears with his finger and brushed my tangled hair from my wet face, as I tried to close my eyes to sleep. The door opened suddenly, and *yang fu's* shadowy figure stepped in. "Get off the bed," he ordered me.

"*Da ge*," I cried, pulling him closer to me and burying my face against his chest.

"Are you listening to me?" my stepfather said, his voice rising again.

"Leave her alone. She's sleeping in here with me," *da ge* answered sternly.

"No, she's not." A few Mandarin words followed immediately, but he cut himself short of finishing his sentence.

Enraged by what *yang fu* had started to say, my brother stood up and faced him in the dark. "How dare you imply I would do such a thing to my own sister?" *da ge* shouted.

"Yiwen did." And with that, *yang fu* turned around to leave and closed the door behind him.

It didn't take me long to get over that experience. I talked about it with ease and was never ashamed of what had happened so many times between the ages of five and 15. "It's made me a stronger person," I'd always say, yet I could not be alone with a man without feeling agitated and sometimes fearful.

"But that's only natural," the campus psychologist told me a few years ago.

"It's not that I do not trust men," I explained. "Actually, my best friends have always been guys, and I am able to open up to them. But it feels really uncomfortable to be in the same room, especially in a confined space, with one man. The worst part is, my own father probably falls in this category, too."

The psychologist listened attentively as I continued, "Of course there's my brother and a select few that I feel okay being around." I had a lot of issues to talk to her about, and for the first time since that day back in 1993, I cried again.

My sessions focused closely on the molestation and sexual abuse and its effects on my present life. "I'm more childish than the normal 18-year-old because I feel I have to make up for the innocence I lost. And it's kind of funny because people don't think I know much about sex just because I am a virgin." I smiled a little before adding, "Little do they know, huh?

"I guess my whole view of relationships was molded by that experience. I'm a fool for the romance I am always looking for, which my friends think is insane. I'm actually looking forward to marriage. Perhaps all due to my experiences, I am looking for stability."

I saw her several times and during my last visit, she suggested I get my hands on a book about the accounts of women survivors of sexual abuse called *The Courage To Heal*. I looked it up in the library and only got through the first few chapters because finals came up. It was not the easiest thing to read, so I often put it down after a few pages. About a year later, I bought my own copy, and though I have not had the opportunity to read it yet, at least I will have it when I finally build enough nerve.

I have never been able to tell anyone exactly what Yiwen put me through, and even though I can still clearly recall many incidents of my abuse in Taiwan, the details have stayed within me. Playing 20 Questions with that officer was the closest I've ever gotten to verbalizing what happened. It's been impossible to even write it down.

"Perhaps it's what I need to do to finally let go and move on," I told my friend, Jeff.

"Maybe," was all he said in reply.

It's been nearly five years since the police report was filed, and I've been meaning to read it, but I have never thought I was emotionally and psychologically ready. Still, I felt I couldn't go another day carrying the load of that memory. The intention was always there but never acted upon. That is, until last week when my professor was talking about access to public records. The idea was implanted back in my head, and this time I took the first step of calling the police department.

"Yes," the woman on the other end of the line said. "In most situations, reports are open to the people involved. But there are occasions when they are not."

"How about child abuse cases?" I asked.

"That's a tricky one." She spoke slowly to prolong dropping the bomb of the bad news. "Victim names are not public for most sex crimes, child endangerment, spousal abuse, or interference with civil rights. Access is even denied to the victim and the victim's parents."

"Oh."

She continued past my disappointed response. "But with an approved petition from the presiding juvenile superior court judge and a $12 fee, we can mail you a copy of the report."

My heart started to pound wildly. "A copy?" I never thought I could actually own the piece of paper that documented the violation of my body in exact detail. "What if I just come in with the paperwork? Would I be able to look at it quickly?"

"We don't normally do that because it isn't very time-efficient. But if someone here was willing to pull it out for you, I suppose it would be all right. We cannot guarantee that, though."

The conversation didn't last very long after that. I got off the phone in a confused frenzy and sat motionless for a while, trying to digest the information I was just given. A spark in me had been ignited, and I couldn't stop short of having that piece of paper in my hands. I just had to go the whole way.

I called the juvenile court and requested that the petition be sent to me as soon as possible. About a week later, I held the white envelope in my hand nervously. For awhile, I couldn't get myself to open it. Then, with shaking hands, I ripped open the flap. Inside was a single piece of paper that looked like it came from the same copy machine President Kennedy used in the early 1960s, the county clerk's address stamped in sloppy purple ink on the upper left corner.

Since I had been expecting pages of government paperwork with carbon, this petition came as a surprise. I must admit that I was slightly disappointed, too. I didn't bother reading through it before returning it into its envelope and stuffing it into my backpack.

Several of my friends know what I am up to although I've never mentioned a word about it to my parents in half a decade. They wouldn't understand why I would want to, why I need to open this painful part of my past when it was closed so long ago. At this point, I feel I am protecting them from the details of what had really happened then and so many other times in the last 20 years of my life.

I never knew what molestation was until the DARE program back in sixth grade. Officer Billings (I cannot believe I still remember her name) used to talk to our class about the dangers of alcohol and drug abuse. Then there was a short plug to stay aware that there were people out there who might hurt children like us.

I remember sitting in my small desk, across the room from where Officer Billings stood lecturing the class about being violated and the importance of telling someone we trusted. Long forgotten images flashed in my head, and then I realized that I had been a victim of an evil before I knew it existed. A few months later, Yiwen and his family traveled to the United States for the first time.

We took them to Disneyland, and when we got back home, the boys were assigned to sleep on the hide-away bed in the living room. *Da ge* had a high fever. I gave up my spot beside my aunt so that he could be monitored throughout the night. I volunteered to sleep with Yiwen and his seven-year-old brother, who was asleep in no time.

Tired after an exciting day, none of us changed into our nightclothes as we normally did, and I must admit that trying to sleep in my jeans was uncomfortable. I felt Yiwen's arm reach behind me, slowly unbuttoning my pants. I gasped, and he put his hand over my mouth gently. "Ssh," he whispered in my ear, before he took my hand and slipped them down the front of his pants. I closed my eyes and clenched my jaw tightly.

I saw Officer Billings again the following Friday afternoon for the weekly DARE lesson, but I didn't say anything about what happened. Because of this, the nightmare would continue until Yiwen returned to Taiwan a few weeks later. I told no one, even after he was gone. To this very day, my parents remain unaware that this ordeal started much earlier than they realized.

A few weeks ago, I wrote this entry in my diary:

"I never thought I'd have a chance to own a copy. Never even considered it. Didn't think it was possible, and to think it could actually be in my hands one day.

"At first I thought I didn't want it. Not a copy. But slowly, I saw the advantages: being able to find out the name of the police officer that filed it and then setting the report aside to view when I am ready.

"I've told Jeff about the situation and update him as things come up. I am hoping he'll volunteer to make this mission happen for me because I cannot get myself to go alone, and even if my siblings would, I don't want them to know when I finally have it. They'd surely be curious to read the report, but I would prefer to protect them from the details. They don't need to know, and I know they'd prefer not knowing anyway.

"To tell you the truth, I do not know what decision would be more pleasant to hear. The only reason I am putting myself in this position is because I want to know who that police officer was. I owe him a heartfelt thank you for what he did, for making a difficult task a little easier to bear and making me laugh at the time I needed it most.

"If I had a choice, I wouldn't want to see the report at all. But I don't think I could ever forgive myself for passing up the opportunity, perhaps my only chance, to meet the kind man I had never seen. Of course, that's assuming my request is granted at all.

"The petition will be getting here in the middle of next week. With any luck, I can get a letter from the campus psychologist to advocate my cause. State why I should have access to this piece of paper. Let's just continue to pray and keep our fingers crossed. It may be an uphill battle from here, that's for sure. Then again, I probably should be used to it. It's not like it's ever been easy being me."

5

They Say You Never Forget

Forget

Love

You Bring Out the Filipina in Me

For Joel B. Tan, inspired by Sandra Cisneros' "You Bring Out the Mexican in Me"

BY MAIANA MINAHAL

you bring out the filipina in me
the language born of blood in me
the p instead of f in me
the glottal catch in me
the visayan the tagalog in me
the ancestors in me

you bring out
the murder of magellan in me
the revolution of seven thousand islands in me
to survive 500 years of colonizers in me

you bring out the guerrilla soldier in me
the olongapo bar hostess in me
the mail order bride in me

you bring out the *bahala na* immigrant in me
the god they're so american in me
the yes, i do speak english in me
the tnt green card in me

you bring out the pinay in me
the sass in me smartass badass in me
the proud walker shit talker
third world girl the majority in me

you bring out the *barkada* in me
wolf among sheep in me
the danger the desire in me
the drink til I'm drunk
fuck til I'm good and fucked

you bring out the queer in me
the dyke in me
the brave beautiful butch in me
voracious femme in me
the *bastos* the *bakla*

the *walang hiya* in me

you bring out the wake up
laughing laughing
not crying
in me
my brother
my brother
mahal mahal kita

yes you do
oh yes you do

bahala na: what god wills
barkada: friends
bastos: rude
bakla: faggot
walang hiya: shameless
mahal kita: i love you

The Power of *Han*

BY MARIE G. LEE

Grace Park never liked being Korean very much, and neither did her parents. There was one other Korean family in Oak Grove, the Kims, whom the Parks avoided like crazy. Mrs. Park was even going to stop going to church when she found out the Kims were also religious — but it turned out that they were Methodist, and the Parks had always been good Presbyterians.

Grace knew the Kim's daughter, Sun-Young, who was a grade below her. Sun-Young was a complete dork. She always dressed up, never wore jeans, and if that wasn't bad enough, she carried these stupid Hello Kitty pencil cases. But she was beautiful. She was one of those people who was beautiful without knowing it and therefore was too dumb to use it to her advantage.

Grace hated Sun-Young, partly because she was a dork and partly because she was beautiful and too dumb to do anything with it. The two of them never really spoke, although Grace's friends sort of expected them to.

"Why would I want to talk to such a loser?" Grace said, as she sat with her friends on the bleachers in the gym.

They were supposed to eat their lunches in the school cafeteria, but lunchrooms were for dorks. They had started coming here and hanging out, and little by little others had followed them, including the guys on the hockey team, which was probably the reason why no one stopped them. The hockey players were gods. They ran the school more than the principal and the guidance counselors did. Especially if they were having a good season. This year they were four for five.

Grace had her eye on Mickey Krampotavich, the center. Mickey was supposed to be a senior but had been held back a year. She never knew if it was so he could play an extra year or if it was because he was dumb, or both. She knew, though, that Mickey was out of her league. He was the kind of guy who liked girls who wore tight jeans with high heels and were fast.

In any event, Grace loved Mickey's wavy brown hair and his brown eyes. He was a sweaty terror on the ice, but off it, he was as soft and brown as a field mouse. Once, he'd had a tooth knocked out and he looked like a pirate, if you can imagine a brown field mouse pirate.

The only thing was, Grace had once heard that Mickey sort of liked Sun-Young. She had seen his eyes engage and move when Sun-Young walked past. The thing that comforted Grace was the fact that, even if Mickey liked Sun-Young, he still probably wouldn't ask her out. Guys like him just didn't go out with girls like her. The lines of attachment in high school were like string sculptures: They looked impossibly complex, but when you got down to it, each point had designated lines running to other ones. Sun-Young, with her cowl-neck sweaters and wool pants, wasn't in the lines that ran from Mickey. Grace, who ran with the cigarette-smoking, black-mascara crowd, was. If only she had the courage to do the things one had to do to be thought of as fast.

Mickey was in her World History class. Grace found this class incredibly boring, and it seemed Mickey did, too, since he spent most of his time doodling on his notebook, and during movies, he put his head down on the desk and fell asleep. He wasn't missing anything; the teacher, Mr. Pearich, was senile or something. He liked to ramble and ramble until a pearl of spittle formed on his lip, and it bubbled when he talked. That was the only time the class came alive, when everyone mightily suppressed their urges to vomit.

Grace had hated Mr. Pearich since last month. They had been doing the unit on World War II. He'd shown a movie about the bombing of Pearl Harbor, and then afterward, asked her if she had anything to *add* to it.

Anything to add? At first she thought this was a trick question, some kind of pop quiz to see if she'd done the reading. But there wasn't any reading on Pearl Harbor. When Mr. Pearich asked her if her *parents* had told her anything about Pearl Harbor, then she knew: That dodo thought she was Japanese! Her father had told her it was the easiest thing in the world to figure out a Japanese name from a Korean one: Korean ones were mostly short, one syllable, with sharp intonations, like Park, Lee, Kim. But Japanese names always had a lot of dizzy vowels. Like Miyazawa. Nakamichi. Sony.

She told this to Mr. Pearich, ladling it on pretty heavy that there was no similarity between Japanese and Korean names. It seemed to register only slightly if at all with him. He shrugged.

Now she was watching Mickey Krampotavich eat a sandwich and wishing her friends would quit bugging her about Sun-Young Kim.

"Sun-Young does have really pretty hair," said Phyllis, whose own hair was a little thin on top, but she hid it with elaborate teasing and perms.

"She's a loser," Grace said, again. "Have you ever seen her at a hockey game? No — I think she spends Friday nights pasting stickers of butterflies on her book covers."

Terri, her other friend, opened a KitKat bar. She had recently started going out with Hodge Jones, the goalie, and she was wearing his massive class ring on a chain around her neck. Hodge had recently been going around bragging that he'd finger-fucked her, but Terri hadn't said a word.

"We're not saying you have to be friends with her," she explained. Her eyes were very blue against the stiff black of mascara and eyeliner. "We're just wondering — like wouldn't your parents want you to hang with her? I mean you guys are both, you know, Korean."

"My parents hate her parents, I told you," Grace said, as she watched Mickey throw the rest of his sandwich into his bag, wad it up and then lob it toward the wastebasket. It bounced off the lip and back onto the floor. He didn't bother to go over and pick it up. "The Kims are into all this weird Korean stuff, and my parents just want to be normal."

Someone on the hockey side was making a milk bomb, flattening the top of a carton of milk. It was placed on the bleacher and then Hodge brought his massive foot down on it. It broke with a sonic boom, milk splattering everywhere. The guys laughed like hyenas. Grace and her friends made sure to look horrified. The boys stalked out of the gym, leaving everything behind.

"I feel sorry for janitors, don't you?" said Terri.

"It was your boyfriend who did it," Phyllis told her.

"I know." Her voice was equal parts pain and pride.

In World History, they had gotten to the Korean War, and Grace was bracing herself. Whenever anything came up that had Korea in it, she always felt like people were staring at her or talking about her, although she would never know for sure. For instance, once someone had been telling her and her friends some joke that had the words "made in Korea" as the punch line. It seemed like a vacuum of silence had descended, everyone looking at her out of the corners of their eyes to see how she was going to react, and she knew she had to react just right or people would think she was majorly uptight, or worse, a loser.

She laughed, loud, even though the minute she heard "Korea," her mind had stopped listening to the joke itself and begun to prepare for the reaction. She tried to make the laugh sound sincere, but it came out as a bray.

Now, Mr. Pearich had their textbook open in his huge ham hands. There was a giant picture of Korea, which was sliced in half at the thirty-eighth parallel. He was looking at her.

"So Grace, was your father involved in the Korean War?"

Grace sat stoically. If only Mr. Pearich knew how much her parents hated being Korean, so much that if they'd known Sun-Young's parents would be in this town, they never would have moved here. Put it this way — the word "Korea" was rarely ever heard in the house.

"My Dad was in the Korean War," said Buzz Hardoway, raising his hand to perfect an illusion that he had received permission to speak. "He flew airplanes."

"But we want to know if Grace's Dad was involved as a Korean."

Grace couldn't help glancing at Mickey. She half expected him to be doodling, but he wasn't. He was looking at her, straight at her, as intensely as if she might have been an unmanned hockey puck.

"Yeah, my Dad was in the war," she said, casually. She pretended to brush a piece of lint off her shoulder and looked at Mickey again. He was mesmerized.

"Sure, my Dad got hit by a bomb once, too. He was trying to rescue his friend and he got shrapnel in his brain."

"Was he part of the South Korean Army?" Mr. Pearich asked.

Grace thought for a second. The North Koreans were the communists, right? South Koreans must have been the good guys.

"Yeah, he was with the South Koreans."

"See class, aren't you glad I asked?" said Mr. Pearich, straightening up like a grizzly bear rearing. "We have someone in this room whose Dad was a war hero."

"But my Dad was in the war, too," protested Buzz, now propping his right arm up at the elbow.

"Was he wounded?" asked Mr. Pearich.

"I don't think so. He saw combat, though."

"Well, then it's not the same. And besides, the Korean army didn't have a whole lot of supplies; they only had a few very brave men and that's why President Eisenhower decided we had to send some of our men in there to help them."

Grace envisioned her father lying wounded in a military hospital, all sorts of tubes and jars attached to his arms, nurses with funny paper hats hovering about. But then some old scene from *M*A*S*H* came to her instead. When she thought of her father, mostly she saw him in his Bermuda shorts, pale chicken legs in black socks and dress shoes, out mowing the lawn. Still, it wasn't inconceivable that he was once a war hero.

After class, she noticed Mickey Krampotavich was following her.

"Hey Grace," he said, as he fell in step with her. "That was really neat, about your father."

Grace shrugged, tried to look modest. "It's not like he hangs up his medals all over the house or anything."

"Wow, he has medals?" The look in Mickey's eyes made Grace believe she was probably going to continue digging this hole, even if it meant she'd never get out. It would be worth it if Mickey Krampotavich fell in there with her.

"Yeah, he showed them to me once when I was a little kid."

At the same time, her mind was racing. Did Koreans even give out medals, things like the Purple Heart, Silver Star or Iron Cross? Was that a fraud Mickey could uncover in the encyclopedia? Would he look?

Well, she thought, this is not exactly a fraud. She just didn't know what the deal was, and as long as she didn't know, anything was possible, she reasoned.

"Do you have big plans for the weekend?"

"Nothing too big," she murmured

"Want to go for pizza after the hockey game?"

"Um, maybe."

"I'll call you."

They stayed on the Korean War for the rest of the week. Grace waited until Mr. Pearich prompted her, and then she added a few more details to make her story more interesting. When Mr. Pearich asked her something she couldn't figure out, she said that the memories of the war were very painful for her father so he didn't talk about them much, and when he did, things came out all jumbled. Mr. Pearich nodded with grave sympathy.

Mickey was going to pick her up after the game, after he had showered and returned to his brown field mouse self. He was sure to be in a good mood, since they had creamed their arch-rivals, Red River Rapids. Terri and Phyllis reverently dropped

Grace off back home to wait for him.

"Don't do anything I wouldn't do," Terri chortled as they drove off.

Grace's father was sitting in the living room reading the paper, exactly what Grace expected him to be doing. He wasn't wearing shoes, just his customary black socks.

She sat next to him on the couch, grabbed one of her mother's magazines and flipped through it idly. Then she asked:

"Dad, where were you during the war?"

"Which war?" he asked, from behind the paper.

"The Korean War."

"In Korea, of course," he said, still behind the paper.

Grace pulled the paper down. Her father looked up and blinked, as if he were a little animal whose hiding place had been found.

"Were you a soldier?" she asked. The hope that he had been stirred a kind of love in her heart for him. She looked at his hands holding the paper and imagined the same hands holding a rifle. Of course, he would be very brave. It's the brave ones who can afford to be mild later. Look at Gandhi.

"Hardly." He gave the paper a snap. It crinkled weakly.

"What do you mean?"

"Why do you want to know?"

"It's for a class project," she said. "A graded one." She knew how to get his attention.

Her father slowly lowered the paper. "The war," he said, as if to himself. "What did I do in the war?"

"Exactly," Grace said. Her father's forehead was crinkled like the paper. She could almost feel the painful memories rising to the surface like bubbles in a lake.

"You know the Kims?" he said. "Duk Kim was in my medical school class. I didn't think he was that smart, but when they picked a bunch of people to become liaison officers for the U.N. medical corps, they picked him — I don't know why. So he got to live in those fancy barracks and meet all the famous American generals."

"And you?" Grace prompted, as she sat on the edge of the couch.

Her father stared off in the distance, as if he were watching a movie playing somewhere out the window. "Sure, he got wounded once, but it wasn't that big a deal. He got better medical care than he would have if it was in peacetime."

"But what about you, Dad?" Grace said. She had visions of Sun-Young being in Mr. Pearich's class next year, and what she would say to all the questions he would ask *her* about the War. And what if Mickey Krampotavich got held back another year? He'd be in her class.

"Do you know about *han?*" Dr. Lee asked his daughter. Grace shook her head. If it was a Korean word, her father should know she wouldn't know.

"*Han* is a feeling, a sort of bitterness and sadness. Korea has always existed as a small country between powerful ones — we say it is like a shrimp among fighting whales. When the whales fight, the shrimp naturally gets hurt. This is *han.*"

Two cones of light, like parallel flashlight beams, moved eerily up the carpet, as if to attack them, and then receded. A car was pulling up the driveway. The doorbell rang. Grace groaned.

"I don't get it," she said. "Please Dad, would you tell me quick what you did in the war?"

Dr. Lee looked at his daughter. "I hid," he said.

"You what?"

"I hid. When I was passed up for the liaison officer position, my mother did not want me to be conscripted into the army. So I hid in a secret room at my aunt's. I was like Anne Frank."

"Anne Frank?"

He nodded.

"For the whole war?"

The doorbell chimed again. It was a stupid doorbell, one that played practically a whole song with every press: ding-dong-ding-dong ding-dong-DING-dong ding-dong-ding-dong ding-DONG-ding-DONG.

"I ate nothing but millet for a year — my teeth started to fall out. I had to go to the bathroom into a tin can. When the war ended, I came out."

"Anne Frank," Grace muttered, as she went to get the door. There was a huge silhouette hulking in the light of the porch.

"Hey, I'm ready to go," she said, placing herself squarely in the doorway. Mickey tried to peer around her.

"That your Dad? I'd love to meet him."

"Uh, sure," she said. She realized she didn't have her shoes on, or her coat. She would have to go back in and get them.

Her father had returned to his regular reading position, legs crossed, black socks falling in corrugated ridges about his ankles.

"Hey, Mickey," she whispered, urgently leaning over him. He smelled of soap, but under that, something more insistent that the soap couldn't quite wipe out. "Don't ask him anything about the war, though, okay? He's been getting really upset about it lately, you know, post-traumatic stuff."

"Oh, sure," Mickey said, nodding. "I understand completely. I had an uncle in 'Nam — I know what you're talking about."

"Good," she said with a smile, and ushered him into the house.

She started Mickey talking to her father as she ran to get her coat and shoes. She was thinking of Sun-Young for some reason, and a bitter ball rose in her throat. She pushed it down.

Outside, the cold stars waited sweetly.

You're the One for Me, Leech-Boy

BY MICHI TURNER

My Japanese friend told me that she only dates white guys because she wants *hapa* kids so I asked her who she thought I should date and whether she thought that her rule applied to me, since I'm already half-Japanese. She told me that it didn't matter who I dated because my kids were gonna be fucked up anyway, which I thought was an insult at first, but according to her, people who are a quarter ethnic and three-quarters something else end up being really messed up. I asked my mom if she had ever heard of this stereotype, and she confirmed it by saying, "Yeah, quarter kids. . . they're always dumber than normal kids." I don't think she was intentionally trying to be discouraging, but damn, does that mean I have to avoid dating monoracials so that my children won't be slower than the rest of the kids? Leave it to my mom to make things harder than they should be. Unfortunately, it's always been her neurotic maternal traits that have carried onto me, making my life way harder than it should be, like when I was a kid, I started reading at a pretty young age, and of course she had to push me to the limit so that this intellectual gift could be nurtured and set the stage for future careers in the medical field — so she made me read *all* the time. Instead of Barbie, there was Nancy Drew, instead of Monopoly, there was *Charlie and the Chocolate Factory,* instead of Nintendo, there was *The Cricket in Times Square,* and instead of *E.T.*, there was *Little Women.* Yes, I was always the "un-cool" kid who gave books as presents at seven-year-olds' birthday parties and addition and subtraction flashcards for Christmas, while my friends always tried to make me cooler by giving me Cyndi Lauper albums, Guess t-shirts, or pin-ups of New Kids on the Block. Well, my mom's plan of immersing my childhood in literature backfired when a habit I acquired in the second grade grew steadily worse until eventually my mother just thought I was a weirdo — all her hopes of my achieving Nobel Prize status disappeared. While reading, I felt this intense need to read *every single* printed item in a book, including copyright information, publisher's notes, and even page numbers. For some reason, I had convinced myself that this was the only true way to be able to say that I had read a book. I went through the whole series of *Little House on the Prairie* and *Anne of Green Gables* without missing a single letter or number:

Published by Penguin Putnam, Inc.

375 Hudson Street, New York, New York, 10014, U.S.A.

This is a work of fiction. Names, characters, places and incidents either are the product of the author's imagination or are used fictitiously and any resemblance to actual persons, living or dead, events, or locales is entirely coincidental.

Cover design by Meredith Harte.
Set in Adobe Garamond and Weiss Italic.
Page 34, Page 35, Page 36. . . .

My mother finally gave up on me when I started reading the numbers on the bar codes. And miraculously, I was transported from the bland, mind-numbing world of books to the exciting, fast-paced, mind-numbing world of television. And even though I was only allowed to watch PBS while my friends reveled in a land of MTV, Nickelodeon, VH1, and even HBO, I felt as though I was finally approaching normality, except when everyone would discuss the latest Bel Biv Devoe video and I'd have to retort with "Hey, did you check out that Mathnet episode on *Square One* last week?" I was probably the only one in elementary school who actually kept up with every episode of *The Voyage of the Mimi.*

Despite my mother's attempts to keep me sheltered from the inevitable pre-teen obsessions with popular culture, I did sneak out to see the fifth-grade hit, *Stand by Me,* with friends, which resulted in my new-found crush on Wil Wheaton. And when the stars began to be plastered on the covers of our then-bibles *Bop* and *Tiger Beat,* everyone used to tease me because I liked the guy with the leech on his dick and was too blind to see that River Phoenix was the one who deserved to be worshipped. Now my friends tease me because I have a Macauley Culkin fetish. Not present-day Macauley, not married-too-young and fucked-over-by-his-parents Macauley, but Macauley *then* — red-lipped, blonde-haired, bad-actor-but-it's-okay-because-he's-so-cute Macauley. Macauley from *Home Alone* and *Uncle Buck,* but not *The Good Son,* because who wants to see evil Macauley when you can have Macauley as the prince in George Balanchine's New York City Ballet version of *The Nutcracker?* It's funny, movies like *Casablanca* or *Titanic* don't draw any emotion out of me whatsoever, let alone make me cry, but Macauley's 1992 hit *My Girl* has some secret potion that wrenches the tears out of me. It happens every time, when Vada comes down the stairs and sees Macauley lying in the casket in her living room (because, remember, she lived in a funeral parlor?). And she's crying so hard, because her best friend has just died from too many bee stings, and she goes up to the coffin with little Macauley all white and pasty from the make-up that covers the bee stings and asks him if he wants to go out and play, as if he's still alive, and they have to pull her awkward nine-year-old body, struggling and sobbing, away from her dead best friend. That movie gets me every time, and I can't figure out whether it's because I've never been to a funeral or because the idea of Macauley Culkin dying is so horrid to me. I usually have to fight really hard not to start bawling at that scene by biting my tongue, which I hate, because I used to bite my tongue all the time to keep from swallowing it. I'm surprised my tongue isn't just a torn-up stringy piece of mutilated flesh by now, which I'm grateful for, because who would want to kiss a girl with a tongue that had permanent teeth-marks in it? I'm also grateful for the fact that I've never suffered a tragic, devastating loss, but it kind of makes me feel like I'm in for a really big fall sooner or later. I don't think I'll be able to handle going to a funeral. Plus, I'll probably bite my tongue off.

R

BY ANGELINA FERIL

R

You used You abused
You took for granted
And always expected
>You requested You implored
>You so subtly demanded
>(for gas money, cigarettes, a free meal or two)
>You made everyone feel obligated
>(to give and provide everything for you)
And if they didn't
If they wouldn't give you what you wanted
Guilt was a good way to go
For when you insisted
It was your way or no way at all
>You betrayed You violated
>You assumed someone would get your back
>And you always resented
>When your expectations were not met
You "were hurt" You "were wronged"
You "were persecuted for no reason"
You "were dishonored and victimized"
But truth is not once did you show appreciation
>Appreciation for support —
>Physical, emotional, and material
>Nor the fact that the love and care I
>Showed was virtually unconditional

Sapphire

BY CANYON SAM

Kate and I enjoyed many a day working on Mandy's hexagonal cabin. We'd work shirtless in the mornings on the building site that stood right below the crest of a long, sloped meadow overlooking the valley until about eleven, when the hot summer temperatures climbed to an uncomfortable level, and we'd retreat to Kate's cool cabin on the next hill. It was there at Kate's place in the afternoons where I'd sip homemade lemonade, curled up in the big armchair in front of the picture window, and soak up Lesbiana. I read and read and read, choosing kernels from that treasure chest that was the Womanest library next door. I read *Well of Loneliness* and wept, I read *Edward the Dyke* and chuckled, I read back issues of *Quest* and pondered. I listened to their collection of women's music — Meg Christian, Cris Williamson, Alix Dobkin. Every poem, every photograph, every song was a new discovery.

Kate was busy fixing up and making plans for the house — a cobwebbed, abandoned hunting cabin with only a rusty box-spring bed and two broken chairs to its name when we first stepped across its threshold two weeks before.

Now it was clean but still barren, and Kate — who was not only energetic and talented, but a visionary — had great designs for it. She was also a wonderful cook, so we ate heartily and smoked contentedly every evening in front of the fireplace.

I had quite a crush on my new friend the carpenter, who'd befriended me when I arrived and who, like me, was a recent transplant to Oregon from San Francisco. The nights were especially fitful because we shared the ancient mattress that sank in the center like a crater of the moon, continuously pitching us together as we slept. I couldn't even cling to my own edge of the bed and withdraw; I was compelled to lie right beside her in a quiet, frustrated frenzy of newly awakened sexuality. I was much too shy and inexperienced to do anything about my crush, so most of the time I just looked upon Kate as a young woman looks on an adored older buddy.

When I came out in San Francisco that spring of 1975, one of the things that was most important to me was to meet another Asian lesbian, of whom there seemed to be almost none at the time. When I inquired, one woman's name kept popping up over and over from many and separate quarters, but I never met her. One evening I mentioned this to Kate, and it turns out she had left behind not just a career in the city, but a five-year relationship with — can you believe? — Sapphire. Photo albums and stories poured out about this powerful, attractive Asian lesbian who was somewhat of a legend in San Francisco. Sapphire became larger than life.

These days Kate was in love with a carpenter from Sonoma who had traveled through Oregon that summer. So in love that after a couple weeks without seeing her, Kate wanted to make a trip south to visit.

The morning that Kate's red van, packed up and fueled, finally pulled away from the house, a wave of emotion rolled across my stomach and flushed through my cheeks. My protection and my role model was leaving for two weeks. Suddenly I realized my isolation on this land, my newness to country living, and the skills it required to survive. Mine was a generalized sense of abandonment at being left alone with my new identity at this raw point in my struggle. The cabin and the land were filled with Kate's energy. When occasional visitors came, I would show them the plans for the second-story addition, the new wood burning stove, the kitchen table Kate had built — just like she did for guests.

Every day I got up and went to work. I was building some scaffolding that we'd need for installing the roof on Mandy's cabin, and I was dismantling a fallen chicken coop by the side of the road on the Womanest land next door.

In my free time, I embroidered patches for my faded denim overalls: impressionistic designs with neat patterned centers and etched stitches around the borders. I sewed on scraps of Peter Max material: royal blue background with Sargeant Pepper stars floating by wildly, reflecting my new interest in astrology; swatches of leather and sheepskin fur; and a beaded Indian talisman for the center of my back where the two straps crossed.

My overalls had been given to me by John, a dance friend in San Francisco, after he'd returned from a trip to his native Texas. They had belonged to an 88-year-old farmer who'd just passed away, and John bought them from the man's widow at a roadside sale. They were sun-, wind-, and field-faded — and soft as a rag.

One afternoon I was at the chicken coop pulling out nails and sorting lumber when a big, long car came through the clearing at the bottom of the Womanest meadow. It was white and fancy and seemed to float like a boat. I smiled slightly. It was so easy to miss that turn; people came up here all the time looking for the MacCulloughs or Grant and Glenna's place, only to find women with crewcuts on a hilltop.

I knew this was the case here because this car was spanking new, a late-model deluxe with chrome so shiny sunlight spun off it, and one of those figurines on the hood like on a stretch limo or a Greek yacht. Glinting slivers of sunlight swirled through the cloud of dust fanning into the air as the automobile picked its way up the potholed road. Most of what we saw up this way were rusty VW vans and 10-year-old Valiants; this car was so wide it spilled off the sides of the road.

They saw me and stopped. I was about to tell them they'd taken the wrong turn and ask who they were looking for, when I saw behind the passenger window long black hair and an Asian face. There was a whirring sound like an electric can opener as the blue-tinted glass dropped and released a hit of frigid air, giving me goose bumps. I found it strange, looking face to face with this woman at this moment — not only because it was the only other Asian face I'd ever seen in the state, not even because I realized in a flash this was not a misdirected family but Sapphire come alive from the photographs in Kate's album, but because I found her beauty undeniably captivating and her soft distant manner disturbingly intriguing in a way that others had described but that I had doubted I would ever feel.

I directed them back down and around the long way to Kate's next door, then scurried up the hilly shortcut to tidy up the house. Still being so new to lesbians, every time I met some it was an event of note, and aroused great anticipation, fear and excitement.

"We just moved in," I said, as they climbed out of their boat and looked up at the faded red cabin while I led the way inside.

Sapphire was an imposing figure with a stunning mane of thick, lustrous black hair that swept down the length of her full-figured back. Her presence commanded attention. (Since then I've actually discovered I'm taller than Sapphire, but low cabin ceilings and my own sense of invisibility led me to believe that all lesbians I met that summer were taller and bigger than they actually were.) Nancy, her lover, was heavyset with brown hair and a down-to-earth manner. They were both in their 30s.

I showed them the house with the same pride and enthusiasm Kate did with visitors: the wood-burning stove we'd hauled from town, the stained glass windows we'd hung, the kitchen table Kate built, the bookshelf I had made.

Sapphire was curt, her eyes darting about, taking in everything with sharp, tense glances.

"What did you say your name was?" she asked in a soft but pointed tone of voice.

Where are you from? Oh, the City ... What part of the City? What high school did you go to? What year did you graduate? How did you get to Oregon? How long have you been here? How do you know Kate?

I thought we were conversing at first, but it quickly became apparent I was mistaken. My answers never seemed to improve her mood or serve as an entree to a friendly chat — as soon as I answered one question she drilled me with another, the whole time scanning the room like a cool spy in some dark European movie.

What was with all the questions? When would they be over? Why did she care what year I graduated from high school? (Whatever year it was, I suddenly felt like I was back there in the dean's office.) She obviously wanted to determine my age, get some sort of fix on me. When would she be the charming, charismatic personality I'd heard so much about?

After I said I'd attended Lowell, a college prep public high school in San Francisco, whatever sinking ship I had unwittingly found myself on gasped its last breath. Whatever I thought might be happening before deepened, and a distinct and unkind frost started to chill the hot summer temperatures inside the cabin.

Nancy was more friendly, albeit slightly anxious. I didn't have a clue as to what was happening. Did I say something wrong? Did something about the place offend Sapphire?

Their scruffy little black dog, sniping and growling underfoot and flinging himself around the floor like a flea, was starting to make me nervous. My ankles suddenly felt vulnerable and naked around him. Sapphire strode boldly into the kitchen as if she owned the place. The conversation was over.

Nancy suggested we leave Sapphire alone and take a walk outside. The afternoon was brilliant and warm, and the wild grass hillside was the color of straw.

Nancy was easy and engaging to be with, and before I knew it I forgot the strained interaction indoors. I showed her where we planned to put the garden, introduced her to the prized manzanita tree, and then walked her out to the boundaries of the property, as butterflies danced like stained glass miniatures in the sunlight and bird songs whistled down from the pine trees. The sun shone through my soft denim overalls and warmed my bare brown arms.

When we got back to the house Sapphire said she had left a note and some boxes of food for Kate sitting on the potbelly stove. Then, without another word, they left. They climbed into the long white car, turned it around in the short rocky driveway, and descended down the road through the trees.

When Kate returned a few days later, I told her how inexplicably cool Sapphire had been — that I was puzzled and troubled by it — and did Kate have any ideas about why Sapphire might have acted like that?

Kate looked at me for a long minute with alarm growing in her bright hazel eyes.

"Canyon. . . . Oh, My Gawwwd!" Her long, lanky body drew back in shock and she stared at me strangely, as if she were suddenly seeing me in a new light. "Oh, no!" she screeched in her hoarse smoker's voice, clasping her hand to her mouth.

"Canyon," she said finally, peeling her palm from her grimace of disbelief, her voice low and serious like we'd just made big trouble, "Sapphire and I fought and fought because I wanted to move to the country — I wanted her to come with me. She said, 'No way.' There was absolutely no way she'd ever move to Oregon. 'There are no Asians in Oregon!' she'd always argue.

"Now, six months later she drives up to the sticks of rural Oregon — somehow finds her way back here. I don't know how because she and I have not been in touch all these months. I've never given her my address. And who does she find at the end of a 12-mile dirt road when she comes calling unannounced? This cute young *Asian* woman! *Living* with me! On my new land!"

I still didn't get it.

"She thought you and I were *lovers!* That's why she was acting so weird to you!!" She giggled throatily and popped open the tab of her beer can.

"Remember I told ya, Canyon..." she said taking a sip, "Sapphire's the jealous type."

Since Kate didn't know I had a crush on her, I alone found particular irony in this.

I was sorely disappointed at not having made a better connection with Sapphire. She was the first other Asian lesbian I'd ever met. Actually from what I was able to gather, she was the only one around to meet. I thought we'd have instant rapport — based on our common upbringing in the San Francisco Chinese American community, based on the voluminous reading I'd done about lesbian feminism, about The Movement, poetry about us being common loves and an army of lovers. The concept

"Sisterhood Is Beautiful" was an ideal we strove for in all parts of our lives, like seminarians for virtue. I had harbored secret hopes that I'd find in Sapphire a fascinating, powerful, older Asian sister to look up to — or at least make a friendly acquaintance with.

I pointed out to Kate that she and Sapphire had broken up. They'd split up their property in the city months ago and gone their separate ways. Sapphire had a new lover. They even lived together. So why was she so upset when she met me?

Somehow none of that seemed to matter. Kate shook her head resignedly like she'd seen it all before.

But it was all new to me: I was 19. They were Real Lesbians — 26, 28, even 30. I'd never even had a genuine love affair — they had Relationships.

Thus my first meeting with another Asian lesbian took place not in San Francisco, where there were hundreds of thousands of Asians and tens of thousands of gays, but in the quiet foxtailed hills of backcountry Oregon, where I was just getting my first taste that summer of Lesbian Drama.

They Say You Never Forget

By Angela Rosario

They say you never forget your first crush. Mine was on Sean Miller. Whenever he raised his masculine arm to brush away his reckless blond bangs, my heart would melt right into my gym shoes. He had the body of a surfer god and had earned his place of worship on my wall beside the other legends of our time. But not even Scott Baio or Menudo could compare to Sean's all-American charm. There was something about him that made all the girls frantically check their purses for a mirror when he walked into the room. He wasn't like the other boys I knew; he was much more mature. After all, he was in the eighth grade. And Jenny told me that Melissa told her that she heard that he shaved.

So when Jenny passed me a note in fifth period English asking me if I wanted her to introduce me to him, I just about died. I was so excited I wanted to jump right out of my chair, but since we were in the middle of class, I settled for a muffled scream instead. Mr. Bloxsom swore he never in his life saw anyone get so excited about diagramming sentences. I soon became his favorite.

Jenny set the date for the next day, lunch time. She told me to wait by science class and she would bring him over to meet me.

The next day, I stood outside Room 83, clutching my best friend's arm as the lunch bell rang and Mr. Smith's fourth period physical science class came rushing out the door toward the cafeteria. I closed my eyes, counting down the minutes. He would be coming out of social studies right now. He'd stop to talk to his friend Mike for a few minutes and then he'd be off to meet his best friend Jason by the basketball courts. They'd walk together to the cafeteria, where they'd meet all the other popular eighth graders, a group straight out of an after-school special. There, he'd see Jenny, and she would tell him about me and coax him into meeting me. She'd take him by the arm and drag him out of the cafeteria, past the girls' locker room, back through the basketball courts, and into the science building.

My best friend nudged my arm. I opened my eyes. There they were, right on schedule. Her hand was wrapped around his right bicep, pulling him past room 74, past room 75, and closer and closer to me. His Keds dragged against the tile in protest. My heart pounded as they came closer. The thought of finally meeting my dream man made me want to faint. I dug my fingernails into my best friend's arm. Then I did what every girl would do.

I ran.

I passed Jenny a note in English that day, apologizing and explaining that I had chickened out. She wrote back that it was okay and suggested that I write him a letter first to introduce myself. I immediately whipped out a piece of binder paper and began writing the most important letter of my life, once again impressing Mr. Bloxsom with my overflowing enthusiasm for conjugating verbs. He gave me an award when I graduated.

The next day at lunch, I watched from across the cafeteria as Jenny gave him my letter, nicely folded in the shape of a heart. I watched his eyes as he read the words of my soul, searching for any sign of interest. When he finished, he folded the note back into the origami heart and smiled at Jenny. A good sign.

Then, as if in slow motion, Jenny leaned across the table, reached her arm out, and through the crowd of rustling junior high school students, she pointed straight at me. I wanted to bury myself in my mashed potatoes.

For the next week, I avoided Sean and his friends at all costs, walking an extra five minutes around the school to avoid all of his favorite hangout places. Until one day at lunch, when my bladder couldn't wait that extra minute. I walked toward the girls' bathroom, knowing that Sean and his friends would be hanging around the steps in front of the drama classroom, the drama classroom that happened to be right in the way between me and the nearest bathroom. After a brief argument with my bladder, it won, and I realized that I had no choice but to walk by Sean.

I rolled my shoulders back, raised my head tall, took a deep breath, and headed toward the freshly painted green door, focusing my eyes on the little white letters that spelled out "girls." I was determined not to acknowledge Sean's existence — unless, of course, he acknowledged mine first.

But it was not Sean's voice I heard as I walked by the steps of the drama classroom. It was the unforgettable voice of his friend Jason.

I turned just in time to see the dark-haired chosen companion of the man of my dreams as he rose slowly from his seat on the steps to extend his index finger toward me. His mouth opened and from his lips came the words, "Hey, Chink!"

In less than a second, over a dozen pairs of eyes were glaring my way, including the baby blue pair belonging to Sean. My eyes met his as he sat there motionless while the rest of his friends decided to join Jason in his fun. I turned around and ran toward the green door, leaving behind a chorus of voices chanting, "Gook!" "Chink!" and other miscellaneous noises that were supposed to be Chinese.

I don't remember what I did after that. I wanted to run out and tell them what I thought of them and how immature they were for saying those things, but I couldn't. I couldn't do anything except cry. I think I stayed in that bathroom for the rest of that day. I guess it's true what they say. I had been crushed. And I will never forget.

In Vietnamese

BY DUONG PHAN

During our evening walks,
I teach my Indian boyfriend
words that I'm slowly forgetting
The dazzling stars, the luminescent moon, the calling birds
I clear my throat, swirl my tongue,
and release the word *ngoi sao*
without the Vietnamese accent.
Clearly a mistake, I begin again
This time accented.
He says, *How beautiful* and asks me
to say it once more.
And I do.
His lips move in circles, a word stumbles out.
I laugh.
Mat trang
He repeats the word back slowly to me.
In unison, we say the word
with our crackling voices
unlike the notes from a soft melody.
We laugh and continue on
as we stroll along the street.

ngoi sao: star
mat trang: moon

We Don't Need No Mountain Guru

Where I'm From

A Well-Made Life

BY SHIZUE SEIGEL

Not long after we found *Jiichan* (Grandpa in Japanese) on the roof, he decided he was ready for a rest home. He was 90, after all, and had a bad hip and fading eyesight. Lately his heart had been acting up. Twice, Uncle Tak had had to drive out in the middle of the night to take him to the hospital.

Jiichan loved his little 10-acre farm. Even though he hadn't planted crops for years, he still kept up his vegetable garden. Fruit trees grown from cuttings traded with long-dead friends continued to bear fruit, and roses and fuchsias bloomed in the front yard. And he had plenty to do — fixing water pumps, tightening door hinges, or simply walking the muddy fields amid the ghosts of long-gone strawberry fields and prune orchards.

He always had something to offer us when we visited — ripe tomatoes, corn, bell peppers, persimmons, loquats, Mission figs. . . . After growing season was over, he plied us with Cool Whip containers filled with sugared and frozen raspberries, or plastic miso tubs packed with *umeboshi* (pickled plums). His *umeboshi* were extraordinarily firm, plump and sweet; his secret was to substitute green apricots for plums. In the rainy season, when he spent more time indoors, he fed us new dishes learned from Japanese TV or magazines, elaborately fussy concoctions better suited to Tokyo housewives than to a callous-palmed old man in mud-caked work boots.

I'll never forget the day my mother, Auntie Sumi, and I drove into the gravel yard behind the house for our monthly visit. We went to the back door as usual. (The front door of a farmhouse is reserved for the occasional minister or insurance agent.) The door gaped open, but *Jiichan* was not inside. We peeked into the garage and sheds, calling, "*Jiiichan*! Where aaare you?" Just as we began to get really worried, he strode like a god over the peak of the roof.

"I'm up here," he called as he strolled casually down the sloping roof and slung himself down onto the porch.

"*Jiichan*!" Mom cried, "We were getting worried! What are you doing!"

"I didn't hear you." (His hearing was failing, too.) "The roof's been leaking, so I thought I'd better take a look."

Auntie Sumi clucked under her breath, "It's lucky he didn't break his neck. My goodness, at his age!"

They fussed over him like two grumpy hens while I stood silent, marveling that a 90-year-old man with serious health problems could still handle his own affairs with such casual aplomb.

But that was his last hurrah. Within a few months, *Jiichan* declared it was time he went to a rest home. He wanted one run by Japanese, with Japanese clients and Japanese food. Mom made over 50 phone calls before she found the right situation, in a ranch-style house in town. It was run by a Japanese American man. His Filipina wife was eager to learn Japanese cooking. *Jiichan* would enjoy sharing his recipes.

He made his preparations with good grace, winnowing the accumulations of a lifetime down to a couple of suitcases, but we could see that he had mixed feelings about trading the spacious farm for a shared bedroom and a tiny fenced yard. *"Shikata ga nai,* there's no alternative. It's all for the best," he said. "It's my heart. *Inaka de* (in the countryside), I could die out here, and nobody would know for days. . . ."

After a few weeks, I noticed that he seemed a little depressed. He was losing interest in personal hygiene. He even stopped shaving. As the stubble in his chin grew longer, Auntie Sumi shook her head. "My goodness, he's really letting himself go."

On our next visit, instead of work shirt and boots, *Jiichan* sported a padded Japanese vest and slippers. A wispy little *ojiisan* (old man) beard sprouted from the end of his chin.

Auntie Sumi laughed. "So that's why you stopped shaving!"

His eyes twinkled. "Well, I decided that now that I'm an old man, I should look like one."

I was momentarily relieved, but as the months passed, I noticed that in quiet moments, his eyes dulled like a trapped dog's. He missed the farm, and his remaining friends were too feeble to visit him.

After a year or so, he was moved to a skilled nursing facility. *Jiichan* missed the Japanese food at the home care facility, but *shikata ga nai,* he needed oxygen now. We visited him there just before Christmas. Despite the twinkling trees and tasteful furniture groupings, the spacious sitting room felt as impersonal and transitory as a hotel lobby.

Mom asked how he was. "Fine," *Jiichan* said, but he was subdued and laconic, speaking only when we asked a question. "The place is fine. Not much to do but watch TV. There's only one other Japanese here, and he's too deaf to talk with. The food's okay, but too much meat and potatoes. No rice." He avoided our eyes without seeming to. When I looked carefully, I saw a deep, quiet sadness.

"I love you, *Jiichan,*" I said as we left.

"Hai, hai , so desu ne (yes, so you do)." He nodded distantly, as if saluting the memory of the long-gone times when we used to walk together in the strawberry fields, as if he were looking down a long tunnel towards a place he would never see again.

"He's not going to stick around much longer," I thought. "He's had enough TV." I wasn't surprised that he died a week later.

After the funeral, we visited the farm for the last time. I was overwhelmed by a sense of loss. *Jiichan* and the farm had been a touchstone for all that was Japanese in me. Some part of me had expected them to stay frozen in time, an ageless haven for my heart.

I had spent quite a bit of time on the farm when I was growing up. Bored and at wit's end, I had passed hours leafing through old photo albums and pawing through drawers full of rhinestone shoe buckles, strangely shaped Japanese scissors, and old celluloid fountain pens. One day I found a book the size and shape of a high school yearbook entitled *Mohaveland.* On the cover, a man and a tree stood silhouetted against a dramatic desert sky. On the first spread were photos of rows of shoddy barracks in the searing Arizona desert, with guard towers and barbed wire in the distance. The book was a souvenir of Poston Relocation Center, where my family had been incarcerated, along with 120,000 other Japanese Americans, during World War II. My family had been swept from their sprawling prewar farm on the California coast, leaving everything behind except what they could carry.

Of course I knew about Camp. The family's reference point for time was "before Camp," "during Camp," and "after Camp." It must have been a wrenching experience, but they spoke of it matter-of-factly, without bitterness. *Shikata ga nai,* they said. It couldn't be helped.

Thumbing through *Mohaveland*, I found snapshots of residents from each of the barracks . . . Block 116, Block 117, Block 118. . . . There were photos of the choir, the Young Buddhist Association, *odori* (Japanese dance) performances, and most striking of all — Japanese gardens with stone bridges and lanterns and carefully pruned pine trees. I remember wondering, what sort of people would respond to being uprooted and stuck in a prison camp by building gardens in the desert and memorializing their internment in a yearbook?

My grandparents lived through the rigors of immigration, discrimination, the Depression, relocation camps, the economic death of family farms, aging and loss. "*Shikata ga nai,*" they said. The usual translation is, "It can't be helped; there's no alternative," but *shikata ga nai* connotes something vastly more positive than simple resignation — with echoes of "when you're stuck with a lemon, make lemonade," "living well is the best revenge," or "life is transitory; make every moment count."

Roaming the farm for the last time, I marveled at the richness and creativity of *Jiichan's* life. After the War, my grandparents worked as migrant laborers until they scraped up enough to buy 10 acres, less than a tenth the size of their prewar acreage. *Jiichan* built the house and outbuildings himself, with the help of his sons. A dozen different kinds of cacti grew near the garbage can. They had arrived as 39-cent plants in tiny plastic pots; now they grew on top of each other, squeezing and spilling over themselves, spiny ones, hairy ones, tall skinny ones, with flat paddle-leaves and fat fluted domes. A pile of abalone and clam shells lay near the water tap, souvenirs of coastal forages to gather seaweed and eat black sea snails. The front yard was edged with beautiful rocks, gathered on road trips with his friends. In the shed were more rocks, shelves and shelves of them — examples of the art of *suiseki* — carefully selected for their resemblance to the mountains of Japan, and each set off by a wooden stand precisely carved to fit.

Beneath the apparent dullness and routine of rural life, a self-sufficient and joyful creativity had flowered. The walls of the house were lined with calligraphy, paintings, and plaques crafted by friends in Camp. *Baachan's* (Grandma's) homemade Japanese silk quilts lay on the beds. The drawers of the old, treadle-powered Singer sewing machine were crammed with tatting reels, crochet hooks, bits of lace and fancy-glass buttons cut from worn clothes to decorate anew. In the home-built curio cabinet were handicrafts created from the most mundane materials — lifelike crepe paper flowers and intricately patterned umbrellas and Japanese lanterns painstakingly crafted from dozens of old cigarette packs, folded and glued together.

In the storage room, I found three suitcases. They looked like the old pre-Samsonite cardboard ones, complete with leather edges and metal fittings, except that the bodies were made out of wood. "I made them in Camp," *Jiichan* had told me. "When the War broke out, the FBI came and got all the men in the middle of the night. I didn't even have time to pack a suitcase." (*Jiichan* had spent most of the War in a high-security camp for "dangerous aliens," separated from the rest of the family.) He laughed, "After awhile, they made me a Camp policeman. I was a policeman, but in the middle of the night, I turned into a *dorobo* (thief). I stole some scrap wood and made myself these suitcases."

The suitcases are now stacked in my front hall, handy storage in an overstuffed apartment, the top surface a catch-all for magazines and mail. *Jiichan* is gone, *shikata ga nai,* but sometimes I catch sight of those suitcases, and I'm grateful that I am one of the things *Jiichan* made.

Kim Mi Jin

BY JENNIFER KIM

I can hear myself in different ways:

from the days of Slim in the basketball gym,
to the annoying last name calling
(Kim is not Jennifer!)
which comes out of the mouths of teachers
and distant people,

from the high shrieked Jen Jen,
yelled by a mother holding a phone
between dripping yellow gloves,
to Jennifart with gastronomical problems,

from Jennifer Kim signed on formal letters,
to Mi Jin who will meet her relatives for
the first time, this May.

Comfort Food

BY LILY SUN

When I was about to go off to college, the one thing my mother taught me was how to make white rice. She pulled out the sack of rice grains, showed me how to measure out cups into the pot, how to wash the rice with water to wash off the dust, and how to add water up to the line inside the pot to correlate with how many cups of rice I had put in. She pulled out the rice cooker — a big, old, red Da-Tung one — that had been in the family for years. She showed me how to plug it in and how to put water in the outer pot so that the rice would steam.

She didn't teach me about birth control or sex or about how to treat my dorm mates so that I would get along with them better. She sort of taught me how to do laundry, but she didn't mention how some things shrink in the dryer. She didn't teach me how to deal with drugs or the sort of pressure that made me want to try them. She didn't teach me about older men who'd take advantage of me, or about younger men and how callous they can be. She didn't teach me what I should do when I wake up in the middle of the night with a 102 degree fever and no one else is around. She didn't teach me about how to protect myself from rape, abuse, or violence. But she did teach me how to make rice.

I remember when my brother was born. I was eight at the time and had never in my life seen my father cook. Since Mom was bedridden after the delivery, I walked into the kitchen to witness my Dad busily cutting his old undershirts into pieces and sticking them into the bottom of a gigantic steamer that was sitting on top of the range. It turned out he was cooking oil-rice, a sticky rice dish made with meat, mushrooms, soy sauce and seasoning that is traditionally given out to family and friends to celebrate of the birth of a new baby. Dad was just so happy that my brother had turned out a boy, and since there were no other female relatives around to make the dish, he did it himself. Ten years later, we still joked about him using his undershirts as padding for the steamer.

Driving home from my job interview with *Yolk Magazine* in L.A., I stopped by the Shiao-Mae Taiwanese eatery in Monterey Park to grab some dinner. Walking into the noise- and aroma-filled room, I looked up at the lighted sign above the counter that listed all the tastes of home. I needed a little comfort because the interview had gone so badly. They clearly weren't interested in me. I mean, who could seriously conduct an interview sitting in front of a computer, casually putting the finishing touches on a picture of a model, if they were interested in me? Tommy, the editor, had barely asked me half a dozen questions in the course of 40 minutes. I felt deflated.

So I ambled up to the counter and ordered some *baa-gehn* and some Taiwanese *dan-dan* noodles. I also ordered a *baa-wan*, even though I knew it would be too much food. I didn't care. I wanted to go home, even if it was only through my taste buds; I wanted to absorb a little of what was familiar in my blood through my food. I sat down and looked at the faces around me. They all seemed so familiar and warm, I could almost have been in a noodle shop in Taipei. Earthy in a sincere way, no pretension, no hype. Not at all like the office I had just left, where they were paving the new Asian American way with Color-Macs and Industrial-Deco furniture.

I drove home to San Diego with a boxed lunch and a large cup of shaved ice next to me on the passenger seat.

Exodus from Phnom Penh –
A Cambodian Woman's Personal Memoir

BY DAVY MUTH

EVIL MEMORIES

Pou Sok pulled my hand instead of pushing me into the grave and said, "This is just the Angkar's test, Met Vy." [Angkar is the name the Khmer Rouge gave to its regime.]

Two years passed by slowly. It seemed like two centuries. All the people had to prove themselves by working very hard, and even so, the Khmer Rouge starved us. People died everywhere, in the rice field, on the way to receive their rations, and they even died while they were asleep. Along with all that, we were frightened because the Khmer Rouge executed us at any time, accusing us of being enemies or spies. I went to work every single day, but my mind was always with my children — how could I relax? My two-year-old son was taken care of by my four-year-old daughter for 15 hours a day.

One day my daughter unknowingly picked some poison plants and cooked them with her gruel, which she then shared with her brother. I was ready to commit suicide. I couldn't bear watching my children begging for help. Pou Sok took my daughter to the General Hospital (a General Hospital for the Khmer Rouge only) in the city of Battambang, the provincial capital. My son died two hours later in my arms of vomiting and diarrhea. My sorrow felt greater than my hold on life, but I remembered my daughter. "I have to live. I have another three children," I told myself. I fought my dejection and waited for my daughter to return from the hospital.

I was so thrilled to hear the news when my daughter came back to the village. Unexpectedly, she didn't want to live with me anymore, because Pou Sok told her that she was Angkar's daughter. It was killing my heart to see her sit down beside Pou Sok and sing the Revolutionary songs. Even though I was gloomy and wanted to die, I still assured myself that my daughter would be mine again one day.

MY SANNAYA

Sleeping in my hut alone, I thought I was going to die because I had no one left in my life. I lay very still for a while, not allowing myself to think. But soon, against my will, the vision of my daughter Sannaya ("Promise") and my deceased son seeped into my mind and an uncontrollable trembling racked my body. It remained until the dawn, when I fell into a restless sleep.

I should have felt happy to see my Sannaya having a good life. She had a safe place to stay, food to eat, clothes to wear and a man, the village leader Pou Sok, who carried her wherever he went. Instead, I burst out crying every time I passed Pou Sok's house. Most of the time, I could only smile at her and if I was lucky, when Pou Sok was not there, say, "I miss you so much." She looked beautiful in her new black communist uniform, but her sweet voice in the revolutionary songs was killing my heart. People in the whole village were in such a panic. Besides dying from starvation, more and more people disappeared every day. We knew that the Khmer Rouge executed them, but no one dared to ask or even mention their names. New leaders and soldiers with their families came to stay for a day or two and then left. No one knew where they came from or where they went.

One day while I was working in the rice field with my companions, I heard in the distance what sounded like the echo of artillery fire, or perhaps bombs. My companions told me that they heard a rumor that Vietnamese troops had come. Before we left our work it was pouring hard — rain in April, I couldn't believe it. I passed Pou Sok's house. I did not see Sannaya; instead, I saw many wounded soldiers under Pou Sok's house (his house was built on strong stilts about three meters off the ground). I went straight to the share kitchen to receive my ration. There I saw my Sannaya close by Pou Sok helping the Khmer Rouge give a teaspoon of salt of to each family. She smiled at me and said shyly "ma ma." She gave me a full teaspoon, too, even though I had only one person in my family. I was so thrilled I almost forgot my gruel portion. I went smiling and humming through the slippery mud back to my hut.

My body was soaked with mud up to my knees, but I was so happy to hear Sannaya call me "ma ma." When I got to my hut, I saw my brother Roth climb down from a tree growing alongside. "What are you doing here? How is everyone? Is our mother all right? How is my baby?"

Roth put his hand on my mouth and whispered, "No time to ask, come on, let's go. It's a good time now; everyone's going back to their huts from the share kitchen and we can deceive the Khmer Rouge's eyes."

"How about my Sannaya?" I was genuinely puzzled.

"I'll come back and get her later," Roth assured me.

"No, oh no, I'm not going anywhere without Sannaya."

"Sis, please go, I can't explain to you right now. But I'll explain when we get to the rice field. We might be safe there, Sis."

My only response was to say, "Sannaya, my only Sannaya, I would never leave my Sannaya."

We had to stop because we saw Pou Sok and two soldiers walking toward my hut. I held Roth's hand tightly, I was so shocked. I begged Pou Sok not to kill Roth, but to kill me instead.

Pou Sok looked at me and smiled, "You might get a cold, Met Vy. Go get changed." Then he turned to Roth, "Roth, I think you should go back to your village right now."

Roth's face turned pale. I hid my face in my hands sobbing hard.

"Hey, he has to go back. The Angkar in here has no rations for him. He'll be alive. Hear?" Pou Sok yelled at me.

I hugged that man with relief and happiness in front of Roth. Pou Sok and Roth whispered a little bit, and Roth went with the two soldiers and Pou Sok back to the share kitchen.

I was cold and my whole hut was wet because the wind had blown away some of the palm leaves that roofed my hut. My only blanket, mosquito net and another pair of pants were soaking wet. I sat down, crying and trembling. I felt warmer and warmer. Around midnight I was shaking, not from cold or fear but from yellow fever. I heard noises, people walking with lanterns and ox carts. An unexpected meeting had been called.

"Come to the meeting, everyone. The Angkar will have plenty of food and fruits for all of you. The people from three villages can get to know each other." I was thrilled to know that my family would come to the meeting and I could get to meet them. I wondered why the Angkar let us see the inside of the huge share barn used for stocking thousands of sacks of rice. Pou Sok came to my hut while the announcer continued their propaganda. I felt very weakened, and as I saw Pou Sok's face, a fit of shaking seized me and I started vomiting. My intestines emptied themselves in one convulsion, as if the contents had been blasted by a powerful force. When I tried to stand up, I collapsed.

When I woke up again, I lay beside Sannaya in Pou Sok's house. To see her sweet young face peacefully in repose felt like magic medicine. I lifted my fatigued hand to feel her, but she woke up hearing noises from the share barn about 200 meters from the house. She quickly sat up and called his name, "Pok Sok, Pok Sok." (Pok means father in the peasants' language.) She wept softly.

"Sannaya, it's me, your mama," I called, but she had already walked toward the door. Pou Sok lifted her up and cradled her tightly to his chest. Her eyes closed again. "Oh, my God, she needs him that much," I realized as I lay back to think of a way to die.

"Met Vy, why don't you wait here? I'll come back later," urged Pou Sok.

Shortly after Pou Sok left with Sannaya in his arms, other Pol Pot leaders came and they insisted on putting me into an oxcart. Luckily they thought I was a Khmer Rouge comrade. I was horrified to see the leaders shooting those soldiers with serious injuries. The oxcart line did not move in the share barn direction. I panicked, and I had to know what to do. I asked the soldier leading my oxcart for permission to relieve myself. I jumped off without spirit. I could not find a place to hide. I crawled till I found a hole that used to be a grave. A loud blasting sound came from the village. I quickly squeezed myself into the hole.

While I made myself comfortable, I heard a familiar crying voice — I tried to turn around and a piece of sharp wood pierced deep into my left thigh. I couldn't move. It was very painful, and I was stuck. As I peered out of the grave, I saw my brother Roth; his hands were tied behind his back and two soldiers were beating him with their rifle butts.

"Kill me now, you pack of savages!" Roth shouted, but the last few words were drowned in a sudden burst of noise from exploding bombs. In the reflected light of the flames, I could see Roth's body covered with blood. His right leg was completely scorched. The left leg of his trouser was in shreds.

I was overcome with emotion. I tried to call Roth, but my voice disappeared in the blasting noise. When Roth fell down on the ground, I saw those Khmer Rouge soldiers run away. Then I saw Vietnamese troops and the new Cambodian soldiers, who freed me from my grave. As they cleansed my wounds, I turned and saw a swollen face with perfect shining black rings around his eyes and dried blood scattered all over his smiling face. It was my beloved Roth.

Roth told me that Pou Sok had warned my family not to go to the meeting. He then returned to the house and found me gone. He clutched Sannaya to his chest and ran into the barn believing that I must have gone to the meeting. The Khmer Rouge bolted the doors, and opened the roof and then dropped grenades and bombs onto the innocent people. Pou Sok and my lovely Sannaya were buried among thousands of other fresh victims of this cruel and hideous war.

THE ENDURING PAIN

During the Pol Pot regime, farms were frequently organized as slave-labor camps, with constant supervision and meager rations of rice or gruel. My mother and I each lost two children during the time of this communist regime because of the starvation.

Four years passed by slowly with evil memories. Things were changing again. In 1979, the Khmer Rouge were busy fighting with the Vietnamese troops. I escaped the village and was reunited with my mom's family. It was a miracle of prophecy when I found my mother and children again. Unfortunately, my father, like my husband Hong, had also been taken away. My father had been a famous surgeon in Cambodia. I admired my mother; she did not show any of her sorrow about the loss of her loved ones, whether to her own children or to the Pol Pot people. We never saw her tears, but I heard her once, when she lay down near my daughter. She was weeping softly.

We were happy to hear that the Vietnamese troops came to rescue us from the Pol Pot soldiers. However, it did not seem that they ever would leave Cambodia to go back to their country. I saw unjust things done more and more often. When the Pol Pot forces ambushed the unarmed farmers, the Vietnamese troops were conveniently absent. After our harvest, they seized our rice by the truckload and transported it to Vietnam. They did not let us marry Cambodians; we were expected to marry only Vietnamese soldiers. The Vietnamese occupation seemed like the Pol Pot regime to me, since the latter killed our men in front of our eyes while the Vietnamese did it by taking them away ostensibly to be trained as soldiers — but Vietnamese soldiers had rescued us from the horrors of Pol Pot.

The Vietnamese troops were in our country. I was reunited with my family. I went to search for Hong in Phnom Penh, but he had completely vanished, so I began to think about leaving Cambodia. I did not know where I wanted to go, but all I wanted was to leave that land. My mother was mad; she did not want to leave our country. I had already made up my mind. I begged her until one day she said okay, hesitantly.

We decided to leave our own land. We prepared to leave the Khmer Rouge behind, but we had nothing. We had to do something to feed our empty stomachs, so my mother decided to bake cakes to sell. Markets had appeared again, but this time no one had money. Instead we traded and bartered our clothes and jewelry for rice and meat.

Around the middle of June 1979, we left our country. I remember my mother saying to us, "Life is stronger than death. This is the last we will see of our country and our shelter." I led my family into the jungle. Bad luck followed me; two brothers and a sister died during our escape.

It was green everywhere; the wild bamboo grew extravagantly because of the heavy rains of the last week. We were wet up to our knees from the morning dew. The wild flowers in the forest smelled like perfume, and sometimes it made me feel like crying. There were five other families traveling with us. My family of 11 members was the largest. None of us had time to appreciate the gorgeous view because we were so worried about the dangers that could befall us at any moment.

We had to hide from Vietnamese troops and the Heng Sam Rin soldiers of the new government of Cambodia. We also had to hide from the dreaded Pol Pot soldiers whose home was the jungle. When we traveled, everyone in my family walk-stepped — they had to step exactly where I stepped to avoid the land mines and leftover grenades or bombs.

When we stopped and relaxed, we collected leaves or roots to eat. We cooked rice only for my youngest brother, my youngest sister and my daughter. The rest of us ate rice soup with lots of leaves. Sometimes, we did not know which leaves were safe to eat, so we mimicked the eating selections of animals in the forest. We slept in hammocks hung from tree branches. When we got ready to leave, I stood up with my eyes closed. I prayed that I would not be seen by the enemies, thankful the wild bamboo was high and thick.

Fourteen nights I counted after my family left Battambang Province. I was so scared, but I never let anyone know. Our rice was almost gone. Two people who came with us were sick; my sister had yellow fever and my mother fell down and broke her right wrist. We decided to stay at least for one day by a small pond. My brothers and my sisters felt sorry for my mother. They thought everything was miserable because of my decision to leave our country. My mother stared at them and said they should not blame me, and they should respect the older sister. I cradled my mother's wrist as I applied poultice to ease her pain.

My sister and my brothers gathered some wood and began to build a fire while I went down to the pond to get some water. Halfway to the pond, I heard an extremely loud exploding noise. I turned around and ran back toward my family, screaming, "No! No, not them! Please, me." It was silent for a second, then my cries mingled with those of my family. We did not care that the enemies might hear us. I was thrilled to see my mother sitting up with my daughter. Then I was frozen like a statue because I realized that two brothers and a sister were gone. As the dust began to clear, I could see pieces of flesh and pools of blood covering the area where they had been building the fire.

My mother began to hysterically bang her head against the ground. My other brothers and sisters hit their heads against the trees. They turned toward me with their angry faces. They started to break and tear our belongings. One of my brothers shook me and screamed that I was a killer.

"Sis, aren't you happy now that you forced us to come to a place like this to die?" one of my sisters shouted at me.

I had no answer; I could not think. In my heart I could only repeat, "Oh, my God, I killed them. Why? Why? How could I kill them like this? My dearest God, why didn't you kill me instead?" I knelt down beside my mother and tried to stop her from banging her head against the ground. I asked her forgiveness with my begging eyes. I blamed myself; because of my decision, my brothers and my sister were dead.

Now, 20 years have passed since Hong was taken away, but the void in my heart remains. Often I have asked God, what I had done in my last life to deserve so many heartbreaks? I never stop thinking of my absent family, and through all of my days the pain endures. Sometimes, I think that these terrible things must have been only a dream, but I still wake up in the middle of the night and know that it was real.

Shooting Pineapples

By Corrine Leilani Domingo

*I*nside is better than outside,
  you said over school lunch,
    my fork piercing the yellow chunks
      of our island dessert. It was our first day back
      from summer break, and I envied
        your browned face, the heavy sculpt of your arms
        that was not there the last time.
    I sat office-white and gaunt,
      hungrily eating the fruit you would not touch.

They have eyes, you said,
  shuddering how knives extracted
  brown o's into waste bins. Conveyor belts
  moved the sightless into blades, sticky rings
  sealed into steel cans vacuumed by machines
  set on high. At 15, your first job.
You liked the shade of the factory
better than the hot sun
the company made you stand under,
that baked your face to a wrinkle.

Inside, outside,
the smell
was everywhere.

  Under thick-gloved fingers, at night under nails.
  A sweetness cursed for following
    on flannels and hair.
    It coated your girlfriend, who left,
      then the cash wad dealt on pay day
        that too, departed.

      But there were secrets learned
        during the ten-dollars-an-hour days,
          how centipedes and spiders bred
            under the spiny patch, and how the leaves
              were feathers ready
                to cushion the tired.

That afternoon, we drove into the field,
    across dirt roads carved by tires
heavy from harvest. The No Trespassing sign
    was splashed with mud from recent rains.
            Suddenly, you cried, Look!
        whipping out a BB gun, the barrel
        aimed at the patch that wavered
        in the wind gust off the Haiku cliff.

            This is for the stings, you said,
        the track marks below your elbows,
                red as the shot earth.
            This is for the bites, now yelling,
            the welts on your pale fist
            puffed on your trigger finger.
        You tried to knock them down
        their leafy perch, pinballs bulleting
            young fruit with silver.
        Then you put the gun down,
        the carriage empty, your eyes wet,
        stepped out of the car and reached
                into the patch,
    plucking a pineapple with bare hands,

                grasping it as you fell
            back first, eagle-spread onto
        green blades. The leaves carried you
            weightless as the air.
    For minutes you never touched the ground.

            When we arrived home
            you gave me the fruit,
        silencing the afternoon with a finger
                to your lips.

    Mother laughed at the prickly green
    cradled like a football in my arms.
        she said it was not yet ripe,
    that it was plucked too young;

        Once picked pineapple
    does not ripen further.

Blue Fairyland

BY SASHA HOM

My name is Wol Soon Ann. I was born somewhere in the South of Korea in a place called Anyang, a place that did not approve of bastard children. It is a place I was in only once, when I was first born. Though many times later I have returned in my dreams. I know Anyang through these dreams and the stories I make up.

My name is bastard child. I was born in the winter. The snow blanketed the soil in a thick crunchy layer, muffling the sounds of my mother's labor so that I could slip out like a wet secret. On the third day after my birth, my mother wrapped me in blankets and a woolen knit hat. She placed me in a basket and left me on the doorstep of a wealthy man's house. I imagine her heaving a big brass knocker and then disappearing into the snow like a fleeing rabbit. Perhaps she was crying; perhaps she was relieved. She left a note on the basket with the date of my birth. Just like in the cartoons, I thought. The orphanage named me Wol Soon Ann. Maybe I had other names before that — baby names like Sweetie, Pumpkin, Muffin. I do not know.

My name is Sasha Gabrielle Hom. My adopted parents couldn't decide what to name me. My mother wanted to name me Fanny or Lulu, impractical names for a round Korean baby. She settled on Sasha because my mother had heard someone calling their child "Sasha" in an empty museum. She said it sounded like the wind echoing off the cement walls.

My name is Tom So Lan, because the child must have a Chinese name, even if she is Korean living like a Chinese American. My grandmother named me before she was murdered, before my grandfather passed away, before I even knew what it meant to be a Chinaman's Korean baby in a country that belonged to neither one. The Chinese believe that when you are troubled, or grieving or dying, if your "personal" name is spoken into your ear, it will draw out the sorrow and the pain. My grandfather's name was Richard, my grandmother's name was Doris. I do not know either of their "personal" names. I wonder what they whispered to themselves as they slipped away, what name my grandmother imagined was being whispered to her as she lay slipping away in a basement closet.

My name is Sasha Gabrielle Hom. My uncle tells me I should reclaim my "original" name. I do not know what he's talking about.

My name is Sasha Hom. When receptionists and bill collectors ask me to spell my last name. I say, "H-O-M." They say, "And?" I say, "That's all," but I think, stupid white people, even though I cannot see their faces. My name is Sasha Gabrielle Hom. My name has been on many mailboxes, school rosters, checks, bills, invitations. It has been written on love letters, hate mail, recommendations, eviction notices, airplane tickets and veterinary bills. My name is Sasha Gabrielle Hom, but I imagine that when I die many names will be whispered into my ear from ghosts and loved ones I never knew.

I went to preschool 15 blocks away from home. My mother would ride me on the back of her bicycle, a purple two-speed with a tattered basket in front and a yellow child's seat on the back. She rode me to school every morning until I got to be too big. I was a big-boned child with a heavy round head, and my mother was petite, with wrists like hollow birch trees. We began periodically tipping over onto lawns, or into a bush of rosemary or ivy, before she began driving me to school in the tan VW bus. The "hippymobile" was yellow and had homemade paisley curtains, a round rainbow sticker on the back window, and a loose screw causing the horn to blast sporadically for minutes on end. The incessant honking was so embarrassing that I'd bury my face beneath my arms while my mother, oblivious to my embarrassment, sang Joan Baez songs at the top of her lungs in an attempt to ignore the honking.

My preschool was started by communists. Jane Fonda was one of the founders. The school was in a small building behind a house with a crooked tree in front. It was a brown-shingled building with green trim, similar to many of the houses on the tree-lined blocks in Berkeley. On the first day of school the teachers allowed us to make up a name for the school. We decided on Fairyland. The teachers smiled. They exchanged glances and said, "How about a color. Why don't you put a color in the school's name, like the color of a rose or a heart." The children, perplexed, all looked down at the carpet, a blue industrial rug that smelled like dried vomit and baby powder, and in unison we squealed, "Blue!" The teachers frowned, except for Manuka who smiled with the hint of laughter beneath his beard. I'm sure the teachers would have preferred a name for the school that reflected their politics, such as Red Comrades or even Red Fonda, but Blue Fairyland it was.

At Blue Fairyland I loved to write in enclosed spaces. During nap time, Manuka would let me read books instead of sleep. I wrote stories also. I'd hide in the tunnel in the playground and write stories in its cool echoey emptiness instead of napping in the house with the rest of the kids. Once, I found a huge cardboard box behind the rug store on Ashby Avenue and carried it three blocks to my house. I put the box inside my closet beneath a tiny window. The box was nestled among old stuffed animals, broken hangers and fallen clothes. Posters and pictures of dogs were taped on the walls. I would sit inside the box, inside my closet, and write.

This is what I wrote: A 10-page illustrated novel about the adventures of my dog and cat; two spiral notebooks filled with information about my neighbors that I had observed from peeking into their bedroom, kitchen or hallway windows, as well as from climbing on their roof and looking through the skylight; a story about my life as a dog; complaints about my enemy, the red baron. I believed I was a cross between Snoopy and Harriet the Spy, and that everybody surrounding me worked for the Red Baron: *"po3Ono.4010 World War Flying Ace checking in"* is how I would begin each entry in my little notebook. I wrote about my friend Sierra, and how she always got candy for Easter — jellybeans, cream-filled Cadbury eggs, and sugar eggs with windows you could look into like a glass-bottomed ship and see edible candied worlds.

I wrote in the smallest spaces that I could squeeze into. In elementary school I sat underneath my desk sucking on chicken bones I had saved from last night's dinner, reading books and writing funny stories. I wrote in a cupboard that I'd sneak into before grammar lessons, or I'd jump out the window and read books in the well beneath. At the numerous Chinese dinners I had to attend with my entire family I'd pass on the roast duck, fried fish and numerous chicken dishes, and sit underneath the table with the tablecloth covering me like a mosquito net, and read or write in my Hello Kitty notebook. My mother used to say, "The world is filled with shit so ignore it whenever you can."

In fourth grade, I switched schools and had to take a bus every morning, and began wearing my keys around my neck on a shoestring with bells attached. My classmates would hear the jingling of the bells and keys as I walked by and say, "Here comes Sasha." They thought I sounded like a dog when I walked.

I have been a dog-lover ever since I was two. Once my mother turned her back on me while she was shopping for shoes. She frantically searched for me, hoping to find me crawling amongst racks of shoes. Instead she found me in front of the store curled up in the soft belly of an Italian mastiff, a dog that looked as if it could swallow me whole, or suffocate me with the weight of its extra folds of skin. Since then, I have carried dog biscuits in my pockets and a dog encyclopedia in my hand so that I could identify all the breeds I saw while riding on the bus. I believed I should have been born an Argentine Dogo, not a human being.

During recess, I wedged myself between a bench and a fence, and I used my keys to try to drill a hole into the bench. I believed that once the hole was deep enough I could fit my key into it perfectly, turn the key and unlock the invisible door to the imaginary world where I believed I belonged. Surely God must have made a mistake to put me in a foreign place, in a foreign world amongst people who did not look like me, or even imagine like me, with a family who did not share the same blood or ancestors as me. I was not only adopted into a foreign family, but into a foreign world. "I'm on the wrong planet," I thought. So in every public restroom, closet, or cupboard that I could fit in, I would knock five times on the top of the door, twice on the bottom, and wait for that invisible door to open.

Fourth grade was when reality began to seep into my small spaces. It was when life began to feel like something unfamiliar, something that needed to be thought about, navigated through, accessed. The world was shit, but I was having a hard time ignoring it.

Fourth grade was when I first learned that I wasn't white. I had always known that I was the "Chinese, Japanese, dirty knees, look at these" kid, because that was what the kids used to sing to me while pulling up or down at their eyes, depending on the taunt. But it wasn't until fourth grade that I was able to distinguish how I was different from the white kids. The girls' bathroom was always damp and cold, and I think it was made out of cement or hopelessness. I remember going to pee one day and hearing two black girls talking. One girl said, "Did you know that white people just sit on the toilet seats. They don't put seat covers or toilet paper down or nothin'!" "That's nasty!" said the other girl. And that was when I knew I wasn't white because I always put paper on the toilet seats first. Even if the toilet paper was in squares and I had to lay each square down one by one, dancing around and holding my crotch while the sheets inevitably slipped into the bowl or onto the floor. To be white meant that you didn't have to patiently lay down each square sheet of toilet paper, that you could put your own white butt on the white porcelain seat and not get hit for it if your mother was around.

Fourth grade was when Russ stabbed Darnell, and for months afterward I could swear I saw blood spots on the gray cement of the school's floor. Fourth grade was when I first saw a bullet that wasn't in my Daddy's gun, except these bullets were long and pointy like a witch's finger, and when I first saw crack, and a fight between a kid and a teacher, and when I used to bring caterpillars in boxes to class. Fourth grade was when my grandmother was murdered and I developed a speech impediment and had to go to speech therapy and miss music class. Fourth grade was when I stopped writing stories.

I learned how to swim at Malcolm X Junior High. There were three P.E. teachers: a man with a metal plate in his ass, a 250-pound woman whose son had drowned in a river, and Mr. Wallace, a 64-year-old virgin. Mr. Wallace was my teacher. He was so out of it that he never noticed that half of the class, including the boys, were not participating because they were having their "menses." He also never noticed when a girl was pinned against the steps in the kiddy pool and being raped by three boys. We used to say that Mr. Wallace was so out of it that that was why he was still a virgin in his '60s.

I loved the way the world sounded when you were underwater. It was as if you were in a different place or a different dimension, where you could see the wavering images of people on the other side, but you couldn't make out their expressions or facial features, and they couldn't reach you without getting wet. It reminded me of being little and feeling safe in a cardboard box, and of believing in a different dimension that made you feel at home, even if that dimension was a body of warm water and muffled sound.

There was a rat epidemic at Malcolm X. It got so bad, what with the rats walking down the halls with us and eating lunch in the grass with us, that they had to close the school to fumigate. Just before that I was swimming one day, and I looked over and saw a rat swimming next to me. I screamed, "Rat Swimming in the Pool!" and everybody jumped out so quick it was as if somebody had shat in the pool. Everybody except Mr. Wallace. He was left treading water absent-mindedly as the rat paddled closer and closer to him.

I told my mother about the rat in the swimming pool. "Everybody has a rat story to tell," she said, and then she told me about the rat in her house when she was a little girl. "When I was little," she said, "our house was infested with rats. Most of them we never saw, we only heard their scurrying feet between the boards in the walls and floor." I imagined the house my mother grew up in as a tiny shack with holes in the walls bursting at the seams from too many children. "There was one rat that I saw periodically," she said. "I named him Binky. I made up stories about Binky that I'd tell my younger brothers and sister at night. Instead of TV, I'd tell my siblings stories about Binky the rat." My mother was the oldest of five. "And then one day my mother borrowed the neighbor's cat and we found beheaded Binkys all over the place for weeks."

I think that what has kept me writing is the fact that my mother has faith in stories about aliens and ghosts and rats named Binky; the fact that she tells me that she lied to me when I was a child by telling me that I was just imagining that I saw a hand go through my bedroom wall and wave to me, and that she saw it too; the fact that she believes I did come from the stork, not an international adoption agency, and that the stork was the silver bird of miracles. That I am special. It is my mother's belief in the imaginary that has kept me making up stories and living them. And sometimes when I go home and she babies me, makes me *jook* and steamed pigs' feet, brushes my hair roughly, or trims it too short, I feel like a little girl again. I remember what it feels like to cry at the bottom of the bathtub because you don't want to get out, and I remember what it feels like to be homesick while lying in your own bed. I remember how to close my shades, sit in the closet writing stories, and shut the door to monsters, bad ghosts, and the rest of the world. I write to go home, to find home, and to make my home in a blank page, forgotten memory, or a question that I will never know the answer to. "The world is shit, why not tell a story."

Magellan's Got Nothin' on My Lola

By Pia Cristina Infante

My lola
swings
from Fullerton to the Philippines
in stories told
from a green lawn chair

My lola
wears
skin soft and dark
a ripe avocado *bulaklak*
plucked from the Bulakan
where the carabao
speak only Ilokano

My lola
smiles
baptisms of brown
spilling secrets even lolo never
knew
like how to wrap *suman*
smooth
in velvet leaves from banana trees

or how to run laps
'round a fast flood of ash
in the race against Mt. Pinatubo

My lola steps
between lives
crosses thousands of blue ocean
miles
swims to Pampanga and back
in two seconds flat
same trip
took Magellan
a rough ten years
but you don't read about
Erotida Rodriguez Infante
in the *History of the Pacific*

Magellan's got nothin' on my lola
and if that sucker ever reads this
poem
he better blush when he says
my lola's name

Daily Affirmation

BY DONNA Y. CHIN

"*China, china,*" they'd call out from their windows on my way home from school. Picking up my pace, I'd try to ignore the voices from above. Still minding my own business, I'd hear them get louder. "*China, china,* ching chong, ching chong!" Their voices would ring in my ears and resonate as I felt the heat and rage build up inside me.

I wish they would just leave me alone. Don't they have anything better to do? I don't even speak Chinese! "*China, china!*" Their taunting put me right back inside that junior high classroom at I.S. 170.

It was seventh period, and I had Social Studies with the ever-so-boring Mr. Weinstein. I sat in the very first row, too far forward, so I had to turn my chair to see the teacher. As I drifted off into a pleasant daydream, my eyes stared off into space.

"What the fuck are you looking at, *China?* You better watch it, or I'll fuck you up!" interrupted Dolores. Totally stunned and shocked back into reality, I immediately buried my face and started to cry. Mr. Weinstein hardly stopped his lesson to reprimand Dolores, who only replied, "She better learn to keep her eyes to herself, or I'll mess her up!"

Choking on my tears, I tried to calm myself down, although I could feel my face burning. Turning to face forward, I felt my fear shift into anger. Why didn't Mr. Weinstein do anything? Why was it okay for her to threaten me that way? She didn't even know me! Little did I know then that Mr. Weinstein *should* have done something. It was not okay for Dolores to threaten me the way she did. Nor did I know then that 10 years later, I would travel to China to study abroad only to get a similar, yet exact opposite, slap in the face.

"*Where are you from?*" they'd ask me in Chinese. "*Singapore? Malaysia?*" They'd try to guess. "*Oh, America?*" they'd unbelievingly reply after I told them. Yes, I am from America. No, no, not all Americans are white. My ancestors were from China. "*So, why don't you know Chinese?*" they'd ask, and that would be my cue to give them my well-rehearsed explanation, using the two years of college Mandarin I knew.

The same interaction would occur every time I'd go out, meet new people, go shopping, catch a cab. Like the kids in my neighborhood who'd tease me for being Chinese, in China I was getting teased (or rather grilled) for not being Chinese enough. I came to term it "daily affirmation." A constant reminder to continually ask myself: Who am I? Where am I from? Where is home?

Today I try not to take these questions for granted, but I do not need these types of encounters to confirm who I am. I am Chinese American. I was born here, my parents were born here, and my grandparents were born here.

I am who I am. Who are you?

China: Chinese girl in Spanish

Harangue Directed Toward My World Studies Teacher and Network Executives

BY KLARA YEIJIN KIM

I open my textbook to page 122
to find
Clara Barton
Napoleon Bonaparte
Franklin Delano Roosevelt
i don't belong here.

My people didn't fight in the
Civil War
Vietnam War
World War I
and II
we were picking azaleas
and eating of rice and life

I turn the TV on to see
Asians with thick accents
Chinese cooking shows
and M*A*S*H showing

Korean peasants (portrayed by
Japanese actors)
begging Americans
for help
The first and only sitcom based on
Asians was canceled
after one season
(due to low ratings)
no one got the joke.

You tell me this is my history
that i should feel pride for these
well-documented caucasians
tell me this:
i see the word "Korea" in the
index once
i see "France" 29 times

i don't belong here

A Horse Story

BY ROBERTA UNO

Editor's Note: After Japan bombed Pearl Harbor and the United States entered World War II, the president signed Executive Order 9066, incarcerating 120,000 Japanese Americans, two-thirds of whom were American-born citizens, in 10 hastily built internment camps. Santa Anita Racetrack in Arcadia, California, was a relocation center where people where taken before they were shipped to the camps.

C amp was a place rich kids got sent to in the summer when their parents wanted to get rid of them. War was something black and white on the Million-Dollar Movie starring John Wayne. Santa Anita was a racetrack where they ran the Strubb Stakes. In those days . . .

At 12, Dee was one of those horsey girls, that breed of adolescents devoted to the almost ritual worship of anything with four legs, fetlocks and a mane. Her brother Doug would say, "Horse crazy now — boy crazy later," and dismiss his sister's devotion as something almost normal. Her mother would shut the door to Dee's room tight when the relatives came at Thanksgiving and laugh nervously, "Oh, that's just Dee galloping around her room — she's a horse nut. They all go through some phase. With Doug it was Spiderman. Excuse me — Dee! Cut out that racket in there and come out here like a lady!"

Her Dad would just shake his head and say, "Its all Papa's fault — the old man used to fill her head with those crazy stories when she was a kid. She still talks about *Ojiisan* and the things they did as if they were real. Honest, Emi, if he hadn't been my father and I didn't have to respect his words . . ."

Christmas mornings were never the same after *Ojiisan* was gone. The last one with him had been like all the ones before. Dee, a child of eight, was there before anyone else, bright-eyed, intoxicated with the lights and colors and packages. *Ojiisan* came down last as always, and as always Dee waited for him, scolding him as he entered the room, nearly knocking him over, "Grandpa, hurry! I want my pre-sent!"

"Yakamashi desu, neh," he chided, settling into his chair. "OK, OK, it's time now, OK — look under the tree and find the magic rope now." He smiled, touching her head and closing his eyes as if deep in thought.

She scrambled to look, ignoring the toys and department store boxes held out to her and Doug's cries as he tore through his own packages. Her father, holding out a silver box, glared unconsciously at the old man, who stroked his beard and continued to smile as if he could see with his eyes closed.

"Kazto, honey," her mother soothed in a placating voice, "calm down."

"Calm down? I'm calm. I'm calm," her father snapped then turned and lowered his voice apologetically. "You know how he aggravates me sometimes, Emi — look at him just sitting there, just because he's old and can get away with it."

"But you know how much he loves the girl," Mama reproached him, softly attempting to avoid an argument, especially on a holiday.

Kazto began to open his present and muttered under his breath, "It's just that he's going to tell her another one of his senile tales and we'll be hearing about it for weeks!"

Dee found the magic "rope." *Ojiisan* always hid it with great care in the branches of the Christmas tree. A tiny thread, this year it was red, and she followed it as it wound down the trunk of the tree, burrowed under the carpet and snaked out of the room.

"Grandpa, I found it! I love it!" she cried, racing back in triumph and carrying a ceramic horse with a red thread trailing from its right foreleg.

"Honto?" Ojiisan woke with a start, a wide grin creasing his face. "What's all this noise, little monkey?"

"Tell me about my horse, Grandpa, tell me, is he a racer? *Ojiisan,* where is it from, what kind is he?" She scrambled to the arm of the chair and pushed the horse into his waiting hands. "Look Grandpa, he's spotted."

"*So desu,* he's an Appaloosa," the old man announced, ceremoniously loosening the tiny thread from its leg. "But first I'll tell you about the magic rope — why is it red?"

Dee thought and fingered the other magic ropes, threads twisted into a fine knotted necklace inside her nightie. Papa's tall tales, Mama always said. Daddy was more emphatic; he called them the old man's crazy lies. But Dee knew one of the strands she wore around her neck was a tassel, which hung on a scroll in Japan, a scroll written by the Emperor himself honoring Grandpa's deeds. Another thread was from the rope Grandpa used to pull a wagon when he was indentured with a band of Chinese workers on the railroad. And she knew he wasn't lying by the sadness in his eyes when he had given her the thread he said was pulled from the wide salmon-colored obi belt of a young maiden, who, he said, taught his heart heavenly joy, a long, long time ago. . . .

No, these were not stories, Grandpa knew more than anybody. Since she was little, *Ojiisan* had woven the delicate strand with his quick fisherman's hands, adding a new color and tale each year. Five years, five colors entwined.

"Do you remember what the colors mean?" he questioned, removing the rope from her neck.

Dee watched the sureness and nimbleness with which his seemingly frail fingers moved and began to recite, "Purple is dignity — the color of royalty, the color of honor. White is truth — you said, *Ojiisan,* it is the color of death because it is pure like our souls, right? And pink is happiness because it's the color of cherry blossoms."

"And the cheeks of little girl monkeys." *Ojiisan* pinched her, then feigned a confused expression. "I know this brown one is for patience . . . but what is the green?"

"Hope, Grandpa, like the leaves in spring after winter — did you forget already?" she fidgeted, examining his thin silver beard, which she thought made him look like a two-legged billy goat.

"Maybe I should give you another brown rope, neh, *saru-chan?*" he smiled, gathering her two small hands in the warmth of his. "Red is courage strength, *Dee-chan,*"he revealed. "It is the color of blood, life, anger — like the koi flags on Boy's Day. You know those banners, hai?"

He began to weave the vermilion thread into her multicolored strand. "Koi fish are red because they swim upstream, like boys must fight sometimes to be men. . . . You are not a boy, *Dee-chan,* but I give you this color because there will come a time . . ." She drew on his palm with her finger, following the well-traveled map.

"Listen, *Dee-chan,* listen now. You must remember all the colors, but most important this last one. *Ojiisan* had to have courage, many times." He bent his head to her ear and said in a low voice, "I was in prison once . . ."

"Jail? You're a jailbird?" Dee turned her full attention on him with new interest, trying to see him as a bank robber or kidnapper.

"Papa!" Kazto interrupted, red-faced. "What nonsense are you telling that child? Honest, some things are better left unsaid, and why on Christmas of all days? For Chrissake, Papa."

"OK, OK, Kazto." *Ojiisan* deferred to and then ignored his son's exasperation. "Just remember — courage . . . and anger too." Dee met his gaze squarely as he quickly reached for the horse, cutting off any questions. "*So desu,* now I will tell you about the Appaloosa. *Ojiisan* is part Nez Perce Indian."

"Oh, Jeez, Papa, why must you fill the girl's head with lies?" Kazto broke in again.

Ojiisan turned 90 degrees and faced him fully, his gray eyes narrowed and becoming almost ice blue. "Is your father a liar, Kazto, my son?" he challenged in a clear imperious voice, dragging out the "my son." Dee looked in silence from one to the other and her Mama began rustling wrapping paper nervously.

"Uh, of course not, Papa. I just, that is . . ."

Ojiisan cut him off with a wave of his hand and announced to the room, "A long time ago, there was a bridge between this land and our home, Asia. Many, many people walked this bridge because it was too cold in Asia and they liked to eat corn more than rice. They crossed the bridge looking for a warm place to grow corn. Then there was an earthquake and the bridge broke. Our family is from the tribe that stayed on the other side. *So desu,* this is why I say, yes, I am Nez Perce Indian. You say this is a lie, Kazto-san?"

"Oh, Papa, you're sense of history is so distorted." Kazto shook his head.

"*Yakamashi desu* — enough disrespect!" *Ojiisan* raised his voice as Kazto turned deep red and Emiko hurried to pass him another present. "Now, *Dee-chan,* you listen," he continued with great authority. "We Nez Perce bred the fastest horses in the land. Fast, fast . . . no *hakujin* could catch us. This magic rope is from the blanket of the chief's horse — we were fierce, brave — same spirit as samurai. . . . Did I tell you about when I was a samurai in Japan?" He glared at Kazto for a fleeting moment.

"Emiko — it's all because of Papa she's such a . . . a . . . fanatic 12-year-old and all she can think about is horses, horses, horses." Dee had to bite her tongue to keep from snapping back at her father. A fanatic, huh? She pressed closer to the living room door as he continued, ". . . and now she wants to go to Santa Anita racetrack, of all places."

"Well, he was your father, Kazto," Mama was saying, but Dee found it hard to hear all the conversation over the drone of Johnny Carson on TV. She attempted to inch the door open a little just enough to see Mama doing her manicure and Daddy having a beer, his "nightcap"as he called it. "Why didn't you raise her to be more feminine anyway?" he asked, appearing to be talking to Johnny as his eyes stayed glued to the set.

"Me?" Emiko answered indignantly. Then, choosing to ignore the question, she added, "She'll grow out of it soon, Kazto. Maybe it would be best if we just took her. Then she'll forget all about it." Dee looked quickly back to her Dad, whose eyes were still riveted to the TV.

"Emiko, you know how I feel about that place. I won't have a daughter of mine set foot there. I cannot allow —" It was all so unfair and one-sided, Dee couldn't stand it anymore. She blurted out, "Pleez, Daddy it's the only place that has morning workouts open to the public. They don't charge anything, oh, pleeez Dad — "

Kazto gagged on his beer, "Where did you come from? Good Lord, were you eavesdropping? Young lady, I ought to turn you over my knee."

"Oh, pleeez, Daddy," she went on, "just this once and I promise, I'll never, never, never ask again."

Emiko frowned and interceded, "Papa, it's not unreasonable, really it isn't." Then, turning to Dee, she admonished, "Really, honey, you shouldn't listen in on people talking."

Dee's eyes dropped, "I'm sorry, Mama. It's just that I want to go so bad."

"And hang out with hoodlums and gamblers." Kazto shook his head with finality. "Look Dee, I know more about these things than you. I know those kind of people, I was your same age when . . ." He paused as a troubled look clouded his face.

Dee squinted. Daddy at a race track? She knew he didn't like horses, but she never knew he was a gambling man.

"But it's different, Dad, these are workouts — they start at 6 a.m. — it's too early for hoodlums to wake up. Pleeez, Dad, don't worry, there's no betting in the morning," she assured him, "just this once, and I promise —"

". . . you'll never ask again," her mother completed her sentence wearily. "Kazto, dear, just to get her to promise that, I'd take her anywhere. You remember when she was little and begged us to let Papa take her to the races at Hollywood Park, and she promised never to ask again. Well, has she?"

"Races, workouts, what's the difference?" Kazto slumped in his chair.

"I promise, Daddy, I'll never ask to go to any racetrack again, ever, anywhere, no matter what. I'll stay in the house for the rest of my life —"

"Oh heavens, what a threat!" Emiko exclaimed. "Take her, Kazto. She'll keep her promise. It will be good . . ." her voice trailed off, ". . . for all of us, besides."

Kazto winced and turned the TV off. "I don't like the idea, but Emiko, if you think . . ."

"Oh, thank you, Daddy, thank you, thank you, thank you." And Dee was out of the room before he could change his mind.

Santa Anita Racetrack was eerie in the early morning fog. The backdropped San Gabriel Mountains rose like the backs of deep blue dinosaurs stretching in the dawn light. From the moment they entered the park, an unusual silence fell over both her parents, but Dee was oblivious, racing and galloping and sucking in all the smells — the fresh-turned sod, the hosed-down pavement, the crisp morning filtering over the mountains. Within seconds she was on the rail and her mind filled with thoughts of Grandpa and her visit to the races so many years before.

There had been too many people and the horses looked like ants from the grandstand. It had taken forever between races. She had gone to get a soda and some drunk had stumbled over to her at the concessions stand.

"Hey, you a Hawaii girl? I love little Hawaii girls — you know the hula-hula cootchie coo?" he leered. She ran back to *Ojiisan* crying, but she wouldn't tell him what had happened because she was afraid he would take her home.

She just whimpered, "I can't see, Grandpa. Can't we go stand up front?" He had pushed and elbowed his way to the rail for her and perched her on it where they stood between two gamblers chanting, "Oh sweet Jesus God, be good to me this time," and "C'mon, y'motherfuckin' fool, ride that damn nag."

Ojiisan just put on his Japanese ears and pretended not to understand. Dee did the same. They had fought for that rail and were not going to give it up.

But now she had the whole length of it to herself. With her elbow, she wiped the chill dew from the smooth railing and propped herself against it happily. Peering into the fog, which still hung thick over the track, she became aware of a distant low thunder and a steady pounding, which she felt in her stomach more than heard. She shivered, and her breath caught in her throat as a great striding beast leapt out of nowhere, his hooves flailing forward recklessly, tearing the ground in huge bounds, the air charged with the steam of his deep snorts and the cooing and cursing of his rider's urgings. As suddenly as he appeared, he vanished. Dee watched as powerful haunches propelled the apparition into a wall of mist; only a diminishing pounding remained, echoed by her own heartbeat. She glanced back in her excitement to see if Mama and Daddy had seen the same thing, only to find them huddled over a thermos of coffee looking miniature and blank in the grandstand. She turned and hung even further over the rail.

"Hey, sugar, watch it!" an exercise boy warned as he brushed by. Dee fell in love instantly. The next time he circled by her, she all but hung by her toes trying to capture the whole feeling of the powerful bay horse with the white blaze and the rider who had called her "sugar" astride. The youth laughed as he passed and reined the giant in, circled back and called out, "You writin' the tote sheet this mornin'?" she nodded, yes, grinning.

"Who's the odds-on favorite?" He took off his mud-spattered goggles and winked. She blushed and pointed back at him without a word.

"You like horses, huh?" He circled his mount, which was fidgeting and would not come to a walk.

"I love them!" Dee blurted out. "My Mom and Dad brought me here because I begged and begged and promised if they let me come here today, I would never ask again. My Daddy doesn't like gambling." The horse stretched its neck trying to grab the bit between its teeth, and the boy frowned and spat out his gum.

"That's tough, sugar. In that case you better take in everything. You want to see the stable area?" Dee couldn't believe it, she couldn't even speak, she just nodded and nodded and nodded 'til the boy broke out laughing, and his mount threw his head high into the air with impatience.

"I'll leave a pass at the gate for you and your folks." He spun around as the bay bolted at his own shadow lengthening in the morning light. "What's your name?" he shouted, fighting as his mount moved out from under him.

"DEEEEEEEEE!" she cried out after them and watched hooves and chunks of dirt and flight leveling out to touch earth.

Kazto and Emiko looked sick when she raced back to them with the good news.

"But you promised, Daddy, you said I could have my way today if I never asked again — pleeeeez."

Kazto seemed incapable of speech. It was her Mama who answered quickly and firmly, "OK, Dee, you're right, Daddy promised, we'll go with you." Before he could respond, Dee was dragging him by the hand and Emiko was trailing after.

Dee's ecstasy in the stable area was uncontainable — being so close to the magnificent animals, which had been just a blur of sound and smell and color as they brushed close to the rail. Her eyes glowed as she watched the sleek horses being groomed so lovingly, their coats gleaming burnished chestnut, bay and ebony, the pungent odor of the liniment, the shimmering stable colors — she breathed it into her very toes. She ran loops around her parents and broke away from them, looking back. They seemed even smaller then they had dwarfed by the huge grandstand.

"Look, Daddy, look at the machine that walks the horses!" she exclaimed upon seeing a group of horses, tail to tail, wrapped in gaudy purple, green and yellow stable blankets. "Quick Investment," "High Life," "Drinks at 7." She read the names emblazoned on their sides. "Gawd, poor horses, what awful names, don't you think that's terrible, Daddy?" Kazto nodded back vaguely, his eyes moving from stall to stall. As they moved deeper into the stables, Dee's impatience grew.

"C'mon, why are you so slow?" Daddy's face was lined with a weariness made sharper by the rising morning sun. Dee saw him reach out to touch Mama's shoulder and stumble, he swayed for a moment and shook his head. A baffled expression came over him, and Mama suddenly appeared to be leading him, almost holding him up as he walked straight ahead, placing one foot carefully in front of the other.

"Mama, come on, make Daddy hurry!" Dee cried as she abandoned them and ran off to inspect a row of shining well-oiled saddles. She touched the cool smoothness and beauty of the worn leather. They were so perfect. She ran her hands over the polished fittings and started back to show Mama. Daddy could be such a drag sometimes, she wished they had left him at home.

"Mama, come quick —" She turned to call her and saw Daddy stooping over as if he were looking for something. Suddenly his body crumbled in half and he dropped to his knees, a weird, half-amused smile on his face. Mama stood over him, whispering inaudibly trying to pull him to his feet.

"Daddy! Daddy — what happened?" Dee ran to them, embarrassed and afraid. Kazto was laughing and grimacing at the same time — a low deep rumble that swelled like the moan of a wounded animal. Dee felt a fear worse than when they told her *Ojiisan* had had a heart attack and might never come back.

"Kazto, honey, get up," Mama begged. But it was too late; he was slapping his thigh and laughing without sound.

"Right here, Emiko, yep, right here — Number 5 Seabiscuit Lane. Hey, Dee, did you know your good old Dad lived in that stall right over there? That's right, me and Bachan and the three little ones," his eyes gleamed. "Rent free, hey you can't beat it. . . ." He shuddered as if startled from a bad dream, shadows still looming. "That's right — eight paces by eight paces — five of us in that son of a bitch horse stall. There was still horse shit on the ground when we moved in —"

"Daddy, Daddy, what are you talking about?" She started toward him and pulled back without knowing why. "Mama, what's Daddy saying? Mama —"

Emiko held on to his arm, "*Shikataganai,* Kazto, please, for our daughter's sake . . ." He jerked his arm aside in one short violent motion and turned on her.

"YOU, Emiko, YOU insisted we bring her. You said it would be good for all of us — I told you I didn't want her to come to a place like this, I never wanted her to know —"

"Daddy, shhh," Dee hushed him, feeling eyes turned their way. "Don't talk so loud, you'll scare the horses."

"Scare the horses, scare these animals?" he boomed. "I'll tell you about scared animals — scared animals who let themselves be led into horses' stalls to live packed in next to each other like sardines. You don't want to scare the animals? What about the guard towers that were there and there and there?" He pointed to the empty grandstands and flung his arms open. "And barbed wire everywhere? Who cared about scaring animals then? Who cared about scaring a boy whose papa was dragged off to prison with no trial — four years we didn't see Papa — who cared about scaring an old woman who would cry late at night when she thought all her children were asleep? I didn't sleep, Emiko, I heard her, I heard Mama crying. . . ."

Dee and her Mama just stared gape-mouthed like carp, their lips opened and closed around soft air bubbles. Dee heard sounds as if underwater. Phantom soldiers came out of nowhere, and the lane suddenly filled with Japanese ghosts shuffling quietly, a soft spongy mute herd.

Dee reached inside her shirt for her knotted strand and struggled to remember exactly what Grandpa had said. She looked at curious onlookers and for the first time in her life, she hated. She hated all of them for knowing. The thought that perhaps they, like her, did not know, crossed her mind, and her hatred grew at something greater and unknown. Everything shining and gleaming and polished lost color and became prison gray. *Ojiisan* had been here? *Ojiisan* had lived in a place made for an animal? *Ojiisan* had been sent from here to a place worse still, to a jail like a thief or a murderer? It was true, though; hadn't he said last Christmas, "I was in prison once. . . ." Dee felt deep humiliation and pain and wanted to run, wanted to close her eyes and fly like some great thoroughbred racehorse, flattened to the ground and disappearing in speed.

But her eyes were open, and before her were her own parents, earthbound and two-legged. Mama stroked Daddy with a tenderness so loving and fierce, Dee didn't even realize it until they were all holding each other, Mama saying softly, "*Shikataganai,* Kazto, we're all here together, we're all here together," over and over. Dee looked up and saw a growing crowd of puzzled stable hands and grooms staring at the weeping huddled Japanese family in the middle of Seabiscuit Lane, and she didn't care. After a time, the three gathered themselves and turned and walked away with dignity. For the first time, Dee felt her Daddy's arm around her as firm and as strong as Grandpa's.

Camp would never again be a place rich kids got sent to in the summer. War would never be celluloid black and white. And Santa Anita was a racetrack, but it had also been a camp during the war. Now Dee knew. And she knew why *Ojiisan* had added the red strand to the braid around her neck. Courage, strength, anger . . . The time had come.

This Is My Story

BY MARIKO DREW

This is my story
This is who I be
It's about battles and glory

And trying to be free. . .

We live in the Mission, but me no habla Español!
But I know my city, I feel its heartbeat, and La Mission, she's mine.
I've seen her soft underbelly and her hard callused shell
How many times have I awoken to find myself runnin' trippin' down the
stairs to see what the wailing was about, or who's gun it was,
or who crashed on our blood stained corner
How many times have I lay deathly still in my bed not daring to breathe
— waiting, listening for the rattle of the ivy covered iron gate
in my back yard
I heard him, he's in my backyard, he's climbing my stairs,
he's waiting for me to fall asleep
Will he get me or my mom first? Where should I go? Out the fire escape?
Should I yell and scream?
Dreams of robbers and murderers and rapists, crazy gangsters at the park
where mom went to jog —
No! Don't go there mom, it's not safe, they'll get you.
"Oh, don't be silly."
Night creeps into a beautiful day — birds screaming outside my window
— Get up! Get up!
Foot steps onto the dirty broken concrete as I walk the Mission streets,
past the Mission style villas and stucco houses, families resting on their
doorsteps, crying babies and blaring Salsa music.

Low riders rumble by. Bum Ba Ba Bum Ba Ba,
it all seems to be the same song.
The sun exposes the smoldering cigarette butts, used condoms, bottle
caps, the dealing of the night before put away for the breakfast eggs
and hash browns filling in the gaps
Those who are lucky return home to sleep as the sun's fingers poke in
through their bright cloth window shades.
Colorful murals of ancient faces peer out from scenes of repression and
struggle. Cesar Chavez is looking over me. He's watching his people.
Old Mexican women pat tortillas and chit chat
in the back room of a Taqueria.
All these smiling happy wise people — they're mine.
These broken streets I pound everyday — they're mine.
La Mission — she's mine.
Ain't nobody gonna tell me she ain't!

An Excerpt from...

A Cab Called Reliable

BY PATTI KIM

We finally arrived back at the store, and Father backed the truck to Good Food's front door. He opened the bars, unbolted the top, middle and two bottom locks, pulled open the door, and pushed the screen back, hooking the handle on a rusty bent nail. I crawled into the bed of the truck and waited for him to bring the cart so I could load and he could roll the boxes and sacks to the back. But he didn't come out like he usually did with a smile or a burp or a scratch. He didn't come out. So I called him three times. When he didn't answer, I worried, remembering how Angela's father got stabbed. I climbed out of the truck and looked inside.

My father was on his hands and knees picking up the quarters, dimes, nickels and pennies that had spilled out of the cash register when the burglars cracked open the drawer. He collected the coins into the King Edward cigar box. The chairs were knocked over onto the middle of the floor. Tables turned.

Greasy posters of cheeseburgers and french fries hanging by one corner. Cigarette cartons torn and stepped on. Clean napkins scattered on the floor, like they had been thrown up in the air by gloved hands. I could see them having a party in here. One with chunks of ham and roast beef, one with a carton of beer, one with the slicing machine coming in and going out of the hole they had drilled in the middle of our wall underneath our sink next to our steam table in front of the grill. The only things left in the back were opened sacks of cornmeal, mousetraps and the stink of horse manure from Mr. Selby's limo service. They were renting our horse, carriage and rider by the hour because the weather was so pleasant nowadays.

When a path was finally cleared, I wheeled the cart around from the storage room to the back of the truck. My father was mopping up the eggshells. I loaded the cart with stacked boxes of bottled orange and grapefruit flavored RC. I rolled the cart to the back. He was still mopping up the eggshells. I unloaded the cart and rolled it back to the truck. Sylvany Spanish onions wheeled to the cooking room; Kings potatoes leaned against the onions; the crate of collard greens in the refrigerator. He picked up the napkins, dusted them on his thighs, and collected them in a pile. I loaded the cart with turkey wings, ham hock and the slab of bacon. I rolled the cart to the freezer and unloaded. He was taping the greasy posters back up on the wall. I rolled the cart back to the truck, unloaded the boxes of Snickers, Milky Way, Three Musketeers, M&Ms and five boxes of Juicy Fruit, the gum they love to chew, and wheeled them to the counter. He was looking into the hole, shaking his balding head, and touching the edges of the circle they made. I wheeled the empty cart to the back storage room and leaned it against the wall underneath the light switch.

I swept the floors, while he tried to cover up the hole by nailing a piece of plywood over it. I swept the corners, underneath the tables and counters, and around his stooped body. We wouldn't be able to total up the week's worth of sales on the cash register. I mopped. I poured Clorox and Ajax into the bucket of hot water, dunked the mop in, and without wringing it, dripped the water onto the floor. I scrubbed the corners, underneath the tables and counters and around his stooped body. I wrung the mop and soaked up the soapy water from the wet floor. The mop slapped.

I washed and rinsed the four coffeepots, using rags rubber-banded around the tip of a tong. He was still nailing the piece of plywood over the hole. I dried the coffeepots and returned them to the coffeemaker.

I scraped the week's worth of grease into the large can that held a month's worth of grease. I shut it and wobbled out to the alley with it. When I returned, he had finished nailing the piece of plywood over the hole. I rinsed out the toilet bowl. I emptied out the trash. I beat the dust out of the welcome mat.

My father spoke in Korean. *"Ahn Joo-yah, let's go home."*

He locked the four bolts and let the door of bars clank shut. It shut, and we heard liquid quickly streaming. When we looked into the alley, there was an old black man peeing next to our can of a month's worth of grease. When my father quickly turned me around and pushed me toward the truck, I heard the man say he was sorry, but he couldn't help it, you know how it is. My father said he was sorry and hey man you can finish, take your time. The man zipped up and walked to the end of the alley.

My father sat on the driver's seat and fiddled with the gear before starting the ignition. I looked at him and said, "What the hell is his problem? Can't he find another hole to land his pee in?"

He didn't answer. He drove over a curb, barely missing the NO PARKING sign that was bent in a 45-degree angle.

"Dad, who does he think he is?" I screamed.

My father told me to quiet down.

"It's bad enough Mr. Selby's horses shit there, why does he have to hang his dick and piss in our alley? I can't stand this. It's making me sick. It's bad enough we get robbed, why does he have to add on to our misery and leave his urine in our alley? That's illegal, do you know that?"

He opened the glove compartment and took out a napkin to wipe off the sweat beading on his head.

In Korean he said, *"Ahn Joo-yah, please let's drive home quietly."*

I wanted to tell him the robbery and the urine were absolute injustices, we were wronged, and the guilty would eventually have to pay their karma debt. All of them. For stabbing Angela's father, for holding Yoo Jin's mother at gunpoint underneath the toilet, for shooting off Mr. Hong's ear for a couple of hundred dollars and a bag of chips, for calling Mrs. Kim a stingy money-hungry chink because she refused to give her customers cleaning for free or because she charged extra for boxed shirts, for making me write badly to save myself from being accused of copying out of a book, for telling me to go back to where I came from (how can I return to my mother's womb?), for stretching their large, long, curly-lashed eyes at me while singing about my being Chinese and Japanese, for making me want to look, walk, eat, sleep, talk like them, for expecting me to sit quietly in the back of the classroom, for making me repeat my question two or three times because no one could hear my voice squeezed out of a throat that always had clay caught in the center except when it was speaking to Father. When I spoke at Father, my throat opened up and clever words, sentences, paragraphs came to me. It was because I believed I knew better than he.

He had pushed his socks down to his ankles because the weather was warm, and the vent above the pedals blew air. The vinyl seats were sticking to my thighs. The sun reflected the off the side of a high-rise made of mirrors that twinkled, blinked and winked at me as if trying to dazzle me to keep its secrets. We were driving across a bridge over a river. The wind beat in and made noise. But it didn't keep me from hearing my father's breathing, which was his pathetic plea: *Ahn Joo-yah, Ahn Joo-yah, you have to save your poor father. You are the reason I do this. I cannot do this for long. Study hard, place first in your class, become a doctor or lawyer, take care of me, make money, make my suffering pay off, make my sacrifice worthwhile . . . .*

A man on a 10-speed carrying a blue knapsack on his back pedaled past us as my father slowed down to exit the bridge. As he switched gears, I saw my hand zigzag and tremble next to his, bound at the wrist by steel rings.

Duty caught me by the throat, keeping me from beating my forehead against the bathroom floor as my mother used to do while she chanted and wailed: *Why did you bring me to this awful, awful country?*

We Don't Need No Mountain Guru

After Ruth Forman's "Young Cornrows Callin Out the Moon," for my sister Natala

BY SHEILA MENEZES

We don't need no mountain guru, no *bindis*
no mysterious incense swirls neither
cuz we got Episcopalian church on Sundays
stainglass windows/concrete walls/red wine/stale wafers
and mom readin the Tao of Pooh on
     car rides to Santa Barbara

     we don't need no sitar or tabla records
     cuz we got the jingle of mom's gold bangles
     and dad singing elvis

  yah we got mangoes/tamarind/*burfi* treats/*gelabis*
  then seven-up for a tummy ache
we got *pooris* and coca-cola at the Santa Clara Pasand
and crab curry on New Year's Day

     yah me and my sista got fried *papadums* and dad's *biriani*
     yoghurt to calm our tongues from the zap of hot spice
     then tv dinners with daddy watchin Dallas
     and on Saturdays he fries up pancakes
     that spell out the first letter of our names

     we don't need no mountain guru
     no *bindis*/no mysterious incense swirls neither
  cuz we Indian no matter what/we American too
but we don't need no mom calling us *pumpkin* or *precious*
cuz mummy call us *bundoo* or *boochi*
  we don't need no jars of cookies
     we got jars of pickled lemons
          squished in sunlight on the windowsill

and we got asteroids on dad's computer
and G.I. Joe cartoons right after mom's stories
'bout cobras on couches in hot hot Tirapur
yah we got mom
eyes outlined with *kohl*
toes in red red nailpolish
pullin our hair
into pigtails and *kondais*

we got sandalwood elephants on every table
dreidels n transformers n hot wheels
we got aloe vera for burns
and a creaky patio swing

so we don't need no mountain guru
no *bindis*/no mysterious incense swirls
no *pumpkin* or *precious* neither
cuz you got me and I got you
and we got mom n dad
and India n America
and that's just the way
I like it

bundoo: little bug
boochi: little caterpillar
kohl: black eyeliner
kondai: hair pulled back into a bun

CHAPTER 7

Cute
Asian
Girl
This

Girl Power

Cute Asian Girl This

BY YUNJONG SUH

Don't ask me where I'm from again and again

ask me to teach you how to stir fry

and how wide I can open my eyes

snicker karate chopping ching chong

if you want to live long

because I do know

taekwondo

Girlfriends

By Barbara J. Pulmano Reyes

Smart as any boy
Even smarter
Cooler than any white girl
And much more beautiful

Though we haven't got much money
Just the cool things we learn and believe
That scare people to death
Make them fall in love with us
Hate rape and beat us

My girlfriends and I are funky and cute
Tough Pinays who didn't grow up
In Daly City

With pierced navels nipples and tattoos
With college education going far

At night we still dream
Of fairy tale weddings and babies
The part of the story
Where we live happily ever after

It's the woman in us
That gives us dreams
Visions and prophecies
Our mothers' and grandmothers' blood
Runs undeniably warm beneath our skin

In Response to the Queer Sister of Color

who sed "help a sister out and translate these little chinese pictures"

BY PIA CRISTINA INFANTE

Contrary to what
you may have heard
about Asian women
I am not always nice

Contrary to what
images may come to mind
about Catholic raised Filipina
women
I am not necessarily patient or
forgiving

Contrary to what
you may think you know about
politically active Filipina dykes
I refuse to further participate
in a minority politics
which perpetuate
the Myth: american racial
consciousness is two-
toned/black and white

If you are another sister of color
/A queer sister of color/
contrary to what you
may expect from a queer asian-
ambiguous sister
I cannot embrace you
until YOU
                              SEE
                                        ME

and that means
it is your job
not mine
to educate yur self out of
ignorance
so, please
figure out/before you ask
me/that
No,
I don't read Mandarin
And neither does my sister.

In the Back of My Mind

BY SOTHAVY MEAS

The world is full of crap. Crap women must deal with

Asian people really eat dogs. Take on risks, they make you stronger.

Conquer your fears before they get the best of you.

Long Beach has the largest population of Cambodians, next to Cambodia. Many of them, with the help of the government, get to live in small, cramped houses and apartments of the eastside.

Don't just follow. Question Authority. Don't let a MAN rule your life.

Never let pride get in the way. HE can be right. Don't regret. Deal with it.

Men are sensitive sometimes. NEVER leave the toilet seat up.

Some girls still want to be like Barbie. Make yourself your top priority. The world revolves around you. Women are stronger.

Never wear polka dots and stripes together.

Stop growing up so quickly and enjoy everything.

Go SKINNY-DIPPING.

Excess isn't good. Especially chocolate. Drive at the speed limit.

Live with your parents, not for them.

Maré Is a Diva, *di ba?*

For all strong sistahs, especially Meg, Liza, Arleen, Maria, Alyssa, Lauren,
Dawn, Carmen, Michelle, Diane, Ethelyn, Linda, Joanie, & Auntie Dorothy

BY EMILY PORCINCULA LAWSIN

We call her "Maré,"
As in "Comadré,"
our sistahfriend.
Not "SIS - TER," my friend,
but "sistah-friend,"
said all-in-one.
She's the womyn
who defies us –
U - S -
of A - stereotyped popularity,
of a
bubblin', babblin'
B - I - T of a CHiquita
banana yellow-face white bread
MEN - tality.
In totality,
it ain't no Wonder.
She crushes the violent patronizing of
miss saigon-like lyrics and
flushes them down the toil–
it's not enough.
So she conquers the street,
telling a wart-nosed cop that
"Under Municipal Code Number 2-6-5-6
we can wage a massive protest"
provided she keeps us on the move.
Maré is a diva.
So instead of walking us in traditional circles,
she sends us in lightning movin' spirals,
like tornadoes whipping unshielded storefronts.
She is a diva, *di ba?*

di ba: Tagalog for "Isn't it so"

O-o,
Maré is more than a

W - O - M - B - man.

With her saber-like tongue, gleaming brown skin and charcoal eyes,
she burns fire into
the souls of Pinoy folk,
makin us look back
at womyn legends of the P.I:
(NOT including Imelda, the crooked shoe queen, of course)
so we study Magandá,
meaning "beautiful,"
who was stronger than Eve,
the first diva of all divas,
who killed a bird that mocked
at the bamboo of her man.
And Gabriela (Silang)
of yesterday and today,
a true revolutionary,
the real, live Womyn Warrior,
before Kingston made it fiction.
But Maré is more than a teacher, *di ba?*
She's the Mother of all lands
that resist using our bodies
as bases of war.
She is like a book of ages
and time that can't stand still.
She is a roaring river
who don't need to beg to be heard.
She is the strong waves of HERstory,
of our revelations,
of our liberation.

Maré is a diva,
Yes.

— *1994, Los Angeles, California*

The Pinay Experience

By Jacky Casumbal

the pinay experience . . .
youthful arrogance
perfect angel or perfect menace?
Raise 'em high
with that two finger reply!
Don't ever deny your pride.

i'm that girl with the pen
talking to my uncle up in heaven
and my lolo and his lola . . .
with words that can only be said
to the non-dead
in my heart.

see that veteran standing tall?
though he's hunched over
on his cane and all
he knows what's up
he's seen it before
giving "his" country all of his pride
for that world war.

knowing a bit of history
has helped me see —
our ancestors so brown
struggled with their faces to the ground
and echoed in their ears a colonial sound.

that farmer works his hands and knees
all day
without any kind of pay.
that may have been some hundred
years ago
but when one brown person is in pain,
we all feel the blow.

while that break dancer's breakin',
there's a poor momma wakin'
to the sound of her baby
no more than 16 years younger.

no, no, she's a straight honor student
this girl's nothing else but prudent
she's the object of all the parents'
dreams.

so where do i fit in?
(am i in-between?)
— unseen —
i lie here stressin' over being a calm,
collected pinay
when anger's on my mind
and that sense of identity can be
so hard to find. . . .

so what's up youth?
do we really hold the truth
REFLECT,
NEGLECT,
PROTECT,
INFECT. . . ?

or do we throw bread
when we can't be fed
what we believe?
(i'm right with what i perceive!)

naw sistah, you've got it all wrong!
that ego of yours won't last you long
respect your people, give them space
cuz then again, united we should be —
the filipino race.

My Pinay Nanay

For Mom & all Filipina American mothers, especially Irene Suico Soriano's

BY EMILY PORCINCULA LAWSIN

My mother has many names:
"Mama," "Mommy," "Lola," "Grandma,"
"Tia," "Chang," "Manang," "Emma," "Emang,"
But I just call her: My "Pinay Nanay."

MY PINAY NANAY,
    She can speak
    Ifugao, Ilongo, Ilocano, Waray, Cebuano, Pampangueno,
    Spanish, Tagalog,
    AND
    English,
    Thanks to the three Pinoy men she married
    And the thousands of U.S. troops stationed in her island province.

MY PINAY NANAY,
    She can whip up a dozen lumpias — vegetable and Shanghai,
    Roll it/paste it/fry it/see you joke with it like a cigar
    or boto/penis
    And whirl a boomerang bakya/slipper at you
    AllInOneBreath.

MY PINAY NANAY,
    She can cook a feast for seven in as many minutes,
    Spread the table with
    Fresh mongo beans/seafood/pinakbet/chicken/beef/pork/adobo/
    plus tokwa/tofu/chicharron sizzling on the
    side/lasagna trays of pancit noodles:
    Bihon/Canton/
    Lug-lug/AND Malabon/vats of tomato-pasty menudo/ machado/
    peanut kare-kare/dinuguan (chocolate meat — ha-ha!) /
    AND for dessert: platters of steamed puto/suman/cutsinta cakes/
    baked bibingka/biko/deep fried cascarron/donut holes/
    bowls of sweet ginataan
    with ping-pong-ball-sized-bilo-bilo dumplings
    JustLikeYouLikeThem/and STILL ask you,
    "Are you hungry? You better eat!"

MY PINAY NANAY,
    She can, with one hand, twirl a hundred-pound lechon over
    a fiery roast pig spit
    While smoking a Marlboro backwards,
    Guess a mah-jong tile's face with one finger — always her middle
    — sliding underneath, (*Boom!* "Ay, Mah-Jong!")
    Fill the house with smells of fried garlic rice, longaniza sausage, and eggs,
    So the Pusoy poker players will come back
    With much "tong" to pay for your 18th birthday debut.

MY PINAY NANAY,
    She can sew First Communion dresses and Eddie Bauer jackets
    Without a McCall's pattern,
    Net, pierce, gut, chop, and can Alaskan salmon with a blind eye,
    Write round-trip tickets to the Philippines,
    And cuss out the neighbor Jones kids
    For throwing firecrackers down her white stone chimney,
    All with her Tondo accent and 9th grade education.

MY PINAY NANAY,
    She can sic the cops on the son-in-law who beats you,
    Lead a hundred-member march to the Mayor's Office,
    Demanding he give the city its historic Jose Rizal Park,
    Turn the corner to the Seattle School District's pad,
    And shout in nine different languages
    for Bilingual Education NOW,
    Then act like she doesn't speak a lick of English
    on a Metro Bus.
    So a greedy seat hog will scoot on over.

MY PINAY NANAY,
    She's got more power — more PINAY POWER —
    Than all our childhood role models put together:
    Wonder Woman, Charlie's Angels' Kate Jackson,
    and even my favorite,
    Betty Rubble (it's the hair).

MY PINAY NANAY,
    She's down.
    She's brown.
    She's the Pinay
    SUPERFLY.

The Princess in the Palace of Snakes

BY CHITRA BANERJEE DIVAKARUNI

Growing up in Calcutta, I was poor. My aunt, who was not poor, said this was because my mother had married foolishly. You were the best looking of us all, she'd say to my mother when we went to visit her. If only you hadn't listened to That Man.

That Man was my father, who was never there. I remembered him vaguely as deep laughter and the smell of cologne, as warm hands that threw me up in the air and always caught me. As the empty space in the wide bed in which my mother sometimes wept.

Already my life was surrounded by the basic elements of the fairy tale: beauty and a foolish heart, love and poverty and betrayal. Being a child, I liked that.

During those hot Bengal afternoons while my uncle was at work and my cousins, who were older, were still at school, my mother and my aunt sat under the slow-whirring ceiling fan. They drank iced *lassi* and ate fragrant *supari* and sighed over the past, that magic time when all things had seemed possible. They left me to my own devices. I liked that, too. I would go into the office-room, which was out-of-bounds for children, and take from my uncle's table a round glass paperweight in which air bubbles glowed and shimmered. All afternoon I would run down the marble staircase to the ground floor, cool and dim as the bottom of a lake, and slowly climb back up, holding the paperweight in front of me. I was the princess in the underwater palace of snakes, carrying the jewel that allowed me to rise to the surface of the lake.

This is her story:

The princess lives in an underwater palace filled with snakes. We do not know who she is, or how she came there. Do not feel sorry for her. She is happy enough. The snakes are not horrid creatures, as in Western tales, but beautiful, green and yellow and gold. And gentle — they feed her and play with her and sing her to sleep. She has never left the palace, has never wanted to. But then, she does not know that there is more to the world than these sinuous beings, this dim green light, these cool walls built of shell and submarine stone.

As you might guess, there is a prince in the story. And his friend, the minister's son. Wandering in the forest, they happen upon an *ajagar*, a mythic snake with a jewel on its head. It attacks them; they kill it and take the jewel, and when they bring it to the lake to wash it clean, they are astonished to see the waters parting, a marble staircase appearing. They go down it and find the princess. She falls in love with the prince, of course — innocent and unadvised, what chance does she have — and for a while all three live happily in the palace of snakes. (The snakes, I think, are less happy; but on this, the tale does not comment.)

Soon the prince wants to take his bride-to-be back to his kingdom. He sends his friend to bring an entourage worthy of escorting her: elephants with gold umbrellas, soldiers with silver spears, drummers in turbans of red silk, palanquins of rosewood and sandalwood. And while they wait for the entourage to arrive, he tells the princess stories of the marvelous world above the lake.

The prince must have been skillful — too skillful for his own good — for one day, while he is sleeping, the princess decides she cannot wait any longer to see the wonders of this new world. She takes the jewel, the waters part, she walks up the marble stairs.

The story goes on to how she is lured away and captured by an evil king who wants to marry her; how, with her gone, the snakes in the palace turn on the sleeping prince and trap him in their poisonous coils; how, together, she and the faithful minister's son trick the evil king and find their way back to the lake. The prince is rescued, they go to his kingdom, and the tale ends with a sumptuous wedding.

But I am caught by that moment of ascent when the princess saw for the first time the glint of gold light on green mango leaves. When she heard a *kokil* cry its song from a jasmine bough, when she smelled the sweet red earth, the clean blue sky. I think it was afternoon then. The long jagged shadows of coconut trees must have shivered on the water. Perhaps in the distance, woodcutters, on their way home, were singing a peasant ditty. She breathed in that strange melody and felt it begin to change her, cell by cell. Never again would she be satisfied by the wordless songs of her serpent companions.

This was the moment I played over and over in my aunt's house, not knowing why I was drawn to it.

I did not know then that the power of the moment lay in the princess's dual vision, the innocence of child-seeing that creates a world newly, the adult consciousness that compares and understands and remembers. I didn't know that the tragedy of the moment lay in that, too; as she stands in the lake, looking up at air, she is part of two worlds but wholly of neither. For the rest of her life, she will belong nowhere.

Those Calcutta afternoons, when our visit was over, I would leave my aunt's house reluctantly, gazing back at the marble staircase that rose out of the magic lake. I couldn't wait to come back next week so I could be the princess in the snake palace again.

I didn't know then that I would live her life in earnest soon enough — at least that one heart-breaking, heart-thrilling moment of it — when I left India to come to America.

InvAsian Contributors

Jennifer Ahn performed "Absolution," her first published piece, in New York City with Peeling, an Asian American performance group.

Born in Okinawa, Japan, **Catherine Bitney** is a multiracial Vietnamese American. After graduating from the University of Maryland, she worked for the National Organization for Women, fighting for queer rights and against hate crimes.

Eliza Y. Chan, president of Asian Women United of California, is a veteran public relations professional specializing in international corporate communications and crisis management. A U.C. Berkeley graduate and CORO Foundation fellow, she represented Asian Women United at the United Nations Fourth World Conference on Women in Beijing, China, in 1995.

Asian Women United board member **Joannie C. Chang** was born in Taipei, Taiwan, raised in New Jersey and now lives in San Francisco. A graduate of Bryn Mawr College and New York University School of Law, she is the director of employment and labor projects at the Asian Law Caucus and also serves on the boards of the Chinese Historical Society of America and Kearny Street Workshop.

Donna Y. Chin, a teacher in a New York City Chinatown/Lower East Side public school, graduated from Smith College and is pursuing a master's degree at Hunter College to teach English as a second language.

Marilyn Chin's books of poems include *Rhapsody in Plain Yellow, The Phoenix Gone, The Terrace Empty,* and *Dwarf Bamboo.* She co-directs the M.F.A. Program in creative writing at San Diego State University.

Born in Calcutta, **Chitra Banerjee Divakaruni** came to the United States more than 20 years ago and resides in Northern California. She has published four volumes of poetry – *Dark Like the River, The Reason for Nasturtiums, Black Candle,* and *Leaving Yuba City* – and three novels: *The Mistress of Spices, Sister of My Heart,* and *The Vine of Desire.* Her first collection of short stories, *Arranged Marriage,* won the American Book Award in 1996.

Anida Yoeu Esguerra identifies herself as a non-hyphenated Cambodian Malaysian Muslim American woman. She founded Mango Tribe, an Asian American women's interdisciplinary performance ensemble; Asian American Artists Collective, a nonprofit

Biographies not available for all contributors

arts organization in Chicago; *Monsoon Magazine,* a literary arts journal at the University of Illinois; and I Was Born With Two Tongues, a pan-Asian spoken-word group.

FRANCES LEE HALL, broadcast television producer, writer, and actress, won honorable mention in the San Francisco Film Arts Foundation's short screenplay contest for her adaptation of "Don't Forget the Whiskey." She won an Emmy Award for "The Art World Meets the Internet" for TechTV.

SASHA HOM, adopted from South Korea by a Chinese American family, grew up in Berkeley and lives in San Francisco. Her work has appeared in *A Ghost at Heart's Edge: An Anthology of Adoption Fiction and Poetry, The Sun,* a literary magazine, and *Hip Mama.*

PIA INFANTE describes herself as "a brooklyn-based queer pinay educator poet currently directing youth-led media activism with We INTERRUPT This Message." She was featured on the S.L.A.A.A.P. 2000 (Sexually Liberated Art Activist Asian People) mock Bollywood poster called "Fearless Love."

KELLY EMIKO IWANABE attends Edison High School in Huntington Beach, California, where she is student body vice president and a member of the varsity tennis and swim teams. She was 14 when she wrote "I Used to Be."

NORA OKJA KELLER, author of the novels *Comfort Woman* and *Fox Girl,* was born in Seoul, Korea, and now lives in Hawai'i with her husband and two daughters. She is the co-editor of *Intersecting Circles: Prose and Poetry of Hapa Women* and *YOBO: Korean American Writers of Hawai'i.* Her column, Small Moments, appears every Sunday in the *Honolulu Star Bulletin.*

Asian Women United of California co-founder, past president, and board member **ELAINE H. KIM** was born in New York, raised in the Washington, D.C., area, and now lives in Oakland, California. She teaches Asian American and comparative ethnic studies at U.C. Berkeley and has written and edited several books on Asian American literature and Asian American women.

JENNIFER KIM, a second-generation Korean American, was born and raised in Ohio and lives in Los Angeles. She has won several awards for her writing and her work with PBS and the UCLA Asian American Studies Center in children's media production.

KLARA YEIJIN KIM, a Korean American living in Chicago, wrote "Circles" when she was 14.

PATTI KIM, born in Pusan, Korea, immigrated to the United States when she was three. She has published several novels and now lives in Riverdale, Maryland, with her husband and daughter.

Born and raised in Stockton, California, **AMY LAU** is a graduate of U.C. Berkeley, where she received a bachelor's degree in English and Mass Communications.

EMILY PORCINCULA LAWSIN, born in "She-attle," Washington, has published poetry and essays, is an oral historian, has performed on radio and stage across the United States and in the Philippines, and has taught Asian American Studies at UCLA, Cal State University Northridge, and the University of Michigan. She is a trustee of the Filipino American National Historical Society.

MARIE G. LEE, born and raised in Hibbing, Minnesota, is the author of several books for children. Her first novel, *Finding My Voice,* is an autobiographical novel about growing up Korean American in Bob Dylan's hometown.

JOYCE S. LIU lives in the San Francisco Bay Area where she performs and teaches music, a legacy from her paternal grandfather, who sang Chinese opera, and her maternal grandmother, who sang torch songs and played the piano.

LYNN LU is a freelance writer and book editor. Her work has appeared in *Ms.*, *Sojourner, AsianAvenue.com,* and in the anthology *Dragon Ladies: Asian American Feminists Breathe Fire.*

SHEILA MENEZES, a first-generation American of Goan and Anglo-Indian descent, is a U.C. Berkeley graduate who lives in Oakland, California. For two years she was program coordinator for June Jordan's Poetry for the People.

MAIANA MINAHAL, born in Manila and raised in Los Angeles, lives in San Francisco. She studied poetry at U.C. Berkeley with June Jordan's Poetry for the People collective, and her work has appeared in *Poetry for the People: A Revolutionary Blueprint; Take Out: Queer Writings from Asian and Pacific America;* and the anthology *Screaming Monkeys.*

DAVY MUTH arrived in the United States from Cambodia in 1982. In the next seven years, she earned a G.E.D., A.A., B.A., M.A., and a teaching credential. In 1999, she received a doctorate in multicultural and bilingual education, and now is an elementary school principal in a Seattle public school.

Asian Women United board member **SUSANNA NG-LEE**, born and raised in Hong Kong, came to the United States to attend college. A U.C. Berkeley graduate, she works in human resources management, specializing in classification, compensation, and recruitment. She also serves on the board of Family Bridges, an Oakland social service agency.

MARY-JOCELYN ("MARI-JO") A. ORTEGA emigrated from Manila when she was 10. A U.C. Santa Cruz graduate, her poetry has appeared in several publications, including anthologies produced by the International Library of Poetry.

REBEKAH FARRAH QIDWAI, a Pakistani American woman living in New York City, studied creative writing at the New School and ethnic studies at U.C. Berkeley.

AIMEE PHAN wrote "Tree" when she was a junior at UCLA. She currently lives in Iowa City, where she is a student at the Iowa Writers' Workshop.

BARBARA J. PULMANO REYES, a U.C. Berkeley graduate, was born in Manila, Philippines, and raised in the San Francisco Bay Area. Her work has appeared in several publications, including *Babaylan, Liwanag Volume Two,* and *Maganda.*

ROWENA ROBLES recently completed a Ph.D in ethnic studies at U.C. Berkeley and wrote her dissertation on race and public school education. Now based in Los Angeles, she plans to continue teaching, writing and representing women students of color.

Asian Women United board member EVELYN IBATAN RODRIGUEZ is a second-generation Pinay who was born in Honolulu, raised in San Diego, and now is a sociology Ph.D. candidate at U.C. Berkeley studying culture, gender, and immigration.

An Asian American of Chinese and Portuguese descent, Sao Paolo-born ANGELA ROSARIO graduated from San Jose State University. Her work has been published in several online magazines, including *DisOrient Journalzine, Plugged Magazine,* and *II Stix.*

FRANCES KIM RUSSELL, a Korean-Irish hapa who recently graduated from U.C. Santa Cruz, is a member of the San Francisco chapter of Hapa Issues Forum, a national nonprofit organization that celebrates the mixed-race Asian American experience.

FAM LINH SAECHAO is a Mienh American who was born in Thailand and now lives in Richmond, California. She co-edited and contributed to two anthologies by young Mienh Americans, *Quietly Torn* and *Quietly Reborn.*

CANYON SAM, a San Francisco writer, performance artist, activist and, in 1977, founder of the first organized group of Asian American lesbians in the United States, has published fiction, nonfiction, and drama. She currently is working on a book, *One Hundred Voices of Tara: An Activist's Spiritual Journey Among Tibetan Women,* and on a film of her first one-woman show, "The Dissident."

SHIZUE SEIGEL is a third-generation Japanese American writer and graphic designer living in San Francisco. She formerly was editor of *Nikkei Heritage*, a quarterly publication of the National Japanese American Historical Society, and English editor of *The Beam*, a free monthly bilingual tabloid for Japanese Americans and Japanese-language speakers in the San Francisco Bay Area.

JANE SINGH, a second generation South Asian American, grew up in Northern California. She teaches in the Asian American Studies program at U.C. Berkeley and serves as an Asian Women United board member.

SUSAN A. SUH, born in Nebraska and raised in New York, now lives in Los Angeles. "The Girl Who Lost Her Face" is her first published story.

YUNJONG SUH, a media activist born in South Korea and raised in Connecticut, lives in the San Francisco Bay Area and is a producer for WINGS (Women's International News Gathering Service).

LILY SUN, born in Taiwan and raised in the United States, earned an M.A. in English literature at the University of Minnesota.

MARI F. TOM, the author of *Hikaru of Monsoon*, has a master's degree from San Francisco State University in special major, which emphasized creative writing, Asian American studies, and English literature. She is interested in Japanese animation and its adaptations in American popular culture.

ROBERTA UNO, artistic director of New WORLD Theater and a professor of theater at the University of Massachusetts at Amherst, is the editor of several publications, including *Unbroken Thread: An Anthology of Plays by Asian American Women*.

DOLLY VEALE, a veteran of the movement against the Vietnam War and the movement to establish ethnic studies at U.C. Berkeley in the 1970s, was a founding member of the Revolutionary Communist Party, USA, and is its San Francisco Bay Area spokesperson today.

LILIA V. VILLANUEVA, past president of Asian Women United of California, is co-author of *Philip Vera Cruz: A Personal History of Filipino Immigrants & The Farmworkers Movement* and co-editor of *Making More Waves: New Writing by Asian American Women*.

GRACE M. WOO started writing "The Cockroach" while she was in high school and finished it after completing college.